MEDIEVAL DUBLIN II

I ndilchuimhne ar
Phádraig Ó hÉailidhe (Paddy Healy), 1916–2000,
cara Átha Cliath ó dhúchas agus i ngníomh

Medieval Dublin II

Proceedings of the
Friends of Medieval Dublin Symposium 2000

Seán Duffy

EDITOR

FOUR COURTS PRESS

Typeset in 10 pt on 12.5 pt Bembo by
Carrigboy Typesetting Services, County Cork for
FOUR COURTS PRESS LTD
Fumbally Court, Fumbally Lane, Dublin 8, Ireland
e-mail: info@four-courts-press.ie
and in North America for
FOUR COURTS PRESS
c/o ISBS, 5824 N.E. Hassalo Street, Portland, OR 97213

A catalogue record for this title is available
from the British Library.

ISBN 1–85182–607–6 hbk
ISBN 1–85182–602–5 pbk

This book is published with the active support of

Dublin Corporation
Bardas Átha Cliath

Printed in Ireland
by Betaprint, Dublin.

Contents

List of contributors

PHILOMENA CONNOLLY is an archivist in the National Archives of Ireland.

SEÁN DUFFY is a Fellow of Trinity College, Dublin and Chairman of the Friends of Medieval Dublin.

MARGARET GOWEN is an archaeologist and a Director of Margaret Gowen and Co. Ltd.

BENEDIKT HALLGRÍMSSON is an Associate Professor in the Department of Cell Biology and Anatomy, University of Calgary, Canada.

JAMES LYDON is a Fellow Emeritus of Trinity College, Dublin, where he held the Lecky Chair of Modern History.

ANN LYNCH is a Senior Archaeologist with Dúchas: the Heritage Service.

JESSICA MCMORROW has recently graduated in history from the University of Washington, Seattle.

AILBHE MACSHAMHRÁIN lectures in the Department of History at NUI, Maynooth.

CONLETH MANNING is a Senior Archaeologist with Dúchas: the Heritage Service and President of the Royal Society of Antiquaries of Ireland.

BARRA Ó DONNABHÁIN lectures in the Department of Archaeology, University College, Cork.

CLAIRE WALSH is an archaeologist and a Director of Archaeological Projects Ltd.

BERNADETTE WILLIAMS holds a PhD from Trinity College, Dublin on the Franciscan annals of medieval Ireland.

Editor's preface

This volume contains the proceedings of the second annual Symposium on medieval Dublin, organised by the Friends of Medieval Dublin, and held in Trinity College on Saturday 13 May 2000. All the papers presented on that day are here published, and it would be difficult to overemphasise their importance. Margaret Gowen's paper is of historic significance: on the basis of radiocarbon dates from excavations at the site of the church of St Michael le Pole, she reveals the earliest evidence yet produced from the Christian era for human activity in the environs of the later town. Ann Lynch and Conleth Manning directed very substantial excavations in the mid-1980s on the site of what was for many centuries this country's most important building, Dublin Castle, and their findings are given a detailed airing here for the first time. Apart from the Castle, we know a great deal more about the town's earliest earthen defences, and the massive stone wall built by the Hiberno-Norse to encircle it, thanks to the excavations conducted by Claire Walsh at Ross Road, where she also uncovered the magnificent remains of the Anglo-Norman mural tower called after the lord of Trim, Geoffrey de Geneville, who died in 1314: these data too are presented below for the first time.

Geoffrey would have known well his namesake, Geoffrey Morton, mayor of Dublin in 1303–4, one of the most colourful and canny individuals ever to occupy the office; the ups and downs of his career are meticulously pieced together below by Dr Philomena Connolly. This can be done in part using fragments of information from chronicles written in the medieval town. Although versions of some of these have long been available in print there has been little 'scientific' analysis of precisely when, where and by whom they were compiled; the answers are now starting to emerge through the work of Dr Bernadette Williams, who demonstrates below the contribution to the annalistic record made by Dublin's Dominican friars. The town described in these annals bore little resemblance to that which the Anglo-Normans overran in 1170: Professor J.F. Lydon discusses below, however, the extent to which Anglo-Norman Dublin adapted the town's earlier Norse structures and system of administration. The classification of the ethnic background of the latter community, the 'biological identity' of Dublin's Ostmen, and their relationship to other Viking peoples elsewhere in Ireland and abroad, is the pioneering project upon which Drs Barra Ó Donnabháin and Benedikt Hallgrímsson have embarked, and they present some of their remarkable data in this volume.

Finally, we have found room for a further three important additional pieces not on the Symposium programme: Dr Ailbhe MacShamhráin presents a timely reassessment of the famous battle of Glenn Máma fought between

Brian Borúma and the Ostmen of Dublin on the very eve of the second millennium; Dr Barra Ó Donnabháin examines some intriguing evidence for the practice of cranial surgery in medieval Dublin; and Ms Jessica McMorrow has kindly given permission to print the text of an undergraduate essay produced under my supervision which provides a very valuable introduction to the lives and role of women in the medieval city.

The Friends of Medieval Dublin are very grateful for the financial assistance again provided by Dublin Corporation towards the costs of publication, and to the Department of Medieval History at Trinity College, Dublin, for covering the costs of the 2000 Symposium. As the City Manager, Mr John Fitzgerald, stated at the launch of *Medieval Dublin I*, we are all 'Friends of Medieval Dublin' now, but the editor would like to take this opportunity to thank individual Friends, in particular Terry Barry, Howard Clarke, Mary Deevy, George Eogan, Stephen Harrison, Helen Kehoe, and Stuart Kinsella, all of whom contributed to the planning and/or running of the Symposium, and Linzi Simpson, who also helped enormously in the editing of the archaeological papers. Eamonn McEneaney of the Waterford Museum of Treasures kindly facilitated with the cover illustration, and, finally, Michael Adams of Four Courts Press has been as supportive as ever, and clever enough to pass on the lion's share of this year's work to the ever-efficient Martin Fanning.

SEÁN DUFFY
Chairman
Friends of Medieval Dublin

Paddy Healy: an appreciation

Paddy Healy, archaeologist, local historian and friend, has died after a long life devoted to Ireland's past. Through his work on archaeological excavations in Dublin city and elsewhere, his meticulous collection of information, his support of various societies and his encouragement to younger generations, his influence has been widespread and invaluable.

Born in Canada of Irish emigrant parents, Paddy moved with his family to Dublin at the age of five. After schooling in Haddington Road and Marino he studied building construction in Bolton Street College where his subjects included land surveying and technical drawing, both of which were to prove important in his later career. Following his graduation he worked as a silkscreen printer in Modern Display Artists while he took night classes under Sean Keating at the National College of Art.

During the Emergency Paddy served in the army, following which he worked as a painter and decorator for a time. An important change came in 1949 when he joined the staff of the Land Commission as a surveyor. After eight years with the Land Commission he moved to work with the Forestry Division, again as a surveyor.

Since his teenage years, Paddy had been interested in history and archaeology, initially in the Dublin area and later throughout the country. His years as a surveyor afforded him the opportunity to get to know the antiquities of the Irish countryside first hand and his professional eye ensured that he understood their layout and construction. He took his interest further in his spare time, joining the Royal Society of Antiquaries of Ireland in 1950 and in 1952 he began to attend Professor Sean P. Ó Ríordáin's lectures in archaeology in University College, Dublin as an occasional student. He joined the UCD Archaeological Society, becoming its Vice-President, and here he met many fellow students who were to become his friends and colleagues of later years.

His contact with the college led him to work as part of Professor Ó Ríordáin's team on the excavation of the Rath of the Synods at Tara during his annual holidays from his surveying job. Here he quickly found a niche using his skills as a surveyor and draughtsman while building up excavation experience. In the summer of 1967 he joined Breandán Ó Ríordáin's team on the second excavation at High Street in Dublin. At this stage Paddy made a major decision to abandon the security of his job with the Forestry Division to work full-time on archaeological excavations, despite the lack of certainty that work would always be available. Hence, in April 1968, he became a full-time member of the excavation team at High Street as chief surveyor and draughtsman. He went on to work on excavations at Winetavern Street in 1969, Christchurch Place between 1972 and 1979 and, from 1976, Fishamble Street.

When the work on the Wood Quay site became controversial, Paddy stood firmly on the side of archaeology. His quiet but determined manner was a great source of encouragement to his colleagues as he sat in on the Wood Quay site, and he was the author of a poem written about the controversy and sold to raise funds for the campaign.

During the 1970s Paddy Healy acted as a contract archaeologist providing advice and working on excavations. Most importantly, he provided lists of monuments and sites of archaeological interest in Dublin county in the mid-1970s to assist in the preparation of the county development plan and the action area plans which proceeded the development of the western new towns of Tallaght, Lucan/Clondalkin and Blanchardstown. These lists were major works involving detailed knowledge of published and unpublished information and needing close familiarity with the monuments on the ground.

In more recent years Paddy continued to work on excavations, including those at the Viking cemetery at Islandbridge in Dublin and the nearby Bully's Acre at Kilmainham.

Over the years he had written papers and articles for a variety of journals and other publications including several in which he described for the first time archaeological monuments and artefacts which he had discovered. Some of these were early grave slabs from the Rathdown area of south Dublin and north Wicklow and these became the topic for his MA thesis presented to the National University of Ireland, Galway under the supervision of Professor Etienne Rynne.

Paddy, in turn, was the subject of a publication when no less than twenty-nine colleagues and friends contributed papers in his honour for publication in a book *Dublin and beyond the Pale*, edited by Con Manning.

Paddy's involvement with societies and other organisations was never passive and amongst those to benefit greatly from his membership were the Old Dublin Society, the Royal Society of Antiquaries of Ireland, the Dublin Archaeological Society, Friends of Medieval Dublin, the Irish Architectural Archive and the Rathmichael Historical Society.

Paddy Healy was laid to rest on 11 December 2000 in the cemetery at Mount Venus in the Dublin Mountains, close to historical and archaeological sites that he had investigated and overlooking the city which he had loved so much.

ROB GOODBODY

(This appreciation first appeared in *The Irish Times* on 29 January 2001; the Friends of Medieval Dublin wish to record their gratitude to the latter and to the author for permission to reprint it here.)

Excavations at the site of the church and tower of St Michael le Pole, Dublin

MARGARET GOWEN

I'm down in a hole at St Michael le Pole
Where scientific research has just started
But all I can find is a rare peace of mind
And the bones of the faithful departed.

(written in 1981 by Paddy Healy,
to whom this paper is dedicated)

ABSTRACT

This paper describes the results of a limited pre-development excavation undertaken in 1981 on the site of the church and graveyard of St Michael le Pole, at Ship Street, Dublin 2. The site is perhaps best known for the confusion surrounding the tradition that it once possessed Dublin's only Round Tower, so famously illustrated by Gabriel Beranger in 1766. Six locations were the subject of test excavation. One of these revealed the partial remains of the twelfth-century church and was extended during the excavation to expose and record the surviving fabric of the church, which was found to incorporate the foundations of an integral Round Tower-type belfry. Numerous burials were also revealed. A small number of these, along with additional evidence for activity, were found to pre-date the church. Finds included a fragment of a jet bracelet and a glass bead droplet, both probably of Early Christian date, together with a range of medieval and post-medieval ceramics and other small finds from the graveyard soil.

INTRODUCTION

The site of the church and graveyard of St Michael le Pole lies outside the enclosed medieval walled town to the southwest of Dublin Castle and to the northwest of the large, early ecclesiastical enclosure defined on its western side by Stephen Street (fig. 1, after Clarke 1978). The site is bounded by Ship Street Great, Ship Street Little, Bride Street, Chancery Lane and Golden Lane (NGR O15233; fig. 2). The excavation work was undertaken in 1980 by a group of ten

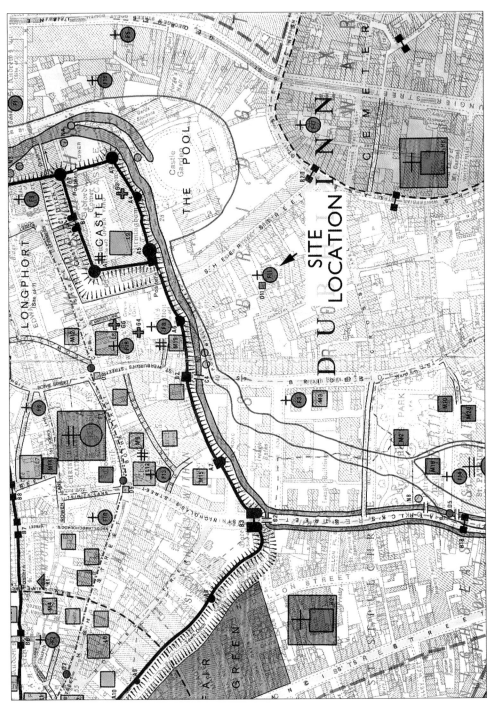

1 Site location placed on Clarke's map of medieval Dublin (1978).

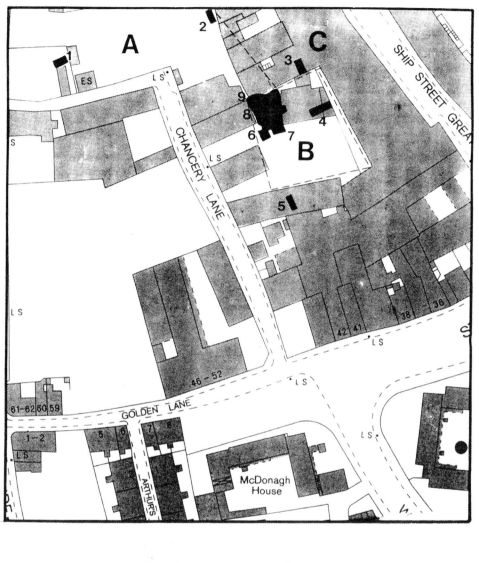

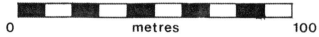

2 Site location and cutting layout.

freelance archaeologists who had all worked on the excavations at Wood Quay and Fishamble Street. It was conducted under licence, held by Kieran Campbell, to the then National Monuments Branch of the Office of Public Works (licence ref. E217) on behalf of Dodder Properties Holdings Limited to fulfil the requirements of the planning authority in advance of proposed development. On completion, the remains of the church and associated features were covered with heavy plastic sheeting, the burials were reinterred within the church foundation walls and the site was backfilled. The portion of the site that possesses the remains of the church and associated features has remained undeveloped to this day and is located to the north and west of the Woodchester Buildings on Stephen Street and Ship Street Great. On completion of analysis and recording, the finds (E217;1–921) were deposited with the National Museum of Ireland.

In the following text, the test excavation cuttings, which did not produce evidence directly related to the church, are described in summary only. Each produced evidence of an unrelated nature. The focus of the paper is on the remains of the twelfth-century church, the important evidence for pre-church activity on the site and evidence that can be linked to historical records.

HISTORICAL BACKGROUND

There are few records relating to the history of the site of the church and graveyard of St Michael le Pole prior to the late seventeenth century, but earlier references do exist and these have been researched by Simpson (2000, 17–19). There are several seventeenth-century and later descriptions of the church and tower on the site, though these are not all in agreement. As a consequence, there was some confusion, and debate, about the nature and date of the tower from that time until excavation revealed its foundations.

The church of St Michael le Pole was located in the southern suburb, outside the city walls. The toponymic *le Pole* or 'the pool' refers to the dark pool, or *Dubhlinn*, that gave its name to Dublin city. This was a large natural pool formed by the tidal action of the river Poddle, remnants of which can be seen on Speed's map of Dublin, dated 1610. This pool was evidently a very important topographical feature, naming the city but also naming many of the major buildings in the southern suburb. These buildings include the Pole Gate (the mural tower located in the middle of Werburgh Street), the Pole Mills, St Brigit of the pool and St Michael le Pole.

The pool appears to have been associated with the ecclesiastical centre *Dubhlinn*, which took its name from the pool and was presumably located close by. Contemporary documentary sources record the deaths of 'abbots' of Dubhlinn in the Annals of the Four Masters in AD 650 and 785 (O'Donovan 1851), well before the documented arrival of the Vikings in AD 841. The pool was located at the southern side of Dublin Castle, in what is now the castle gardens, very close to the site of the church of St Michael le Pole (see fig. 1 and Clarke 1977, 35). Excavations by Simpson (2000, 14) on the site of the new Chester Beatty Library found evidence of a post-medieval quarry which, significantly, was backfilled with layers of silt, probably original pool deposits. The site of the early ecclesiastical enclosure at Dublin is not known. The curving pattern of Stephen Street, Whitefriar Street and Peter Row, however, is thought possibly to reflect the outline of an ecclesiastical enclosure, removed on its eastern side. Until now, limited test excavation in this area has not produced evidence for early monastic activity (Simpson 2000, 11–19). However, very recent test excavations by Martin Reid and Franc Myles on two small sites on Stephen Street have yielded evidence for burial in these areas (pers. comm.).

The excavations described in this paper identified two phases of pre-Norman activity, the earliest of which suggests activity in the area prior to the arrival of the Vikings in Dublin in AD 841 and the establishment of a presence in Dublin on the banks of the 'Black Pool'. The second phase of activity is also dated to before the twelfth century, suggesting the use of the site when Viking Dublin was at the height of its power.

Early Christian monasteries in Ireland are generally dedicated to their founders, and while the founder of the monastic site at Dublin is not known, O'Donovan has suggested that it was St Mac Táil, a bishop of Old Kilcullen, Co. Kildare (Little 1951, 2). The church may subsequently have been rededicated to St Michael by the incoming Anglo-Normans in the late twelfth century. O'Donovan gives two reasons for this suggestion: the first is the similarity in the names Mac Táil and Michael (but it should be noted that this was not common practice: other churches rededicated by the Normans were dedicated to saints with entirely different names to the founders' names), and the second is a reference in the Annals of the Four Masters in AD 937 to the foreigners deserting Áth Cliath 'by the help of God and Mac Táil.' From this, O'Donovan infers that Mac Táil was the patron saint of the city (Little 1951, 110), though it is much more likely that the saint was mentioned in this instance because he was perceived as having been responsible for the misfortune that had befallen the Dubliners because of their raid on Kilcullen recorded in the same annals for the previous year. There were, in fact, three bishops with that name in the seventh century in Old Kilcullen. The one suggested in connection with this site of St Michael le Pole is Denghus Mac Táil, a nephew or grandnephew of St Pappin of Santry. Clarke (1977, 39) states that Denghus Mac Táil is known to have been alive in AD 650. It is possible that he could have founded the monastery of *Dubhlinn* early in the seventh century. Alternatively, the dedication to St Michael could have been original, as Clarke has demonstrated that there is evidence to suggest that a cult of St Michael was developing in Ireland by the eighth century (Clarke 1977, 39).

Also of relevance is the concentration of churches with pre-Norman and possibly Gaelic dedications near the excavated site; these churches include St Brigit's, St Kevin's and St Patrick's (de Paor 1958, 53). Although contemporary, St Michael le Pole does not appear to have been as important a church as St Brigit's, St Kevin's and St Patrick's in Anglo-Norman Dublin. There were, in fact, two churches dedicated to St Michael in Dublin: St Michael le Pole and St Michael Archangel. St Michael Archangel was located on the west side of Christ Church cathedral and was attached to the priory of the Holy Trinity (McNeill 1950, 7). Even as long ago as the sixteenth century, there was a degree of confusion between both churches. This was demonstrated when Archbishop Alen added 'of Shep street' in the margin of the register of the priory of the Holy Trinity to distinguish between the two churches (McNeill 1950, 48).

Few documentary sources from the medieval period mention the church of St Michael le Pole. A church of St Michael appears on a list of the taxation of the prebends of St Patrick's cathedral dated 1227 (McNeill 1950, 47). A later list of possessions does not list the church (McEnery 1886-96, no. 150), and, unlike St Brigit's, there are no references to St Michael le Pole as a parish church. Although the southern suburb was divided into the parishes of St Michael le Pole and St Brigit, the latter, held by the priory of the Holy Trinity (Christ Church) prior to the arrival of the Anglo-Normans in 1170, was the dominant church (McNeill 1950, 29). St Michael le Pole does not appear to have been wholeheartedly adopted by the Anglo-Normans, although it was in use throughout the medieval period. In 1294, it appears on a new taxation list for the diocese of Dublin under the 'Deanery of Christianity,' along with St Olave's, St Catherine's, St James's, St Mary's del Dam, and St Peter's of the Hill. St Peter's, St Mary's, St Olave's and St James's were also in decline, as they were considered 'not sufficient for the charges.' Interestingly, the churches of St Michael le Pole and St Catherine were listed as 'not worth the service of a chaplain' (McEnery 1886-96, no. 150), suggesting that a chaplain, rather than a resident parish priest, served St Michael le Pole. In the fifteenth century, the sites of St Michael le Pole and St Brigit's are listed together, suggesting that the parishes may have been amalgamated. The lands around the site were held by the priory of the Holy Trinity (Christ Church) prior to the arrival of the Anglo-Normans in 1170 (McNeill 1950, 29). The landholding that included St Brigit's had been received from the ruling Hiberno-Scandinavian family in Dublin, the Meic Turcaill, suggesting that it controlled the ecclesiastical holding of that church.

The earliest record of the church and tower on the site is John Speed's map of Dublin dated 1610 (fig. 3), where the church is depicted with an adjoining tower at its west end. However, Speed depicts all his churches in this way. Bernard de Gomme's map of 1673 (fig. 4) depicts a rectangular enclosure with a freestanding tower, but no church is shown. At that time, the Ship Street area was extensively built up. The parish was united with that of St Brigit's in 1682,

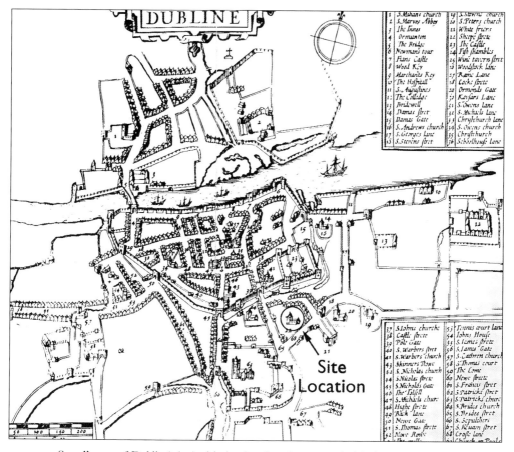

3 Speed's map of Dublin (1610) with the church and tower marked '22'.

and both parishes and the parish of St Stephen's were all treated as one parish
in the Hearth Roll of 1666. As early as 1615, all three parishes were being
served by the same curate. The church was closed by the dean and chapter of
St Patrick's in 1682, and the site was granted to a Dr John Jones in 1706 for a
school on condition ' that Dr Jones do not pull down the monument or tower of
St Michael of Paul's near his schoolhouse in Sheepe Street', suggesting that the
tower was freestanding. The association with St Patrick's at the time may have
led to the incorporation of several early grave slabs into the fabric of
St Patrick's cathedral. It is recorded that Dr Jones built a 'large and lofty
schoolroom with three small rooms at the end and a flight of stairs in the tower
leading to the two upper rooms (*Irish Builder* 1870, 113); the building is marked
on Rocque's map of 1756 (fig. 5).

    An entry in the *Free Press* of 15 August 1778 describes how a Mr Evans
succeeded Dr Jones as master of St Michael's School and goes on to say that the

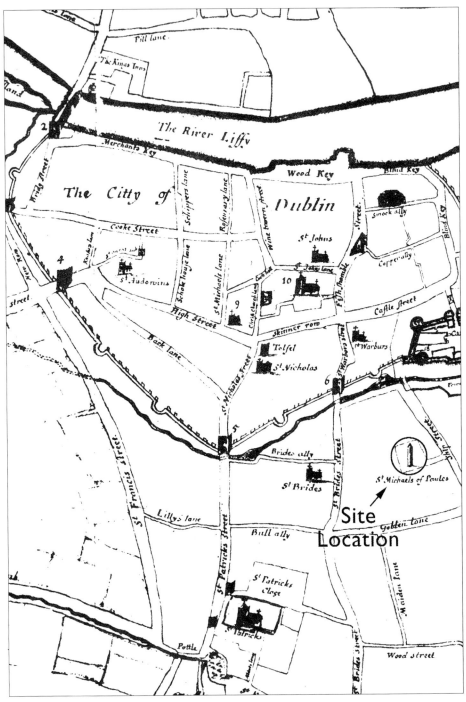

4 De Gomme's map of Dublin (1673) showing a free-standing Round Tower on the site.

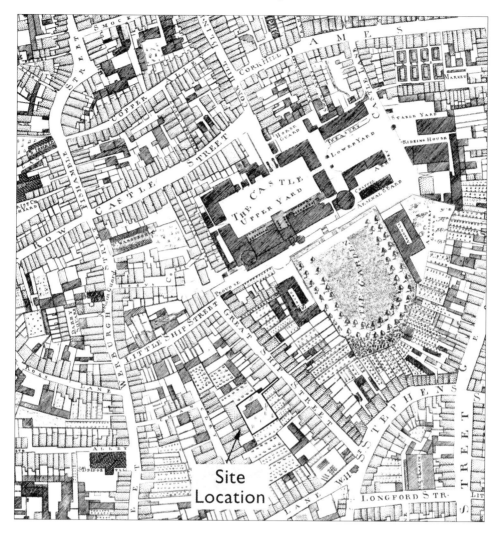

5 Rocque's map of Dublin (1756) showing the ground plan of the first schoolhouse on the site surrounded by a graveyard.

'ruin' of the tower 'was preserved about forty years ago … when it was scaffolded from the ground and well primed with lime and stone within and without, which thorough repairing ever since preserved it from falling'. In 1775, a storm damaged the tower and 'it threatened ruin not only to the schoolhouse but to the neighbouring houses in Chancery Lane'. It was partly demolished 'to the level of the schoolhouse roof', the stones being 'applied to rebuilding the

The Round Tower at Michael a Pools Church near Ship street Dublin, called Michael a Pullibus. Drawn from a Sketch taken A.D. 1751, for J. Grogan Esqr. when a Fellow Commoner in Trinity College. The view looks down Little Ship street towards the Castle, part of which Birmingham Tower appears in the distance.

W. B.

6 Drawing of the tower, dated to 1751.

ruinous wall on the north and east side of the churchyard' (*Irish Builder* 1870, 113). Its removal caused such dissatisfaction in the parish that 'an old inhabitant' wrote on the subject in the *Free Press* (15 August 1778). Before the storm damage and subsequent demolition, two drawings were made of the tower. The earliest, dated 1751, was the work of an unknown artist undertaken for a commoner at Trinity College named J. Grogan (fig. 6). The later drawing by Gabriel Beranger, dated 1766, is the best known and most informative (fig. 7) and depicts the schoolhouse with the tower seeming to break through its roof. At a later date, Beranger described the tower as follows:

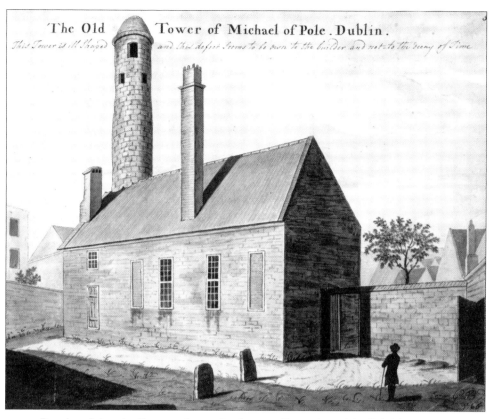

The Old Tower of Michael of Pole. Dublin.

This Tower is ill Shaped and this defect seems to be own to the builder and not to the injury of Time

7 Drawing of the schoolhouse and tower (as shown on Rocque's map) by Gabriel Beranger, dated to 1766.

> ... situated in a yard, at the rear of some houses on the west side of Ship Street, near the castle; it was reckoned one of the most antient [sic] among this kind of structures, as its walls were not perpendicular in line, but so ill-constructed as if the builder had been ignorant of the use of the plumb-line; it was encompassed by a building which was formerly a chapel, but was afterwards used as a schoolhouse; in a great storm we had some years ago [1775] it was much damaged that to prevent accidents its fall might occasion, it was demolished, and this few months after I had drawn it [a later drawing of 1776] this I saved it from oblivion (Beranger in Wilde 1870, 44–5).

Beranger's drawings were later to cause considerable controversy as to whether the tower was freestanding or a belfry tower within the church.

In 1787, the schoolhouse was converted into an almshouse for the widows of St Bride's (Brigit's) parish. It may have been further rebuilt in the nineteenth century, when it appears to have been used as part of a residence for the schoolteachers of St Bride's (Brigit's) parish. Sir William Wilde described the buildings in 1870 as being 'exactly as represented in the drawing [Beranger] of 1776 and the schoolhouse with its tall chimneys presents few alterations'. The tower was completely gone at this stage, and Wilde continues as follows: 'The site of the tower is, however, occupied by a comparatively modern brick building in which reside the teachers. I cannot find in it any trace of the tower' (Wilde 1870, 46–7). Burial had ceased in the graveyard by 1830, when it was 'in a miserable state of filth and decay' (Wilde 1870, 46–7). By 1898, there were only ten tombstones in the graveyard 'over against the side wall of the old church or schoolhouse' (*JAPMD*, IV, 1900). The final phase of building on the site was the construction of a new red-brick schoolhouse for St Bride's Protestant National School in around 1900. Two further tombstones disappeared during this construction work (*JAPMD*, VI, 1906). In 1944, the school was closed and the yard was taken over by Dockerell's. It was demolished in 1975, and the area was cleared for car parking.

THE EXCAVATION

Introduction The site on which the pre-development archaeological evaluation was conducted was large and roughly L-shaped, extending from a narrow entrance at Ship Street to Chancery Lane towards Bride Street (fig. 2). Although largely cleared, it had several standing sheds on its western and southern sides. The supposed site of the church and graveyard, as depicted on Rocque's map (fig. 5), was located in its 'land-locked' southern sector. The focus of the investigation was to establish the nature and extent of the remains of the church, Round Tower, graveyard and any associated remains and to establish in a preliminary fashion the nature of the below-ground stratigraphy in other areas of the site. For this reason, the investigation examined three distinct areas, each with quite different archaeological remains.

The Cuttings
- Cuttings 1 and 2 were opened to record the nature and depth of archaeological deposits at the northern end of the site; Cutting 3 was opened within a garage building as close to Ship Street as possible; and Cuttings 4–9 concentrated on establishing the location, nature and extent of the church and the graveyard on the eastern side of the site. Cuttings 1 and 2 measured 2m by 5m and were located 55m apart. They revealed an accumulation of over 1.50m of medieval soils dating from the post-Norman period up to the seventeenth century beneath 4m of loose rubble.
- Cutting 3 measured 2m by 5m and was located within a shed leading towards the entrance from the Ship Street side of the site, just outside the supposed extent of the graveyard. The floor level of the shed was 1m lower

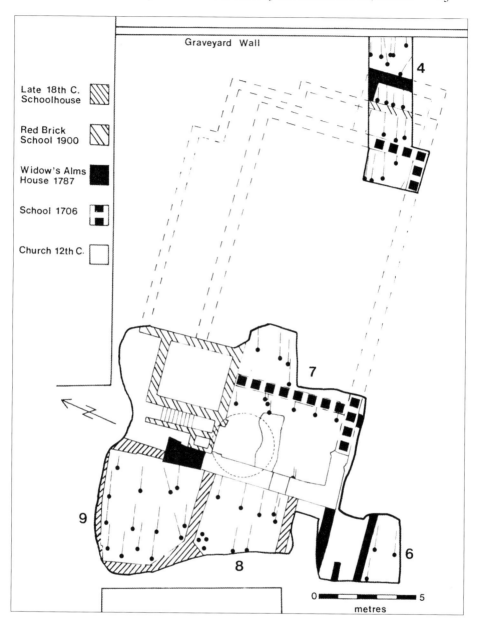

8 Features and burials revealed in Cuttings 4–9, showing the surviving fabric of the church and later buildings.

than the ground (of the graveyard) to the south. The cutting revealed a backfilled rubbish pit cut into truncated post-Norman clays found beneath 1.50m of rubble.

- As expected, Cutting 5 was found to lie outside the graveyard and revealed an accumulation of 0.65m of post-Norman clays overlain by red-brick walls of late seventeenth- to early eighteenth-century date. Some of these walls could be related to the two properties to the south of the graveyard shown on Rocque's map.

- Cuttings 4 and 6 and the conjoined Cuttings 7, 8 and 9 were opened on the supposed site of the church and later buildings. Cutting 4 was opened at the eastern side of the site, extending from the graveyard wall (which corresponded with that depicted on Rocque's map) across the foundations of three post-medieval buildings, all of which were identified (see fig. 8). Eighteen burials were encountered in the cutting; the lowermost did not provide definite evidence for activity of twelfth-century date or earlier. Cutting 6 was opened to the southwest of the church around the spot indicated as 'Site of Ecclesiastical Round Tower' on the first edition (1837) 1:1,056 map of the Ordnance Survey, but no trace of the tower was found.

- Cutting 7 was located to coincide with measurements made, on the basis of Beranger's drawing, from the southeast corner of the schoolhouse remains revealed in Cutting 4. It was extended by the addition of Cuttings 8 and 9. These cuttings revealed the west wall and a portion of the south wall of the church, the supposed foundation of the tower and coherent evidence for a sequence of activity incorporating pre-church occupation and burial, a lintel grave accommodated by, and recessed into, the twelfth-century church wall and a series of later features and burial activity from the twelfth century to the final use of the site by a school in 1906.

The phases of activity on the site Excavation around the west wall of the twelfth-century church revealed five phases of archaeological activity, including two distinct phases of pre-church activity:

- Phase 1 was the occupation of the site before the construction of the twelfth-century stone church. This phase was represented by a group of shallow gullies, cut features and post holes, some of a substantial size, cut through very thin clay deposits and all sealed by subsequent deposits of clay, ash and animal bone.

- Phase 2 was represented by the layers of clays containing ash, mortar and butchered animal bone that sealed the Phase 1 features. Some of these clays were in turn cut by burials that pre-dated the church and were disturbed and cut by the church's foundations. A lintel grave, the only stone-lined grave found during the investigation, was also cut through at its western end by the church wall.

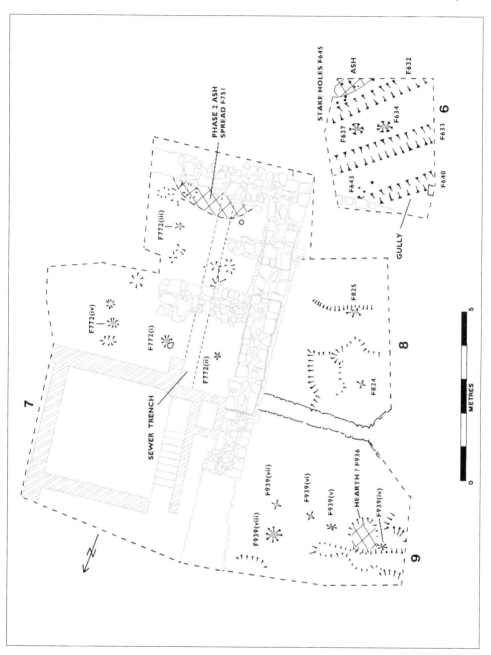

9 Plan of the Phase 1–2 features.

- Phase 3 represents the period between 1100 and the fourteenth century. This is the period in which the church and tower were constructed and in use. The church and tower appear to have been constructed some time around the twelfth century and certainly saw use, if marginal, through to the fourteenth century, after which the western doorway was blocked and no longer appears in the documentary records.
- Phase 4 represents the period between the fourteenth century and the seventeenth century. It appears that the church interior may have become derelict after the fourteenth century, allowing the importation of a soil and its use for burial in what appears to have been a general use of the site as a graveyard. Certainly, burial was as intense within the area enclosed by the church as it was outside the structure. The site may well have continued in use in this way until the seventeenth century, when the walls of the church building and the tower were evidently in sufficiently good structural order to be used as the basis for the construction of the first school on the site.
- Phase 5 represents the period 1683–1981. Three phases of reuse followed the closure of the church: Phase 5a represents the development of the church as a schoolhouse in 1706, Phase 5b relates to the change of use of the building as a widow's almshouse from 1787 and Phase 5c relates to the construction of a new red-brick schoolhouse on the site in *c.*1900.

Phase 1 (pre-church activity)

The pre-church activity on the site was identified in Cuttings 6–9 (fig. 9). This phase of activity, while enigmatic, was represented by well-defined, if shallow, linear gullies and post holes, some of which were stone-packed. The features were discovered both within and outside the west wall of the church and were not found in Cutting 4. By association, they appear to be coeval with the site of the later church. The gullies appeared not to be of structural derivation.

Post holes Fourteen post holes (F772i–xiv) were identified in the area around the west wall of the church, and several further post holes and shallow post hole-like features were revealed in Cuttings 6, 8 and 9 to the west of the remains of the church (pls 1 and 2). In Cutting 7, three of these post holes (F772i, ii and iii; fig. 9) were substantial in size, i.e., up to 0.45–0.50m diameter and 0.40m deep, and were filled with packing stones. Not enough were located within the excavated area to reveal a pattern that might lead to a structural interpretation, though the three found to the northeast of the church wall in Cutting 7 (F772i, ii and iv) formed an east–west alignment, and another three followed a similar, if less strong, alignment at a distance of some 4.50m to the south.

In Cutting 6, two post holes, F634 (0.45m diameter and 0.35m deep) and F637 (0.30m diameter and 0.28m deep), were revealed in association with a number of small stake holes (F643) at the north of the cutting and a second

Plate 1 View of the west wall of the twelfth-century church, the foundation of the tower, the lintel grave, grave-cuts and the pre-church post holes.

Plate 2 Detail of the west wall of the church, the tower foundation and the lintel grave.

cluster of stake holes (F645) associated with a spread of ash (F628). The ash, which occurred at the southeast end of the cutting, filled a shallow depression, and the excavated portion suggested that it formed part of a hearth. A fragment of gold wire (E217:224) was retrieved from the fill of F634.

In Cutting 8, two post holes, F828 and F829, were revealed. F828 was a substantial stone-packed post hole with a maximum diameter of approximately 0.40m and a depth of over 0.20m. F829 was smaller (approximate diameter of 0.20–0.25m) and shallower than F829 and did not have any stone packing.

In Cutting 9, there was one particularly large post hole, F939viii, which measured 0.50m in diameter and over 0.20m in depth. It was associated with four further post holes with an east–west alignment: F939iv, v, vi and vii, which had diameters of 0.24m 0.23m, 0.33m and 0.28m, respectively, and depths ranging from 0.080m to 0.15m. Close to these post holes, and possibly associated with them, was a hearth (F936). This hearth measured over 1.0m in diameter and was composed of ash overlying a thick charcoal spread. A sample of this charcoal yielded a radiocarbon determination (Queen's University Belfast) of 1275 ± 50 BP (before the present), providing a date range of AD 675–779 (1 sigma; 68% probability) or a wider range of AD 663–872 (2 sigma; 95.4% probability) for this phase of activity across the site.

Gullies Three V-shaped gullies (F632, F633 and F640) were defined in Cutting 6. They ran east–west and measured 0.40–0.60m in width and just 0.070m in depth. Further depressions and one further linear feature were revealed in Cuttings 8 and 9 but were not so clearly defined. The gullies in Cutting 6 did not appear to have a structural association and may represent traces of cultivation activity. In contrast, a shallow east–west depression, F940, immediately to the north of the east–west post hole alignment in Cutting 9 could have a structural association.

Thin lenses of archaeologically altered clays (F646, F761, F827, F820 and F947, not illustrated) were associated with these features in all cuttings. These lenses were similar to sterile boulder clay, but some were greyer in colour and contained charcoal flecks and some insubstantial and very thin spreads of ash, none of which could be regarded as *in situ* burning or hearth features. Only one spread of ash, F936, located in Cutting 9, could be regarded as representing a possible hearth, although the spread partially exposed in Cutting 6 may also represent a hearth. The spread in Cutting 9 measured roughly 1m in diameter and had a roughly centrally placed flat-stone slab, 0.28m long.

Phase 2 (pre-church activity)
Sealing and overlying the Phase 1 features and the associated thin lenses of clay soils in Cuttings 6, 7, 8 and 9 was a well-defined composite deposit of friable humic clays interleaved with thick, apparently dumped, ash spreads (fig. 9).

This deposit had one very substantial hearth, F766 (below), and some possible, though ill-defined hearths. While it was extensively cut through by many of the later features and burials, it was clearly identified as part of the same stratigraphic sequence of activity in all cuttings. The deposit was roughly 50-100mm thick, appeared to represent a single sequence of intense activity and largely survived in the area around the church and school walls. It was best defined in Cutting 7 but also survived in a fragmentary manner in Cuttings 6, 8 and 9. In Cutting 8, the spread, measuring roughly 2.0m by 0.6m, was evidently cut by the church wall.

The most notable feature of this Phase 2 deposit was the presence of lime, and possibly mortar, which gave some lenses a distinct greenish hue. In each of the excavated areas, a great number and density of fragmented, butchered animal bones were recovered; much of the bone was also burnt. A small spread of mussel shells was also incorporated into the deposit in Cutting 6. A significant aspect of the bone content in the layer was the nature of its deposition. Many of the bone fragments were found at angular, rather than horizontal positions, indicating either a high level of disturbance and reworking or a simple consequence of a single episode of dumping. In Cutting 7, where the complex was best defined, it was cut through by a great number of later burials. On the northern side of the excavated area, where it was well-defined, it was associated with a large, 100mm-thick red ash spread, F766, which was underlain by a 20mm -thick layer of almost pure charcoal, F751. Both layers appeared to represent the remains of a substantial hearth, which had maximum dimensions of almost 3.0m by 1.50m within the excavated area.

While the combined, composite deposit clearly abutted or may have been cut by the church wall, the intensity of the activity and the high lime-content suggest a possible association with mortar production, and by further association the possible building of a stone structure in the vicinity. The intense activity represented by this deposit cannot be related to the construction of parts of the church itself, as the foundations of the church and Round Tower appear to cut through it in many instances. Its stratigraphic association with the well-defined pre-church lintel burial was unfortunately removed by disturbance caused by later burial activity, though one definite pre-church burial, F773, appeared to cut through the deposit. The date of this deposit is not defined in any manner other than that it postdates the Phase 1 activity and clearly either predates or is broadly contemporary with the construction of the church; however, it must relate to an earlier or different structure on or near the site.

The animal bone assemblage The animal bone assemblage from this deposit was analysed by Dr Finbar McCormick (Queen's University, Belfast), who described it as interesting, if small. The butchery marks, being made with a knife and a heavy instrument such as an axe, were similar to those on bones

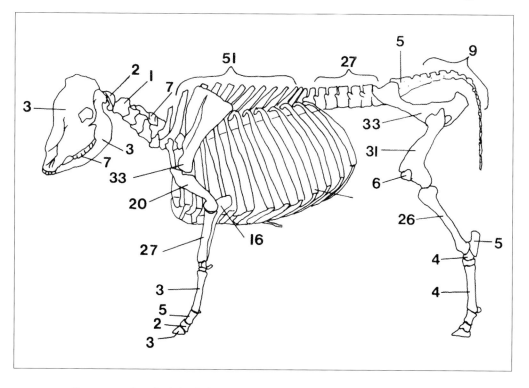

10 Frequency of cattle skeletal elements from a sample of the Phase 2 pre-church layer in Cutting 7: F722/728.

from Viking and other Early Christian sites. The waste elements of the carcass were, however, surprisingly underrepresented in the frequency of skeletal elements found (fig. 10). McCormick noted that, whereas samples from Early Christian and Viking sites indicate butchering *in situ*, the sample from the St Michael le Pole site suggested that the animals were slaughtered elsewhere on the site or that the meat was brought onto the site from outside. He made a very interesting observation that a late sixteenth-century English observer noted that, in Gaelic Elizabethan society, different portions of a cattle carcass were given to different members of the extended family. This observer noted that the head, tongue and feet were given to the smith and that the neck was given to the butcher. All these parts were underrepresented at the site, possibly indicating an early incidence of a practice of this sort. On a more general level, McCormick noted that the age/slaughter pattern was similar to that recorded in the pre-Norman levels at Fishamble Street and that it was very much at variance with that recorded on rural sites. This reinforces his view that urban livestock slaughter was managed on a different basis to that in rural areas during the pre-Norman period (McCormick 1984).

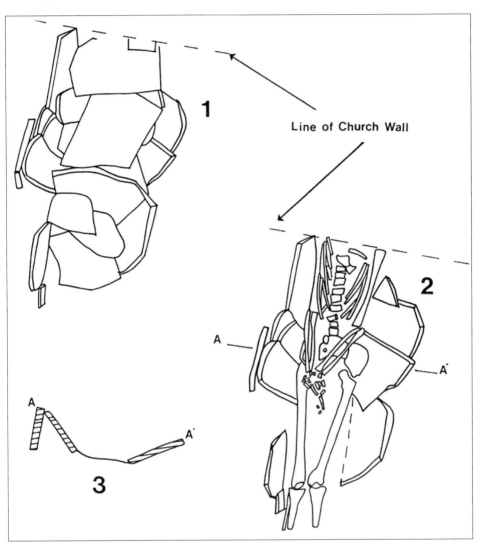

1

Line of Church Wall

2

3

11 Plan of the lintel grave and its burial.

The lintel grave F746 The removal of the lowest two burials, one of which (F767) had been cut through by the west wall of the church, from the south side of the church's western wall revealed a stone-lined and lintel-covered grave, the top of which was accommodated within the church wall and the end of which had been cut through by a modern sewer trench (fig.11; pls 1–3). It survived to a maximum 1.17m in length, extending from the wall face. The grave pit was lined with flat slabs, each measuring 0.25–0.30m deep and 10–15mm thick. The well-preserved, though friable, skeleton survived as a 0.17m long piece, covered

Plate 3 Detail of the burial within the lintel grave.

Plate 4 General view of the earliest level of burials in Cutting 6, to the west of the church wall.

from its scapulas by the church wall and cut at shin level by the trench for the modern sewer pipe. The hands were crossed at pelvis level. The overlying grave (F767) had been cut through by the wall at the point of the first vertebra above the sacrum. Both appeared to have been inserted through the Phase 2 clay deposit described above, thereby dismissing the possible interpretation that the mortar-rich clay with all its food debris might represent a construction level for the church. The later burial (F767) was found with coffin nails along with some very decayed fragments of a wooden coffin. A femur from the lintel grave produced a radiocarbon determination of 955 ± 100 BP (before the present), yielding a calibrated date of AD 999–1189 (1 sigma) or AD 895–1269 (2 sigma), which places the burial date very close to the supposed date of the construction of the church in the early twelfth century.

Other early burials Two further burials (F770 and F773) in Cutting 7 were disturbed by or underlay the church wall, and two burials in Cutting 8 (F820 and F821) were aligned on a slightly different orientation and cut through the thin, Phase 1, spreads of ash and clay. These burials appeared during excavation to pre-date the church, though this cannot be proved to be the case. In Cuttings 6 and 9, no burials could be ascribed a pre-church date with certainty, though F944 was laid at a slightly different alignment to the other burials in the locality

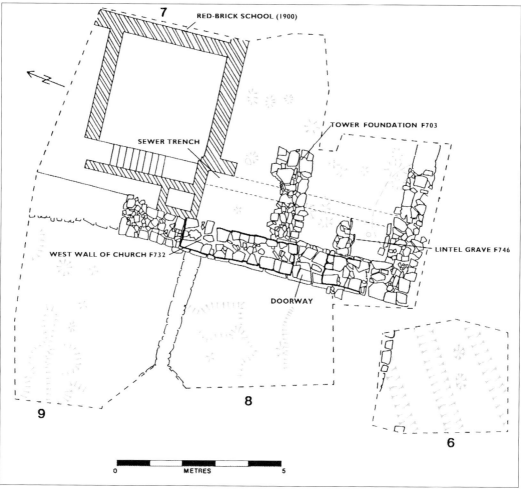

12 Plan of Phase 3 features: the west wall of the twelfth century church; the lintel grave; and the tower foundation.

and was found at the basal level of the excavation cutting through to a level of 0.50m into the basal sterile boulder clay (pl. 4). It should, perhaps be stated that there was no evident phasing in the presentation of the burials as excavated. No burials could, with certainty, be assigned to either Phase 1 or 2, as none could be said to have been clearly sealed by deposits relating to these two earliest phases.

Phase 3 (1100 to fourteenth century)
The church and tower The focus of the investigation on the overall site was to establish the location, nature and extent of any remains of the church and Round Tower (figs 8 and 12; pls 1–3 and pl. 5). Cuttings 7, 8 and 9 were positioned to correspond with the best fit that could be achieved to marry the

Plate 5 Detail of the interior elevation of the west wall of the church illustrating its plinth and blocked doorway.

information on Rocque's map and the position indicated on the first edition of the Ordnance Survey. The excavation in these conjoined cuttings succeeded in establishing that the west wall of the masonry church was the only portion of it to survive. The excavation of Cuttings 8 and 9 clearly indicated that the site did possess the foundations of a free-standing Round Tower close to the western end of the church, as surmised on the basis of the two contemporary drawings. The basal foundation of an internal wall that has been interpreted as the foundation for an internal Round Tower–type belfry was found beneath a much later wall, F703.

Only the west wall of the church survived within the excavated area, and evidence from the adjacent areas excavated suggested that all trace of it had been removed by later buildings. The construction of the 1706 schoolhouse had destroyed the southwest corner, and, on the north side of the excavated area, the much later red-brick schoolhouse had obliterated all traces of the northwest corner. The western wall of the church survived as a 7.30m long, 0.90–0.95m wide section. It survived just one course above a well-defined external plinth of evenly cut, long flat stones that projected out by 100–150mm. The stones were remarkably consistent in size, measuring on average 0.35–0.50m in length, and each was 0.17–0.20m thick. The character of the masonry is best illustrated on Plate 5.

The wall above plinth level was constructed of mortar-bonded masonry, faced on both sides and possessing a heavily mortared, random rubble core – a construction method that was common in the twelfth and later centuries. The plinth was constructed of two courses of stone, beneath which was a rougher, clay-bonded foundation. The stones used on the plinth and wall differed and varied in size (pl. 2), the plinth and foundation having longer, flatter stones (0.35–0.50m long) with large interstices and an evidently more rough construction than the wall above plinth level. Although in general only one course survived, the masonry was characterized by more square and massive well-set blocks (0.25–0.35m wide to a maximum of 0.48m long and 0.25–0.30m high).

The doorway The blocked-up west doorway of the church was found to be slightly off centre (pl. 5). The blocking material was of very small cut stones on the exterior and two large, clay-bonded blocks on the interior face. A sherd of fourteenth-century pottery recovered from this clay may not date the actual blocking event but suggests that it occurred after that time. The doorway was 0.88m wide at its exterior and splayed slightly outwards towards the church interior. It was paved with three flat slabs (average 0.10m thick) on each side, with two smaller slabs in between. Large, blocky stones (0.20m by 0.20m) formed the basal course of the external jambs, and there was a slight, though noticeable inclination inwards.

The Round Tower During the excavation of the church interior, part of the basal foundation of an interior, clay-bonded wall placed at right angles to the church wall was revealed adjacent to the surviving western wall (pl. 2). The area had been very damaged, unfortunately, by the building of the twentieth-century red-brick schoolhouse and also by the insertion of a relatively modern sewer, the trench of which was 0.50–0.70m wide and ran parallel to the church wall at a distance of 1.20m. Burials to the north had also caused significant erosion of the wall's context and fabric. Where the sewer cut through the wall, only one course of stone survived.

What was most notable about this wall was that it had a straight, faced edge on its southern side similar in character to the masonry of the church wall foundations. Its northern face, however, formed a slight curve. However, as it survived only one course high where the curve occurred, it is perhaps dangerous to suggest that the foundation represents the interior of a structure with a slight interior curve. The wall was 0.8–1.10m wide and was 2.8m long, suggesting that the structure was roughly 3.7m square externally at basal level. The masonry survived to a maximum height of 0.6m, where it was keyed into the church wall masonry. Curiously, there was no evidence for a bonding scar above this level, suggesting that an internal doorway might have provided access to the tower interior at this location. Though the evidence is scant, and tenuous, this foundation has been interpreted as the foundation of an integral Round

Plate 6   Ferns, Co. Wexford, the closest surviving parallel to the plan arrangement at St. Michael le Pole

Tower–type belfry similar to those at the similarly dated twelfth-century churches at Ferns and Glendalough (see Plate 6 and discussion below).

Phase 4 *(fourteenth century to* 1706*)*

The graveyard wall, Cutting 4   The church and graveyard were surrounded by a wall of undetermined date (fig. 8). At the eastern end of Cutting 4, a standing red-brick and masonry wall was thought to form the graveyard boundary wall, as it coincided well with the position indicated on Rocque's map of 1756. Excavation revealed that it overlay substantial masonry foundations with a slight external base batter, which, unfortunately, was not fully investigated at the time for safety reasons. This wall, and its heavy masonry foundations, though thought to coincide with that depicted by Rocque (fig. 5), was found to overlie two burials, which, of course, indicates that the graveyard extended further to the east prior to its construction. Neither Speed's map nor de Gomme's map can be relied on for an accurate indication of the size of the graveyard prior to that time.

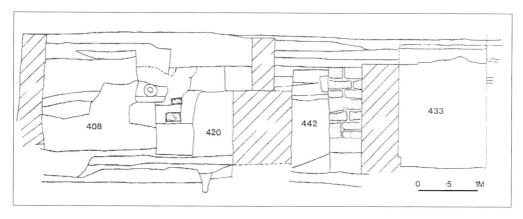

13   North-facing section of Cutting 4, illustrating the graveyard wall (F404) and the extent
     of disturbance of the graveyard soils which occurred across all excavated areas.

The burials Though mixed, the site appeared to have been used for burial purposes prior to the construction of the church and after the closure of the west door and the possible abandonment of the church as a place of worship. It was clear that the burials were interred in an imported clay soil, the ceramic content of which suggested a post-fourteenth-century date. No further phasing in the burial activity could be established with certainty, and there appeared to have been a relatively unbroken use of the site and the church interior until the building of the schoolhouse in 1706. The area outside the schoolhouse appears to have been used as a cemetery as late as 1830 (*Irish Builder* 1870, 113). Burials were revealed in Cuttings 4, 6, 7, 8 and 9. In all areas, the apparently imported graveyard soil was found to be extensively disturbed by later building activity and services. Many disarticulated skeletal bones were encountered in its uppermost levels. The interface between, on one hand, the soils that had been brought into the site for the purposes of burial and, on the other, the stratified pre-church clays was clearly defined in almost all the areas excavated (fig. 13). However, it was found that many relatively late burials cut through earlier interments without care. Clumsy attempts to re-inter disturbed bones or to place them to one side were encountered in some instances.

The only burials that could be dated with certainty were those that underlay, or were cut by, the church wall and hence pre-dated this phase. Others, because of their relatively good preservation and their evident insertion into soil possessing predominantly post-medieval ceramics, were clearly post-medieval in date. In all, ninety-two burials, including the pre-church burials, were found. Fifty-five were articulated and relatively complete. In some instances, the traces of coffins could be discerned as stains in the burial pit fill and by the presence of coffin nails and other coffin fittings. In some instances, shroud pins were also found. The best-preserved and evenly spaced burials were encountered in

Cutting 9 (pl. 4). The burial position was consistent where it could be determined accurately, with the hands crossed and placed in the pelvis region. No particular support or treatment of the skull position was noted in any of the burials. Because the excavation was conducted as a pre-development evaluation exercise, the burial remains were not retained for anatomical study. They were reinterred at the conclusion of the excavation in a position close to the church wall on its eastern side. After the excavation, the excavated church site was surrounded by a new, light, concrete block boundary wall, and its remains and those of the reinterred burials were preserved *in situ*.

One fragment of bone of great interest was retained for examination. It was a disarticulated fragment of a skull with a clean-cut circular disk removed from it. The fragment provided rare evidence for trepanation and is the subject of a special report (Ó Donnabháin, Chap. 5 below).

Phase 5 (1683–1981)

Phase 5a: The schoolhouse, 1706 The masonry walls of the 1706 schoolhouse were revealed in Cuttings 4 and 7, where its southern wall extended from and was keyed into the church wall (fig. 8). At this location, it had clearly been made from masonry derived from the church wall. It was of quite similar-looking construction but was only 0.8m wide (pl. 1). It is perhaps of interest that there was a slight continuity in the building style, in that the south wall of the school also possessed a slight plinth. An interior wall, which could have formed part of the later 1787 almshouse, ran parallel to the church wall some 3.20m to the east, where it survived just 0.38m high and was 0.58m thick. In Cutting 4, the east wall of the schoolhouse survived as a straight-sided, 0.62m wide, 1.95m high structure.

Phase 5b: The widow's almshouse, 1787 When the schoolhouse was adapted for use as an almshouse, an annexe was built on at the eastern side, as depicted on the first edition of the Ordnance Survey. The excavated remains were revealed in Cutting 4. Some adjustment to the structure also appeared to have occurred at the northwestern corner (fig. 8), where the church wall was augmented to form a new northwest corner for the building. The composition of the wall was largely of masonry, but there were red brick inclusions. It was just 2m long and roughly 0.9m wide. At around the same time, the building, incorporating the church wall, was extended westwards. In Cuttings 8 and 9, the red-brick walls and bases of two rooms with back-to-back corner fireplaces appeared to form part of the almshouse or a later extension.

Phase 5c: The 1900 schoolhouse The 1900 schoolhouse was made of smooth, well-fired industrial red brick, and portions of its tiled floor survived in Cutting 4. At the north of Cutting 7, the building was found to have removed all trace of the earlier structures, including the early church wall.

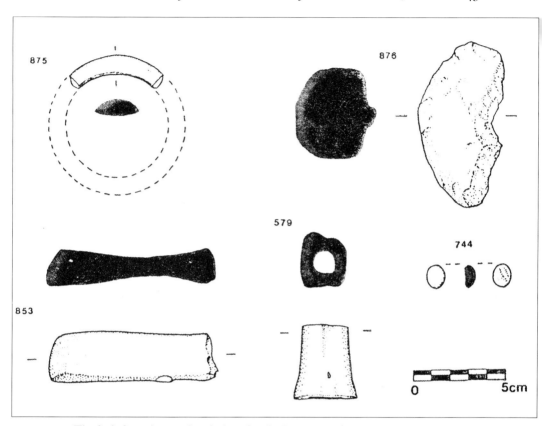

14 The finds from the pre-church clays: 875 lignite bracelet; 876 net weight; 853 hone stone; 579 bone 'cylinder'; 744 blue glass stud.

THE FINDS

Two distinct groups of artefacts were found at the site: those that pre-date the early twelfth century and the church and those of Anglo-Norman and later medieval and post-medieval date.

Pre-Norman finds
A small number of artefacts reinforce the stratigraphic evidence for pre-church (pre–twelfth century) activity on the site (fig. 14). They were retrieved from the Phase 1 and 2 clays and associated features.

Metal, nonferrous
869   Fragment of the upper rectangular in-section shank of a bronze stick pin, just 20mm long. Undecorated, it measured 1.5mm by 2.5mm in thickness.

224   Tiny scrap of loosely tangled gold foil wire, 0.2–0.4mm thick, from
           one of the post holes in Cutting 6.

Stone   Three stone artefacts were retrieved from the pre-church Phase 2 clays
           in Cutting 9.

853   Whet stone, 90mm long, 27mm wide and max. 20mm worn to just
           6mm in thickness.

875   Fragment of jet bracelet, 50mm long, 12mm wide and max. 7mm
           thick. Plano-convex in section and highly polished on both sides.

876   Fragment of a net weight of coarse-grained granite with an hour-glass
           perforation. Max. dimensions 90mm by 50mm.

Bone

576   Bone cylinder/handle cut at both ends and worn smooth from use;
           40mm long and 20–30mm diameter. Found in the pre-church Phase 2
           clay in Cutting 8.

Glass

744   Blue glass droplet recovered from the Phase 2 pre-church clay in
           Cutting 7. Plano-convex in section and 10mm in diameter and 5mm in
           maximum thickness. It has a grooved underside to facilitate fixing into
           a metal setting.

Slag The occurrence of slag on Early Christian ecclesiastical sites is well
attested. Find 881 was recovered from Phase 1 pre-church clay in Cutting 8 and
appears to represent a fragment of a furnace bottom.

Anglo-Norman and Later Finds
Because there was so much burial activity on the site, the post-twelfth-century
finds are almost all (unless stated otherwise) from disturbed contexts and
graveyard soil. Many appear to date from the fourteenth century and later, after
soil was imported to the site for burial purposes.

Metal, ferrous
603   A socketed iron javelin-head 135mm long and 35mm in maximum
           width, with a tang 15–20mm wide. Recovered from Cutting 8 (fig. 15).
           Post-medieval iron finds include a horseshoe fragment (216) a knife
           blade (217), two coffin handles and four coffin plates (none of which
           were recovered *in situ*). Two further iron artefacts from the lower
           graveyard soils are worthy of mention: a small key (415) and a fish
           hook/flesh hook (723) that was almost 100mm long. Over fifty nails
           were found. Most were coffin nails (30 max.), 70mm long and corroded
           to 15–25mm diameter.

Metal, nonferrous Three coins were recovered, two from graveyard soil in
Cutting 4 and one in similar soil in Cutting 8.

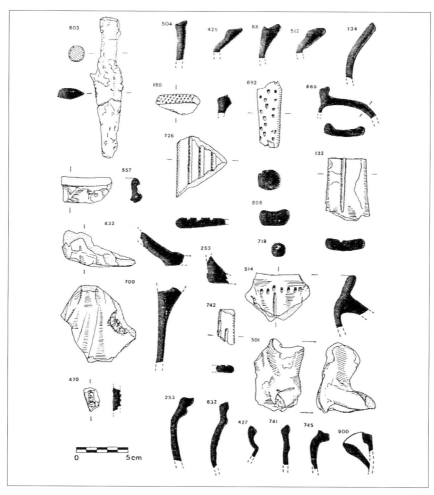

15 Medieval finds: 603 socketed spearhead/javelin head; 504-134 rim profiles of thirteenth-fourteenth-century Dublin Cooking Ware; 180 Ham Green rim; 692 late medieval French jug handle; 669 Saintonge strap handle; the remainder area all Dublin wares dating from the thirteenth-fifteenth-century.

211   Silver coin of uncertain provenance, but probably from the Low Countries. The legend is uncertain, but the obverse side legend corresponds to one already recorded: ' ... moneta nostra,' and it may therefore date to the fourteenth century (Chantard 1871).

215   Irish copper halfpenny of Elizabeth 1, dated 1601.

999   Georgian (Georgius II) halfpenny, dated 1742.

A great number of shroud pins were recovered. All were small, fine and between 20mm and 30mm long with very tiny round or flattened heads.

1000   A gold 'memento mori' pendant recovered in Cutting 7, thought to be
        nineteenth-century in date. Has a central inset of glass and onyx, with
        woven human hair set in between. On the gold surround, in white
        enamel, are inscribed the words 'Dum Memor Ipse Mei.'

Stone

630   Only one very small fragment of a stone memorial was recovered
        during the investigation. Found in Cutting 6 in graveyard soil, the
        fragment is of marble, 20mm thick, with the letters CRE inscribed in
        roman capitals.

The only other stone artefacts recovered were four slate disks used prior to
interment to cover the eyes of the dead. Found in the upper levels of the
graveyard soil, they were 30–40mm in diameter and 2–7mm thick.

Glass Numerous fragments of bottle glass were recovered. Five were from
seventeenth-century 'bag' bottles with deep 'omphalos' bases and obvious pontil
marks.

Clay pipes Over one hundred clay-pipe fragments were recovered, with 32
complete bowls. They were analysed by Joe Norton of Dúchas, the Heritage
Service. Twenty spurred bowls were seventeenth/eighteenth century in date,
nine flat-heeled pipes were seventeenth and early eighteenth century in date and
the remainder were nineteenth century in date.

Ceramics All the ceramics recovered during the excavation were found either in
the graveyard soils or in later overlying fill. They cover a broad date range from
the fourteenth century; some of the Dublin wares may date back to the
thirteenth century. In thirty-seven sherds of local Dublin wares recovered, three
distinct variations (fig. 15) were noted, and there were six sherds of unglazed
cooking ware. The assemblage included four strap handle fragments and several
small rim fragments. Ten small sherds of fine, probably thirteenth/fourteenth-
century Saintonge pots were found. All had pink-buff fabric and all were green-
glazed with the exception of one body sherd, which had a dark buff-coloured
external slip. Eight sherds of Ham Green were found. Find 180 is a rim sherd
with characteristic lattice decoration, and there was one small fragment of a pot
from Bristol.

Tiles Ten glazed pan tile fragments were recovered (fig. 16). Two were from
glazed ridge tiles, three were very small fragments of line-impressed floor tiles,
one thick fragment had an incised line and the remaining fragments were post-
medieval delph tiles.

Post-medieval ceramics The bulk of this material was locally made glazed
earthenware. The remainder consisted of thirty fragments of Blackware vessels;

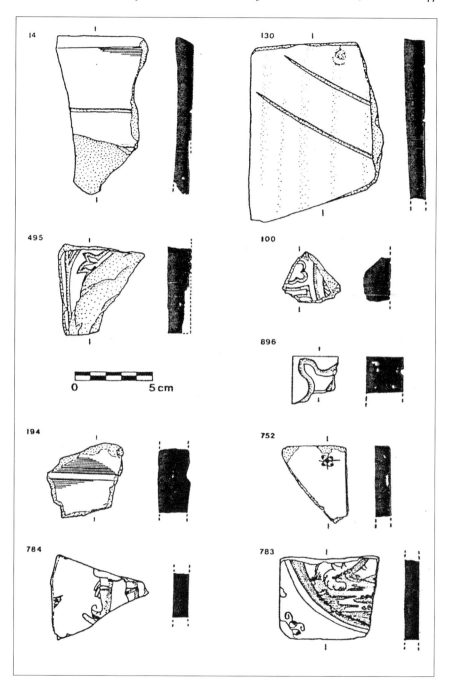

16   14,130 medieval roof tiles; 495,100,896 medieval decorated floor tiles; 194 post medieval floor tile; 752, 783, 784 Dutch delft tiles.

thirty-seven fragments of North Devon gravel-tempered ware; thirty fragments of North Devon Scraffito; seventeen fragments of Staffordshire wares, some of which were from slip-trailed cups; four fragments from a Bellarmine jug; two Westerwald; seven pieces of later stoneware; and numerous fragments of delph, six of which date to the seventeenth century.

DISCUSSION

The excavated features in the recorded location of the church and Round Tower of St Michael le Pole have been interpreted as comprising a portion of the west wall of the church and the fragmentary foundations of an integral Round Tower (fig. 17). The other structures and walls revealed on the site can be related to buildings described in documentary sources and depicted on eighteenth-century and later Ordnance Survey maps. These structures clearly incorporated the surviving west wall of the church and may to some extent define the original size of the church. However, no remains of the church's northern, southern or eastern walls were found during the course of the excavation. Deposits and burials pre-dating the church and tower were also revealed during the excavation, suggesting both habitation and the possibility that an earlier ecclesiastical establishment may have existed on or near the site in pre-Norman times.

Pre-church activity
The discovery of two phases of stratified pre-church remains is particularly important. The Phase 1 remains, represented by structural post holes, linear gullies, hearths and associated clay deposits, are of particular interest, as one of these features has yielded a radiocarbon determination of AD 663–872. The Phase 3 clay deposits, mixed with ash, mortar and a significant deposit of butchered animal bone, yielded a small number of artefacts that can also be regarded as pre-Norman in date. The high lime content in the soil is suggestive of mortar manufacture and may relate to the construction of masonry structures close to the excavated area. This activity cannot be related on stratigraphic grounds to the building of the church itself, suggesting that the building of stone structures on the site may pre-date the construction of the early twelfth-century church. The stone-lined 'lintel' grave, the burial in which produced a calibrated radiocarbon determination of AD 895–1269, presents further evidence for activity on the site prior to the building of the church in the twelfth-century.

While the nature of the settlement is not defined by the historical records, the possibility that the settlement may have been of an ecclesiastical nature is perhaps supported by the presence of several pre-church burials within the excavated area. The focus of early, pre-church activity appeared to be centred on the location in which the church remains were found. The other test

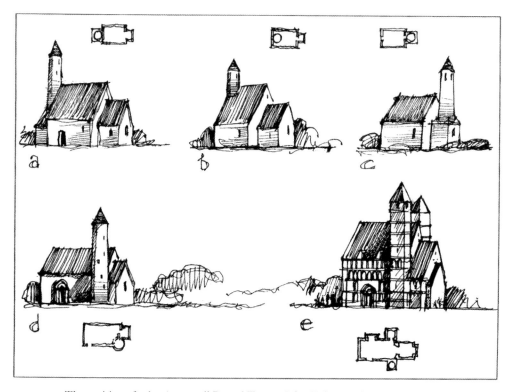

17 The position of other 'engaged' Round Towers (after Lalor 1999).

trenches opened on the site did not reveal any evidence for pre-Norman activity. Of great importance, however, are the results of Mary McMahon's excavation on the large site nearby at Bride Street, which also produced evidence for pre-Norman occupation. One of the pre-Norman burials on the Bride Street site produced a radiocarbon determination with a calibrated range of AD 877–1001. Furthermore, the Bride Street site revealed similar occupation features in its lowest, pre-Norman levels: post holes, a hearth, pits and one linear channel (McMahon forthcoming).

In this context, the significance of the analysed animal bone assemblage from the Phase 2 deposit complex cannot be overstated. It represents a settlement economy that mirrors all the peculiarities of animal carcass management already recorded in the enclosed Viking town and suggests that settlement activity of an almost equally formalised fashion must have occurred in these lands to the south of the enclosed Viking town.

The church and Round Tower
The excavation result finally settled the long-standing controversy as to whether the church of St Michael le Pole had a freestanding or an attached Round

Tower. Gabriel Beranger's description of the tower as being 'encompassed by a building formerly a chapel' (*Irish Builder* 1870, 113), and his drawing of it, were deemed by some to be incorrect (Little 1951, 3; Barrow 1979, 89). Beranger's drawing had perhaps been borne out by the entry in the *Free Press* of 15 August 1778, where Dr Jones's schoolhouse is described as having 'a flight of stairs leading to the two upper rooms'. Margaret Stokes, writing in 1878, accepted Beranger's drawing and suggested eight parallels, including those described below. The closest and most obvious parallel is St Kevin's church in Glendalough, Co. Wicklow. Other internal and external 'engaged' towers occur at Trinity Church, Glendalough; Ferns, Co. Wexford (pl. 6); Kilmacnessan, Co. Meath; Dungiven, Co. Derry; and Templefinnan in Clonmacnoise, Co. Offaly. It has also been argued that the tower at Cormac's Chapel, Cashel, Co. Tipperary, is a development of the form (fig. 17, after Lalor 1999). The twelfth-century church on Ireland's Eye also has a centrally placed integral tower. Almost all of these examples are ascribed to the twelfth century and are described in Brian Lalor's recently published book (1999) on Round Towers as 'engaged towers.'

It seems that the St Michael le Pole tower was probably square in external plan to roof level, then circular for the remainder of its 'seventy or ninety feet' height. It appears also that it had a stone staircase, like Ferns and Glendalough, unlike the wooden loft ladders of the earlier towers. Both eighteenth-century drawings of the tower depict a conical cap, similar to those at Glendalough, though in Beranger's drawing it appears rather rounded. The structural remains of the church suggest a twelfth-century date. While no obvious diagonal tooling was noted on the masonry remains, the stonework, mortar bonding, doorway, doorjambs and plinth configuration can be paralleled in other late pre-Norman churches. By comparison, Ferns was founded around 1150, and Glendalough, Templefinnan, Dungiven and Clonmacnoise are all also of twelfth-century date.

While the site was very disturbed and truncated, many human remains were revealed in the areas excavated. It is likely that a significant number of additional burials still survive on the site in areas not excavated during this investigation. Burial certainly appears to have taken place on the site in the pre-Norman period. At least some of the burials on the site must relate also to the period of use of the church between the late twelfth century and its closure some time around the fourteenth century. The importation of graveyard soil with medieval ceramic inclusions suggests that the interior of the church was used for burial purposes after its closure and prior to its reuse as a schoolhouse in 1706, though the site continued to be used for burial up to the mid-nineteenth century, possibly on a very limited basis. After excavation, the skeletal remains were re-interred and the area surrounding the excavation cuttings and the structural remains of the church was permanently fenced off and remains so to this day.

Dating

The radiocarbon determinations at St Michael le Pole are some of the earliest in Dublin to date. Coupled with the location of the site close to *Dubhlinn*, the pool, they open up the possibility that the site of the church of St Michael le Pole, with its evidence for pre–twelfth century settlement, occupation activity and burials and its Round Tower and twelfth-century church, may mark the site of an Early Christian monastery. Up to now, the particular topographic configuration of Stephen Street and Whitefriar Street has been taken to provide evidence for the Early Christian site that can be related to the foundation of Dublin (Clarke 1978; fig. 1). However, until excavation evidence from the Stephen Street area proves otherwise, the distinct possibility exists that the Early Christian site in question may have existed on or close to the site of St Michael le Pole.

The findings of this excavation and those at Bride Street and other recently excavated ecclesiastical and burial sites in the southwestern part of Dublin city, together with the evident preliminary parallels established for this church with other twelfth-century churches in the Dublin/Leinster region, suggest that further, detailed study might yield very considerable rewards.

ACKNOWLEDGEMENTS

The excavations on this site were undertaken by the Dublin Archaeological Research Team (DART), a group that was formed in the wake of the Wood Quay excavations with the ambition, driven by Nick Maxwell, of setting up an archaeological unit for Dublin; the ambition was not fulfilled. The excavation was carried out under licence to Kieran Campbell with a team that included Thaddeus Breen (historical research), Peter Cutting (photography), the writer, Paddy Healy (surveyor on site), Nick Maxwell (finished drawings of plans), Una McConville, Mary McMahon (ceramics and finds drawings), Michael Moore, Maire Scally-Noonan and Celie O'Rahilly. I am grateful to Linzi Simpson, who has assisted by providing the early medieval historical background text and allowed me to use her considerable knowledge as a sounding board for some of the interpretation presented in this paper, to Dr Seán Duffy for asking all the right, awkward questions and to Mary McMahon for discussion on the possible associations between the results of this excavation and those from the site that she excavated at Bride Street.

Finally, I would like to thank Penny Iremonger and Michael Phillips who assisted in the recent preparation of the illustrations and the final editing of this text.

CITED AND BACKGROUND SOURCES

Barrow, G.L. 1979 *The round towers of Ireland*. Dublin.

Clarke, H.B. 1977 The topographical development of early medieval Dublin *RSAI Jn.* 107, 29–51.

—— 1978 *Dublin c.840–1540, the medieval town in the modern city* (map). Dublin.

Craig, M.J., and Wheeler, H.A. 1948 *The Dublin city churches* Dublin.

Chantard, J.J. 1871 *Imitations des monaies aux type esterlin frapees en Europe, XIII & XIV siecle* Nancy.

De Gomme, B. 1673 *The city and suburbs of Dublin from Kilmainham to Ringsend, 1673*, Ms. Map in the Dartmouth Collection, National Maritime Museum, Greenwich.

de Paor, L., and de Paor, M. 1958 *Early Christian Ireland* London.

The Irish Builder 1870 XII, No. 250, May 15, 113–114 and 274–277.

JAPMD 1900, 1906. *Journal of the Association for the Preservation of the Memorials of the Dead*, 4 & 6, Dublin.

Jennings, S. 1981 *Eighteen centuries of pottery from Norwich, East Anglican Archaeology*. Report No. 13. Norwich.

Korf, D. 1980 *Nederlandse Majolica* Bussum, Netherlands.

—— 1979 *Tegels*, Haarlem, Netherlands.

Lalor, B. 1999 *The Irish round tower: origin of architecture explained* Dublin.

Leask, H.G. (nd) *Glendalough, Co. Wicklow, official historical and descriptions Guide* Dublin.

Little, G.A. 1951 The provenance of the church of St Michael le Pole. *Dublin Historical Record* 12(1), 2–13.

Little, G.A. 1957 *Dublin before the Vikings, an adventure in discovery* Dublin.

McEnery, M.J. 1886-96 Calendar to Christ Church deeds. *Report of the deputy keeper of the public records in Ireland*, nos. 20, 23, 24, 27. Dublin.

McNeill, C. 1950 (ed.) *Calendar of Archbishop Alen's Register c.1172–1534* Dublin.

O'Donovan, J. 1851 (ed.) *Annala rioghachta Eireann. Annals of the kingdom of Ireland by the Four Masters, from the earliest period to the year 1616*. Dublin.

McCormick, F. 1984 Unpublished report.

Petrie, G. 1845 *The ecclesiastical architecture of Ireland*. 2nd edition. Dublin.

Rocque, J. 1756 *An exact survey of the city and suburbs of Dublin* (map).

Shaw-Mason, W. 1814 *A statistical account of parochial memory of Ireland*. 1. Dublin.

Simpson, L. 2000 Forty years a-digging: a preliminary synthesis of archaeological investigations in medieval Dublin. In *Medieval Dublin I*, ed. S. Duffy, Dublin.

Speed, J. 1611 *The theatre of the empire of Great Britain*. London.

Stokes, M. 1878 *Early Christian architecture in Ireland* London.

Wilde, W. 1870 Memoir of Gabriel Beranger and his labours in the cause of Irish art. *RSAI Jn.* 11.

The battle of Glenn Máma, Dublin and the high-kingship of Ireland: a millennial commemoration

AILBHE MAC SHAMHRÁIN

The battle of Glenn Máma and the sack of Dublin which followed, taking place over the new year 999–1000, has been accorded relatively little focus, in comparison with Clontarf, by historians of the later 'Viking Age' in Ireland and Scandinavia. The importance of Clontarf has been appreciated at least since the twelfth century; that particular conflict is at once the highpoint and tragic finale of the Ua Briain propaganda work 'Cogadh Gaedhel re Gallaib' ('The War of the Irish with the Foreigners'), which purports to chart the rise of Dál Cais, the reign of Brian Bóruma and his death in the struggle against 'the heathen'. Clontarf is almost as prominent in Scandinavian saga; it forms an important part of 'Njal's Saga' and presumably featured in the now lost 'Brian's Saga' (Bugge 1908, 55, 59–66; Magnusson & Pálsson 1960, 341; Ó Corráin 1998, 447–52). Quite aside from its survival in popular tradition, Clontarf attracted the attention of medievalists in the earlier decades of the twentieth century, including Goedheer (1938) and Ryan (1938); it continues to be used as a 'marker' by present-day historians (for example Ó Cróinín 1995, 272), and justifiably so, if only because the removal of Brian opened up opportunities for other dynasties. However, scholars appear to have been slower to recognise the importance, in its own right, of the battle of Glenn Máma, and it has attracted rather little discussion. In more recent decades, several commentators have indeed acknowledged that the battle (fought within a day's march of Dublin) represented a turning point in Brian's career; Ryan (1967, 361) and Ó Corráin (1972, 123) have both viewed the battle as a key stage in the conflict between Brian and Máel Sechnaill, a victory which gave him the confidence to challenge the Uí Néill king of Tara for supremacy in Ireland.

Such attention, therefore, as has been accorded to Glenn Máma concerns its place in that contest for ascendancy which many, contemporary commentators and historians alike, have viewed as a struggle for the high-kingship of Ireland. While accepting the importance of its place in this 'broader picture', it seems appropriate here to view the engagement more in the context of its 'Dublin dimension'. There are indications, as is argued below, that Brian had designs on Dublin for some years prior to Glenn Máma as, indeed, had his rival Máel

Sechnaill. The question of Brian's responsibility for exacerbating the unrest which led to Glenn Máma – perhaps through misreading the complex political relationship between the Hiberno-Scandinavian kingdom and the north Leinster dynasty of Uí Dúnlainge – and the extent to which he may have appreciated the importance of Dublin in the context of Irish Sea politics, are among the other issues addressed.

The career of Brian has been widely discussed, and the stages by which he rose to challenge for supremacy in Ireland are charted in several surveys (Ó Corráin 1972, 120–31; Duffy 1997, 31–6). For present purposes, a brief synopsis will suffice. Without doubt, he exercised considerable political power; ultimately, he did force submissions from each of the other provincial kings and from the Norse of Dublin, displacing (and arguably exceeding) the ascendancy long claimed by the Uí Néill kings of Tara and achieving, as has been claimed, a special status. On the occasion of his visit to Armagh in 1005 when, as is recorded in the Annals of Ulster, he deposited the sum of twenty ounces of gold on St Patrick's altar, a note in the Book of Armagh (albeit entered by a partisan) styled him 'Imperator Scotorum', or 'Emperor of the Irish' (Gwynn 1978–9; Duffy 1997, 33–4). However, it seems unlikely that, from the commencement of his reign, he possessed a blueprint for achieving this supremacy. Nor was it the case that he had come from nowhere to challenge for political dominance in Ireland, despite the claims of 'Cogadh Gaedhel re Gallaib', whose authors wished to dramatise his rise to power. From his very accession to kingship, much less by the time of Glenn Máma, his dynasty of Dál Cais was well placed at regional level. As shown more than thirty years ago by Kelleher (1967, 230–41), it is certainly the case that Brian's inheritance from his father and brothers – if it did not quite amount to mastery of Munster – certainly provided him with a firm basis from which to establish overkingship of the province.

The possibility should perhaps not be discounted that Brian's father, Cennétig son of Lorcán, did benefit politically from a strategic marriage with the still powerful Clann Cholmáin dynasty of Uí Néill, as long as the importance of this connection is not overestimated (Kelleher 1967, 230–1; cf. Ó Corráin 1972, 114–15). It happens that Cennétig's daughter Órlaith was married, while apparently still in her teens, to the ageing king of Tara, Donnchad son of Flann. In 941, Donnchad captured the Éoganachta king of Cashel, Cellachán, which probably did help the Dál Cais cause, whether or not that was the intention. That same year, however, the year in which Brian was born according to a retrospective entry in the Annals of Ulster, the king of Tara had his young wife executed for adultery; his apparent willingness to do so might indeed suggest a marriage of convenience with a lesser dynasty, the continued support of which was not crucial for him. It may merely be coincidental, then, that the death of Donnchad in 944 was quickly followed by

1 Map of places mentioned.

a reassertion of authority on the part of Cellachán of Cashel, involving a battle which cost the lives of two of Cennétig's sons.

The question of Uí Néill support aside, however, other circumstances can be discerned which almost certainly facilitated Dál Cais expansion in the early-to-mid tenth century; not least among these is political fragmentation within the Éoganachta dynasties, and the potential which existed to exploit a conglomeration of minor ruling lineages in the lower Shannon basin. The fact remains

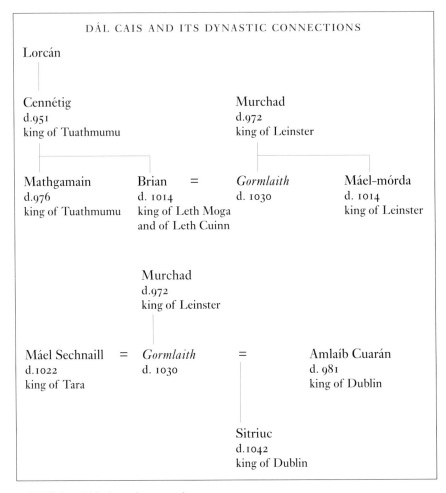

2 Dál Cais and it's dynastic connections.

that Cennétig, at his death in 951, is styled 'Rí Tuathmuman (king of northern Munster)' in the Annals of Inisfallen, and 'Rígdamna Caisil (one eligible to be king of Cashel)' in the Annals of Ulster. Although his son and successor Lachtna, slain in an internal conflict in 953, is not accorded a similar accolade in his obit, he may nonetheless have advanced the cause of Dál Cais. His short reign saw an attack against Clonmacnois which involved the Munstermen supported by 'foreigners', presumably Hiberno-Scandinavians. Later, his brother Mathgamain defeated and subjugated the Norsemen of Limerick and managed to overawe some of the Éoganachta dynasties, but clearly not the Éoganachta of Ráithlenn under Máel-muad son of Bran, whose base-kingdom lay in Co. Cork and who remained powerful in south Munster. Although Mathgamain did not achieve effective control over the province, but was captured and put to death by Máel-muad in 976, it may be noted that the annals style him 'king of Cashel' at his death.

The immediate priority for Brian, nonetheless, was to re-establish the position of his dynasty in Munster, a task which took several years. The annals relate how he suppressed the Norsemen of Limerick, Uí Fidgenti (a kingdom in west Co. Limerick), and the Éoganachta of Ráithlenn – defeating and slaying Máel-muad at Belach Lechta. By 982, he was ready to move against the Nore Valley kingdom of Osraige, in effect a buffer-state between Munster and Leinster. This was apparently a cause of concern for the Clann Cholmáin king of Tara, Máel Sechnaill son of Domnall, who only two years earlier had severely defeated the Norse of Dublin at the important battle of Tara. It required no great imagination to see a foray into Osraige by a Munster overking as a step towards asserting authority over Leth Moga (the southern half of Ireland); this, at any rate, would mean Munster lordship over Leinster – whether or not it was extended to include Dublin. Opting for a pre-emptive strike, Máel Sechnaill attacked the heartland of Dál Cais (in east Co. Clare) and levelled the Tree of Mag n-Adair, which had once been held sacred by the ancestors of Dál Cais and had retained a special significance. Undeterred by such calculated insults Brian, in 983, directed his forces up the Shannon against Connacht, over which Máel Sechnaill claimed sway. The same year, he again harried Osraige, taking hostages. This time he did, as Clann Cholmáin had feared, continue into Mag nAilbe (a plain in Co. Carlow) and took hostages from the Leinster dynasty of Uí Dúnlainge.

It seems that Brian, by this time, had designs on Dublin; he had witnessed the heavy defeat inflicted on the Norsemen by Máel Sechnaill, and perhaps anticipated that his rival might move to dominate the town. In 984, he formed an alliance with sons of Harald, after they had brought a fleet to Waterford. These were representatives of the Limerick dynasty which his brother Mathgamain had earlier banished and, understandably, might have welcomed an opportunity to establish themselves in a new kingship. For Brian, the prospect of dominating a wealthy east-coast trading centre through compliant sub-kings was, presumably, attractive as an end in itself; however, it is possible that, mindful of the close Hebridean connections of his new allies, he already realised the potential of Dublin as a key to the Irish Sea. In any event, Dál Cais and the Limerick Norsemen planned a joint initiative. According to the Annals of Inisfallen, the two sides exchanged hostages and mutual guarantees, in preparation for an expedition against Dublin. A campaign was launched against Osraige and Leinster, and might have proceeded further but for a revolt of the Déisi, a sub-kingdom in eastern Munster (mainly in modern Co. Waterford), which destabilised the province to a considerable degree. It took Brian at least two years to re-establish control; he harried the lands of the Déisi, bringing them to heel, but in 986 found it necessary to imprison his nephew, Áed son of

Mathgamain, and the following year led a hosting across Desmumu (south Munster), taking hostages at Lismore, Cork and Emly. These campaigns occupied his attention during the interval in which his initiative against Leinster and Dublin had lost its momentum.

The late 980s and early 990s witnessed a renewal of the contest between Brian and Máel Sechnaill; the Munstermen campaigned up the Shannon waterway, striking not only at Connacht but now at the Westmeath lakelands. Their achievement, in military terms, could at best be described as a mixed success; on one raid, many of their ships' crews were slaughtered by the Connachta, while on another they reached beyond Lough Ree and into the land of Bréifne. Gradually, they wore down the resolve of Máel Sechnaill. The latter had certainly been active; in 989, he had subjugated Dublin taking hostages and tribute, and then carried the war southwards. In 990, he defeated the Munstermen at Carn Fordroma and in 993, according to the Four Masters, he sacked Nenagh. The very fact that Brian appeared so resilient in the face of these setbacks may have caused Máel Sechnaill to become discouraged. The indications are that Brian was still determined to extend his lordship over Leth Moga and, conscious no doubt of his rival's assertion of lordship over Dublin, had not abandoned his ambitions in relation to the Hiberno–Norse kingdom. In the military sphere, Dál Cais proceeded slowly and with caution from 991 onwards. That year, Brian led a hosting against Leinster. In 995, he constructed extensive fortifications around his home province of Munster, before leading another expedition into Leinster in the following year. This time, he marched to Mag nAilbhe (as he had done thirteen years earlier) in Co. Carlow and took the hostages of the Uí Chennselaig dynasty and of the west of the province in general.

In parallel with these developments, some diplomatic realignments on Brian's part may be viewed in the context of his ambitions in relation to Dublin. It seems that he divorced his wife Gormlaith, whose father Murchad (sl. 972), of the Uí Fáeláin dynasty, had reigned as a nominal overking of Leinster. The separation of Brian and Gormlaith clearly had the potential to complicate political relationships, as her former husbands included Amlaíb Cuarán (d.981), king of Dublin, and Máel Sechnaill, king of Tara. Her offspring included Sitriuc Silkbeard, king of Dublin (Ó Cróinín 1995, 263–4). There was certainly a belief that she used her personal influence against Brian's interests after she returned to her own kindred. Episodes in 'Cogadh Gaedhel re Gallaib' and 'Njal's Saga' credit her with inciting her brother Máel-mórda, and her son Sitriuc Silkbeard, against Brian, prior to the battle of Clontarf (Magnusson & Pálsson 1960, 342, 344); no surviving evidence, however, indicates that she played any such role in the lead-up to Glenn Máma.

Meanwhile, in the early 990s, Brian embarked on his third marriage; to Echrad, daughter of Carlus of Uí Áeda Odba, king of Gailenga Becca (Ryan 1967, 365–6). Given the relative unimportance of his new wife's lineage, the motive for such an alliance might at first sight appear obscure. The explanation, however, probably lies in the geography of politics. While branches of the Gailenga were scattered through counties Meath and Westmeath, Gailenga Becca lay in the south of the Plain of Brega – well within the Dublin ove-kingdom known as Fine Gall (Fingal). It is said that Glasnevin lay in this statelet of Gailenga Becca (Byrne 1968, 393). A difficulty remains, insofar as the ruling lineage of Uí Áeda was associated with Odba, a site which the nineteenth-century scholar O'Donovan located near Navan; however, as the placename merely designates a knoll, it seems reasonable that there was more than one site of that name. Some references to Odba suggest a location in southern Brega, which certainly leaves it possible that the location lay within Fingal. For an ambitious ruler anxious to challenge for overlordship of Dublin, an opportunity to secure a foothold within the Hiberno-Scandinavian overkingdom would, no doubt, have been welcome.

As the 990s came to a close Máel Sechnaill, acknowledging his inability to subdue Brian, appears to have decided to 'cut his losses'. *A rígdál* (royal meeting) was arranged in 997 at Clonfert (more precisely at Port dá Chaineóc, according to the Annals of Inisfallen), and agreement reached on the partition of Ireland into its 'traditional divisions' of Leth Cuinn (the northern half) and Leth Moga. In effect, therefore, suzerainty of the southern half of Ireland was being conceded to Brian by the Uí Néill king of Tara. In certain respects, such a meeting and such a concession was not entirely unprecedented. More than two-and-a-half centuries earlier, overkings of the Uí Néill and of Munster had met at Terryglass to agree spheres of influence along such lines (Ní Chon Uladh 1999, 190–6). On this occasion, however, Dublin was in the equation; Máel Sechnaill gave over to Brian the hostages of Leinster and of the Hiberno-Norse kingdom of Dublin, which he had himself taken in 989. This particular transfer of lordship would have serious import. In the event, it transpired that the 'Agreement of Clonfert' was short-lived; the two kings campaigned together in 998, and took further hostages from the 'Foreigners' meaning, it seems, the Norse of Dublin. Brian then took hostages from Connacht and presented them to Máel Sechnaill – a magnanimous gesture intended, no doubt, to convey that he was the superior ruler. At this point, serious unrest broke out in Leinster and Dublin, which drew the attention of Brian.

The immediate causes of this unrest may well lie in the relationships between Brian and his new tributary kings. It is probable that Dublin, in particular, having resented the overlordship of Uí Néill, was even less willing to yield to Dál Cais (Ó Corráin 1972, 123). Furthermore, it appears that Brian, responding to the mounting crisis in 998, fanned the embers of discontent. Ultimately, however, the roots of the problem lay in the dynastic politics of Leinster and Dublin, the complexities of which Brian either failed to comprehend fully or chose to disregard for the sake of expedience. The north

Leinster dynasty of Uí Dúnlainge had, some two centuries earlier, become divided into rival lineages, two of which – Uí Dúnchada, based at Liamain (Newcastle-Lyons, on the Dublin-Kildare border), and Uí Fáeláin, based in north Co. Kildare – were, in the late tenth century, contesting a nominal overkingship of the Leinstermen. Since the mid 980s, this particular dignity had been held by a member of Uí Dúnchada, Donnchad son of Domnall, who by this time was subordinate to Brian.

For many years, Uí Dúnchada, along with other Irish dynasties adjacent to Dublin, had been severely repressed by the Norse rulers, and remained in their shadow even after Máel Sechnaill had reduced the Norse kingdom's military might and placed it under tribute. When, in 993, a conflict between the Hiberno-Norse dynasties of Dublin and Waterford (Duffy 1992, 96) caused the temporary expulsion from Dublin of its king, Sitriuc Silkbeard son of Amlaíb Cuarán, Uí Dúnchada backed the Waterford Norsemen. Presumably the intention was to secure greater support for their own cause from a new regime. Unfortunately for them, they had made the wrong choice and paid the penalty when, a short time later, the Uí Fáeláin ruler, Máel-mórda son of Murchad, engineered the return of Sitriuc. These two were, of course, related, being uncle and nephew: Máel-mórda's sister Gormlaith, once the wife of Amlaíb, was Sitriuc Silkbeard's mother. Acting as allies, Máel-mórda and Sitriuc pursued a vendetta against Uí Dúnchada (MacShamhráin 1996, 88–9); before the end of 994, they killed Donnchad's cousin, Gilla-céile son of Cerball. Two years later, they slew another of his cousins, Mathgamain, a brother of Gilla-céile. They also killed Ragnall, a member of the Waterford dynasty. By 998, it seems that the situation had deteriorated further. Late in that year, Brian intervened directly and ravaged Leinster. It is not clear whether this action was intended merely to overawe Leinster and re-state Dál Cais supremacy, or had the more strategic purpose of supporting the Uí Dúnchada ruler against his rivals. In any event, it does not appear to have helped matters.

In 999, Donnchad son of Domnall was taken prisoner by Sitriuc Silkbeard of Dublin, again acting in collaboration with Máel-mórda, who assumed overkingship of the Leinstermen. Uncle and nephew then revolted against the overlordship of Brian. Indications are that a delay of a couple of months ensued as the latter, having duly considered his options, mustered his forces. That December, Brian (styled king of Cashel in the Annals of Ulster) led an army towards Dublin. Regarding the composition of this army, it may be noted that only the Clonmacnois set of annals, which may be seen as pro-Uí Néill, mention Máel Sechnaill in connection with the expedition. The Annals of Inisfallen and 'Cogadh Gaedhel re Gallaib', both of which may be accused of being (to varying degrees) pro-Dál Cais, are quite explicit in their claim that Brian's command consisted solely of 'the choice troops of Munster'. It may be significant, then, that the generally reliable Annals of Ulster, in its account of Glenn Máma and its sequel, refer only to Brian and indeed imply that he alone profited from subsequent submissions. None of the sources state that the army spent Christmas on the march, but it might be suggested that it did; for on Thursday 30 December it was intercepted, by the combined forces of Norse Dublin and the Leinstermen, at Glenn Máma where a decisive engagement was fought.

Agreement has never in fact been reached on the location of this important battle. The route taken by Brian's army marching from Munster, clearly a crucial factor in the equation, is of course unknown. The suggestion that he perhaps followed what later became the coach road from Limerick is plausible, but remains unprovable. Nineteenth-century scholars, including O'Donovan (1851, II, 739 n. z) and Todd (1867, cxliii–iv), were tempted to locate the battle-site in the vicinity of Dunlavin, Co. Wicklow. It was later realised that Glenn Máma featured in the itinerary of the tenth-century king of Ailech, Muirchertach 'na cCochall Croicinn' ('of the Leather Cloaks'), who allegedly made a 'Circuit of Ireland' in the winter of 941. Even if, as it now appears, much of the 'Circuit' reflects the achievement of the later Muirchertach Mac Lochlainn (Ó Corráin 2000, 238–50), the position of Glenn Máma in the sequence of placenames indicates a location not far to the west of Dublin. On this basis, Hogan (1910) considered that the site lay in the vicinity of Newcastle Lyons, Co. Dublin, and proposed that it be identified with the Glen of Saggart. Given the propensity for battles to take place in border regions (Ó Riain 1974, 68), it seems reasonable to seek a location close to the perimeter of the Hiberno-Norse kingdom of Dublin. On that account, the suggestion of Lloyd (1914, 305ff), which places the battle at a gap now crossed by the Naas Road on the section between Kill and Rathcoole, is still worthy of consideration. In any event, the engagement took place within an easy day's march of Dublin, as Brian pressed on immediately afterwards to reach the town on the following day.

The sources which offer comment on the scale of the battle indicate that it was no trivial encounter. According to the Annals of Inisfallen, which admittedly tends to represent a Munster perspective, 'formna Gall Herend' ('the best part of the foreigners of Ireland') fell therein. The more blatantly partisan 'Cogadh Gaedhel re Gallaib' bursts into hyperbole (§67), claiming that 'since the battle of Mag Roth to that time there had not taken place a greater slaughter'. It certainly seems that there was high mortality on both sides. The fallen included Harald son of Amlaíb (a brother of Sitriuc Silkbeard) and 'other nobles of the foreigners', amongst whom was one Cuilén son of Eitigén, who apparently belonged to the Gailenga; he was perhaps a brother of Ruadacán son of Eitigén, king of Airther Gaileng, who died in 953 (Jaski 1997, 134). If so, it appears that Brian's efforts to secure the support of the Irish dynasties within Fingal had not been entirely successful. As for the casualties on Brian's side, even the 'Cogadh' acknowledges that 'there fell there multitudes of the Dál Cais', but no details are provided.

In the immediate aftermath of the battle, Brian's forces converged on Dublin reaching the town on New Year's Eve 999. They entered within its defences (apparently without any great resistance) and, as the Annals of Inisfallen attest, on New Year's Day (the Kalends of January) 1000, following an intensive sack, burned both the settlement itself and the nearby wood known as Caill Tomair (it apparently stood on the north side of the Liffey). This plunder of the town, for the second time in ten years, is described in considerable detail in the 'Cogadh' (§68). Allowance must be made here for poetic licence but, even still, some picture can be obtained of the wealth of the trading centre that was Dublin (Smyth 1979, II, 209, 242). According to this account Brian, having plundered the *dún* (fortress), entered the *margadh* (market area) and here seized the greatest wealth. Meanwhile, on the approach of the Munster forces, King Sitriuc had fled northwards hoping to obtain asylum among the Ulstermen. His ally, Máel-mórda of Uí Fáeláin, was captured, in ignominious circumstances according to the 'Cogadh' (§71). At the conclusion of hostilities, the (nominal) overkingship of Leinster was bestowed upon the Uí Dúnchada candidate, Donnchad son of Domnall, who retained this dignity until he was deposed in 1003. Brian, however, asserted his overlordship of the province by taking hostages from the Leinstermen. Before long, Sitriuc Silkbeard returned having found no asylum in the north. The annal accounts concur that he, too, yielded hostages to Brian, while the Annals of Inisfallen add that the latter in a suitably magnanimous gesture, 'gave the fort [*dún*] to the Foreigners'; the implication here is that, from this time onwards, the Hiberno-Scandinavian ruler would hold his kingship from his Munster overlord. Apparently Brian, at this stage, aspired to an even tighter dominance of Dublin than that secured by his rival, Máel Sechnaill, ten years earlier.

There seems to be little doubt that the longer-term beneficiary of Glenn Máma was Brian alone. With renewed confidence, he again moved against Máel Sechnaill, even if his initiatives of 1000–1001 resulted in setbacks; one expedition into Brega resulted in his advance cavalry being slaughtered by the Uí Néill, another foray was reversed in Mide (Co. Westmeath), and the Dál Cais river-fleet was impeded by the king of Tara and his Connachta allies having constructed a barrier across the Shannon. Brian, however, found a way of circumventing this and, early in 1002, brought a large army through to Athlone and took the hostages of Connacht. At this point Máel Sechnaill, finding the support of the northern kings slipping away (Jaski 2000, 227), felt obliged to submit and a new political order was created. The capitulation of the king of Tara left Brian as the most powerful king in Ireland – the first non-Uí Néill king to achieve such prominence. However, it lies beyond the scope of this short essay to attempt any evaluation of his recognised success, in breaking the Uí Néill hegemony and making political supremacy appear an achievable goal (Byrne 1973, 267; Charles-Edwards 2000, 570), much less to contemplate the realities underlying claims to high-kingship of Ireland.

It remains to consider, though, however briefly, the importance of Brian's victory over the Máel-mórda/Sitriuc coalition as a prelude to renewing his challenge to Máel Sechnaill. Presumably, Glenn Máma gave him a psychological advantage over the king of Tara and increased his readiness to break the Agreement of Clonfert. As a result of the battle, he had achieved domination, in a meaningful sense, of Leinster and Dublin. Perhaps he had some appreciation of the potential of Dublin in accessing the Irish Sea area; certainly, in 1011, he brought a maritime fleet to Cenél Conaill (Co. Donegal) – although it is not clear that this included Dublin ships or only those of Limerick. At the very least, he could command the land forces of Sitriuc Silkbeard – and he made good use of them in his hostings from 1001 onwards (Duffy 1992, 95). It appears, therefore, that through achieving effective dominance of Dublin, Brian acquired a military (aside from a psychological) advantage over Máel Sechnaill, which helped him in his endeavours to reach beyond the lordship of Leth Moga. His success in this regard was probably instrumental in tying Dublin into the sphere of Leth Moga for at least a century to follow. When the Hiberno-Scandinavian kingdom was eventually, in 1052, brought directly under Irish control, it was by Leinster and subsequently Munster rulers, a pattern which was maintained until 1118. By this time, however, the compilers of 'Cogadh Gaedhel re Gallaib' were already piecing together the orthodox Dál Cais history of the dynasty's rise to prominence – and Glenn Máma was already part of that past.

BIBLIOGRAPHY

Bugge, S. 1908 *Norsk sagafortaelling og sagaskrivning i Irland* Kristiana.
Byrne, F.J. 1968 Historical note on Cnogba (Knowth), *R.I.A. Proc.*, 66C, 383–400.
—— 1973 *Irish kings and high-kings* London.
Charles-Edwards, T. 2000 *Early Christian Ireland* Cambridge.
Duffy, S. 1992 Irishmen and Islesmen in the Kingdoms of Dublin and Man 1052–1171, *Ériu*, xliii, 93–133.
Duffy, S. 1997 *Ireland in the middle ages* London & Dublin.
Goedheer, A.J. 1938 *Irish and Norse traditions about the battle of Clontarf.* Harlem.
Gwynn, A. 1979 Brian in Armagh, *Seanchas Ard Mhacha*, ix, 35–50.
Hogan, E. 1910 (ed.) *Onomasticon Goedelicum* Dublin.
Jaski, B. 1997 Additional notes to the Annals of Ulster, *Ériu*, xlviii, 103–52.
Jaski, B. 2000 *Early Irish kingship and succession* Dublin.
Kelleher, J.V. 1967 The rise of the Dál Cais, in Rynne, E. (ed.), *North Munster studies: papers in honour of Michael Moloney*, P.P. 230–41. Limerick.
Lloyd, J. 1914 The identification of the battlefield of Glenn Máma *Co. Kildare Arch. Soc. Jn.*, vii, 305ff
MacAirt, S. 1951 (ed.) *Annals of Inisfallen* Dublin.
—— & MacNiocaill, G. 1984 (eds.) *Annals of Ulster to A.D. 1131* Dublin.
MacShamhráin, A. 1996 *Church and polity in pre-Norman Ireland* Maynooth.

Magnusson, M. & Pálsson, H. 1960 (eds.) *Njal's Saga* London.

Ní Chon Uladh, P. 1999 The Rígdál at Terryglass 737 A.D., *Tipperary Historical Jn.*, 190–96.

Ó Corráin, D. 1972 *Ireland before the Normans* Dublin.

—— 1998 Viking Ireland – afterthoughts, in Clarke, H.B., Ní Mhaonaigh, M. & Ó Floinn, R. (eds.), *Ireland and Scandinavia in the early Viking age* 421–52 Dublin.

—— 2000 Muirchertach Mac Lochlainn and the Circuit of Ireland, in Smyth, A.P. (ed.), *Seanchas: Studies in early and medieval Irish archaeology, history and literature in honour of Francis J. Byrne* 238–50 Dublin.

Ó Cróinín, D. 1995 *Early Medieval Ireland 400–1200* London.

O'Donovan, J. 1851 (ed.) *Annals of the kingdom of Ireland by the Four Masters*, 7 vols. Dublin.

Ó Riain, P. 1974 Battle site and territorial extent in early Ireland, *Zeitschrift für Celtische Philologie*, xxxiii, 67–80.

Ryan, J. 1938 The battle of Clontarf, *R.S.A.I. Jn.*, lxviii, 1–50.

—— 1967 Brian Boruma king of Ireland in Rynne, E. (ed.), *North Munster studies: papers in honour of Michael Moloney*, P.P. 355–74. Limerick.

Smyth, Alfred P. 1975–9 *Scandinavian York and Dublin*, 2 vols Totowa, NJ & Dublin.

Todd, J.H. 1867 (ed.) *Cogadh Gaeghel re Gallaib* London.

Dublin: the biological identity of the Hiberno-Norse town

BARRA Ó DONNABHÁIN
AND BENEDIKT HALLGRÍMSSON

INTRODUCTION

Dublin was established as a Viking enclave in the mid-ninth century AD and had taken on the characteristics of an urban centre by the tenth. The large number of archaeological excavations that has been conducted in the medieval core of the city over the last forty years has yielded significant information about the nature of the Viking-age town, particularly after the early tenth century (Simpson 2000). This research has given us a degree of insight into the daily lives of the tenth, eleventh and twelfth-century inhabitants of Dublin that could be described as intimate. The excavations have produced detailed information about the physical characteristics of the town such as building morphology, streetscape and defences (Wallace 1988; 1992a; 1992b) while also elucidating aspects of its economic functions as a centre of production, consumption and as mediator of long distance exchange (Fanning 1994; Wallace 1988). Archaeology has also produced a wealth of data at the level of the individual inhabitant down to matters as personal as clothing (Heckett 1986), footwear (O'Rourke 1988) and sanitary arrangements (Mitchell 1987). These various classes of information have been accessed through the study of the products and by-products of human activities. In this paper, we interrogate another data set that also operates at the level of the individual participant in the past, in an effort to further our knowledge of the dynamics of the Hiberno-Norse settlement. This data set consists of the human remains that were found during the excavations of the tenth to twelfth-century levels of the town.

While the analysis of archaeologically retrieved human remains can produce a wealth of both biological and cultural data, our focus here is on what the skeletons from the Dublin excavations can reveal about the origins and biological affinities of the population(s) from which they were drawn. The material culture record has been interpreted as suggesting that a significant degree of acculturation occurred between immigrant and local populations from the time of the foundation of the town by Scandinavian settlers. Wallace (1992b), for instance, has pointed out that the dominant house type found in early tenth-century Dublin was built to a formula that had been developed prior to the historically documented re-establishment of Norse control of the settlement in AD 917. While this formula may be of indigenous origin, it may also combine elements of Scandinavian, Irish and other northern European building traditions. Remains of similar house types were found in eleventh-century levels in Waterford (Hurley et al. 1997). Interpretations of the architectural data in the light of this more recent evidence have also focused on the exchange of cultural elements between immigrant and local populations in both urban settings. It is also evident from an eclectic range of material culture and other developments from the ninth century onwards, including innovations in art styles and artifact types as well as linguistic borrowings, that a considerable degree of cultural assimilation occurred between the Irish and the Norse (Ambrosiani 1998; Wamers 1998). While contemporary Irish accounts of the Norse portrayed the latter mostly in a very negative light, political and military alliances between Irish and Norse are mentioned from as early as the ninth century (Sawyer 1982) while in the tenth century, such alliances were associated with élite level intermarriage (Ní Mhaonaigh 1998). Even more telling is the use by the Irish annalists of the term *Gall-Goídhil* 'foreign-Irish' from as early as AD 852 (Annals of Ulster). This reinforces the notion of integration between the Norse and at least some elements of Irish society. The biological implications of the use of this term can only be guessed at but the physical admixture of Irish and Norse groups is implicit in the archaeological interpretations that rely on acculturation. It is also implied by a term such as Hiberno-Norse that is commonly used in archaeological and historical discourse to describe the acculturated descendants of the original Viking raiders. The physical integration of populations with such diverse origins as Ireland and Scandinavia should be amenable to testing in the physical remains of adequate representative samples of both groups. The research reported on here set out to establish if biological evidence of admixture could be traced in the skeletal remains recovered during the Dublin excavations and if the flow of cultural elements that has been documented between these early historic populations was matched by a flow of genetic material through mating.

CONSTRUCTIONS OF IRISH AND NORSE

Research agendas similar to that outlined above were pursued in Irish archaeology and physical anthropology in the nineteenth and early twentieth centuries (for example Martin 1935; Morant 1936) during which time the two discourses developed in tandem, with each drawing on and informing the other. The resulting studies are now considered to be methodologically unsound and theoretically naïve because of their typological approach and perspective.

However, the nomenclature of the traditional archaeology survives, a situation that has attendant problems. For example, the use of omnibus labels such as 'Irish' and 'Norse' to describe early medieval societies is potentially problematic, particularly in the context of discussion of the biological relationship between these groups. It simplifies complex situations while promoting a view of homogenous, bounded and self-identifying populations, and projects this into the past. This was the dominant perspective of the traditional archaeology, which organised the past in terms of 'peoples' who occupied specific locations in time and space and were associated with particular sets of material culture remains. This concept of 'peoples' was blended with notions of race developed in physical anthropology. Since the 1960s, there has also been a rejection in the latter discourse of the typological approach favoured in the nineteenth and early twentieth centuries which held that there were Irish or Nordic 'types' that can be identified through the analysis of the skeleton (for example, Hooton and Dupertuis 1955). Similarly, the conflation of biological 'peoples' and specific sets of material culture remains was rejected by the modernist New Archaeology of the 1970s and in subsequent theoretical shifts. For the purposes of this paper, terms such as 'Irish', 'Norse' or 'Viking' are understood as discursive constructs that have emerged out of the historiography of recent centuries which are constantly being reworked and redefined. No matter how perspectives have changed, the terms have been applied retrospectively to peoples whose concept of their own identities was probably entirely different from the meanings invested in them by various discourses in the last few centuries.

The changes in perceptions of the relationship between culture and biology in past societies were summarised by Chapman (1992, 76) who wrote that 'the notion of a finite, biologically defined and biologically self-reproducing population as the basis for an ethnic group is largely fictional'. In the research reported here, we operate from the perspective that ethnicity and ethnic identity are cultural rather than biological constructs. Ethnic identities are often constructed in oppositional terms in relation to groups who are perceived as different, the latter usually being familiar neighbours rather than distant peoples (Barth 1969). In contrast to the inert, typological characterisation of ethnicity held by the traditional archaeology, more recent theorising understands group identities as dynamic phenomena that are constantly renegotiated. There are many examples of individuals and entire groups who have changed their cultural and linguistic affiliations in the space of a single generation. On the other hand, there are also many examples of groups who are characterised by endogamy, strong local continuity and a relatively high level of consanguinity. So the construction and maintenance of identity boundaries is also a dynamic phenomenon: in particular historical and cultural contexts, barriers can be maintained and can encourage endogamy, while in other circumstances they can be permeable. However, the fixing or relaxation of boundaries is not a uniform, predictable process and investigations need to be combined with a sensitivity to particular socio-historical contexts. In this perspective, cultural behaviours such as material culture traditions and language are understood to be transmitted independently of genes, although they can be correlated in specific circumstances. The long term maintenance or lack of cultural or geographic barriers to mating outside a socially defined group will have implications for the biology of that group in terms of levels of intra-group variability. The research reported here is concerned with charting such genetic variation rather than searching for signatures of ethnicity.

CONTEXTUALISING THE DATA: THE SKELETAL SAMPLES

For the purposes of this study, the skeletal material recovered during the Dublin excavations from Later Viking-age contexts was compared with human remains from two sites that are closely related spatially but separated temporally: one predates the Viking-age settlement and one post-dates it. A control sample was also used to facilitate comparisons between the Irish groups. This outgroup was an early historic sample from Iceland. The Icelandic skaldic literature suggests that the founding population of Iceland was of mixed ancestry with cohorts derived from Scandinavia, Ireland and Scotland (Kristjánsson 1998). The genetic makeup of settlement-period Icelanders might reasonably be expected to show some similarities to that of the inhabitants of Viking-age Dublin.

Dublin: Hiberno-Norse
The remains of perhaps eighty early Viking-age burials were found within the bounds of the modern city of Dublin during the two centuries from 1760 to 1960 (Ó Floinn 1998; O'Brien 1995; 1998). Of these, only the few skeletons found at Islandbridge in the 1930s were curated with the result that crucial evidence about the nature of the early phase of interactions between immigrant and local populations was lost. Since the 1960s, skeletal remains have been found in a variety of different contexts during many of the excavations that have been carried out in Hiberno-Norse levels of Dublin. These represent the largest group of Viking-related human remains from Ireland that is available for study. The bulk of this material, and the majority of skeletal remains used in this study, consists of isolated bones that were found scattered in the general matrix of a number of mostly contiguous sites that were excavated in the core of medieval Dublin. Some complete skeletons and portions of skeletons were also recovered. These latter were not found in cemeteries or areas that are likely to have been regarded by the inhabitants of the town as formal areas for the disposal of the dead. Most of the more complete remains came from contexts

that seem likely to have been regarded as atypical at the time of their deposition. The greatest number of these came from the excavations at Wood Quay that were carried out between 1974 and 1976 under the direction of Dr Patrick Wallace of the National Museum of Ireland. The human remains recovered from that site consisted of a mixture of disarticulated bone as well as articulated skeletons or portions of skeletons. Most of the articulated remains represent corpses that were deposited in estuarine mud immediately outside, (i.e., to the north of) the defensive stone wall that was built along the waterfront of the Hiberno-Norse town around the year AD 1100. These remains were subsequently sealed by landfill during late twelfth- or early thirteenth-century reclamation work. Most of these skeletons were found in what are best interpreted as mass graves. The more complete skeletons from Wood Quay represent the remains of at least seventeen people.

Six further individuals of Hiberno-Norse date were found in 1993 during excavations at Temple Lane that were directed by Martin Reid (1994) on behalf of Margaret Gowen and Co. These remains were recovered from a context similar to that described above at Wood Quay. The skeletal remains were found in what may have been a pit dug into the estuarine mud on a sand bar along the southern shore of the river Liffey, *c*.200 m downriver from the walled settlement. The bodies of the dead had been placed in this grave in a haphazard manner, suggesting perhaps that their disposal was a somewhat casual or perhaps hurried affair. These skeletons have produced radiocarbon dates that calibrate to the eleventh to thirteenth centuries at two sigmas (pers. comm., Margaret Gowen).

The twenty-three more complete skeletons from Wood Quay and Temple Lane were scored for this study. A pooled sample of another 70 individuals from the Dublin excavations was also scored. This sample consisted of isolated crania and cranial fragments that were found scattered in the general matrix of the contiguous sites at Wood Quay, St John's Lane and Fishamble St I and II, all of which were excavated by the National Museum of Ireland under the direction of Dr Wallace. On stratigraphic grounds, it seems likely that this pooled sample includes remains from at least the early tenth century to some time prior to the reclamation of the southern banks of the Liffey after the Anglo-Norman conquest in the late twelfth century.

Clearly, this is not an ideal sample to use in characterising the Hiberno-Norse population of the town. However, as is often the case with archaeologically derived material, it is all that is available. The pooled sample probably contains remains that were deposited over a period of two or three centuries. This is a relatively short time span in terms of microevolutionary change and if the sample contains representatives of two populations who had little previous contact, this should still be detectable. Given the numbers of individuals whose remains were available for study (N = 93) and the fact that only a minority of the remains had not been disturbed during the development of the Later

Viking-age settlement, it was not possible to examine diachronic changes within the Dublin sample. Of greater concern is the atypical manner of disposal of those represented in the sample. The mass graves at Wood Quay and Temple Lane were used at a time when formal cemeteries must have been available to the inhabitants of the town. The extramural burial pits in the estuarine mud may represent an expedient response to a calamitous situation of some sort. Some of the human skeletal material found at the base of the thirteenth-century walls of Dublin have been interpreted as representing the display of the remains of executed malefactors and consisted almost exclusively of the remains of adult males (Ó Donnabháin 1995a; 1995b). This is not the case with the skeletons from the base of the twelfth-century wall as these contained the remains of men and women of all ages as well as those of children (Ó Donnabháin, in prep.). This demographic profile suggests that the remains represent a cross section of the urban population, rather than being, for example, a sample of a military force. The identity of the scattered disarticulated remains is also puzzling. Ó Floinn (1998, 137) has noted that the 'ninth/tenth-century Scandinavian settlement at Dublin contained at least four separate cemeteries and a number of single graves which extended over a much greater area of the Liffey mouth than hitherto suggested'. Perhaps the remains scattered in the matrix of the Wood Quay, St John's Lane and Fishamble Street sites could be added to this list of early Viking-age burials. Ó Floinn (ibid.) envisaged a situation in which there were many grave-fields associated with the early phase of the settlement. It seems plausible to suggest that some such burial areas could have been incorporated within the bounds of the expanding town. Simpson (1999; 2000) has interpreted the results of recent excavations carried out a few hundred metres east of the Wood Quay, St John's Lane and Fishamble Street sites as representing an intensification of the pace of urban development in the early tenth century. As was the case in Dublin in more recent times, arrangements related to the separation of habitation and mortuary space may have been fluid during a period of rapid urban expansion.

As a result of these contextual issues, a caveat must be entered regarding the Hiberno-Norse period remains. While it seems likely for the reasons stated above that they represent a sequential sample of the inhabitants of the settlement at Dublin from the ninth to the twelfth century, other interpretations are also possible for at least some of the material.

Cabinteely, Co. Dublin

A sample of 101 skeletons was scored for this study from a total of over 1500 early medieval burials that were recovered during excavations of a cemetery at Cabinteely, Co. Dublin. This excavation was carried out in 1998 by Malachy Conway for Margaret Gowen and Co. (Conway 1999; 2000). Six stratigraphic phases of burial were identified at the site. Radiocarbon dates were not yet available at the time of writing but the earliest phases have been dated by artifactual associations to the fifth or sixth centuries. As a result, the earlier phases of this cemetery provide an opportunity to characterise the local population of the Dublin region prior to the period of Norse contact. As it is possible that the later phases were contemporary with the establishment of Viking Dublin just 10 km to the north of the cemetery, we compared the early and later phases of the cemetery to test for a disjunction that might reflect the addition of personnel from outside the pre-contact population. As the cemetery underwent significant expansion after phase 4, we pooled the data from phases 1–4 and compared those with the pooled data from phases 5 and 6. This also provided an opportunity to test for diachronic change within the population(s) who buried their dead at the site. It is likely that the Norse settlement at Dublin also included the hinterland of the town (Bradley 1988; Wallace 1987). The physical proximity of Cabinteely to Dublin, the presence nearby of evidence of what may be Norse rural settlement that may date from as early as the ninth century (Ó Néill 1999), as well as other circumstantial evidence such as the presence in the area of the decorated Viking stones known as Rathdown slabs and placenames such as Loughlinstown (from the Irish *Lochlannaig*, the Vikings), combine to suggest that the area serviced by the cemetery came under Norse control or at least Norse influence. While we await radiocarbon dates for the different phases of the cemetery, genetic change in the skeletal sample may help elucidate whether or not major population change occurred in the Cabinteely area during the period when the cemetery was in use.

Dublin: high medieval

The site at Temple Lane was mentioned above in the context of the six burials of Hiberno-Norse date that were found there. This site, located *c*.200 m east of the walls of the Viking town, produced two distinct and probably unrelated phases of burial activity: the Hiberno-Norse material that may represent a single burial episode and a cemetery dating from the high medieval period. The latter was located in an area that was known historically to be the site of the Augustinian friary of the Holy Trinity. Architectural remains associated with the friary were found in subsequent excavations carried out to the north east of the cemetery area in 1996 (Simpson 1997). The friary of the Holy Trinity was founded in the late thirteenth century and was dissolved in 1536 (Martin 1988). It appears that some of the monastic buildings survived the dissolution and were incorporated into a series of 'mansions' that survived until the early eighteenth century (Simpson 1997). By the time Speed's map of Dublin was compiled in 1610 the only reference to this Augustinian house was the retention of the name St Augustine's for a street perpendicular to Dame Street (Burke 1990). Speed's map depicts the area formerly occupied by the monastery as gardens of houses that fronted onto Dame Street. It seems unlikely therefore that burial continued at the site for very long after the suppression of the friary.

Excavation of the high-medieval cemetery produced the remains of 59 individuals (Ó Donnabháin and Cosgrave 1994) though, of these, only 33 were suitable for inclusion in this study so it would be unwise to over-interpret the results obtained from this sample. While the remains of both sexes and all ages were present in the cemetery, there was a bias among the adults towards males. This may represent the presence of ecclesiastical burials. Like all other thirteenth- and early fourteenth-century Augustinian foundations, it is likely that Holy Trinity was established by English monks (Martin 1988). The Augustinian province in Ireland was under the authority of the English province and Martin has suggested that in the thirteenth and fourteenth centuries at least, it was 'Anglo-Irish in personnel' (1988, 472). If surnames offer an insight into ethnic affiliations, the friary seems to have had Anglo-Irish personnel in 1379 when there was an enquiry into a murder committed there. Seven of the eight friars charged with the murder had Anglo-Norman or English surnames: Routh, Forster, Clement, Newton, Holm, Holywood and Bodenham (Martin, ibid.). The demographic profile of the skeletons from Temple Lane suggests that it is likely that the cemetery was also patronised by the inhabitants of the town. According to the traditional historical narrative, the Hiberno-Norse population was expelled outside the city walls in the aftermath of the Anglo-Norman invasion in 1170. While it is debatable as to how comprehensive this expulsion may have been, there can be little doubt that Dublin must have been subjected to significant gene flow from England and from other possessions of the English crown. The expectation then would be that the population burying at this cemetery would differ from both the Hiberno-Norse sample and the pre-Norse inhabitants of the region

Iceland
The entire curated collection of adult crania with observable traits that has been recovered from archaeological contexts in Iceland (N = 403) was scored for a companion study (Hallgrímsson et al., in prep.). This skeletal material is drawn from a large number of locations covering the entire island and is stored at the National Museum of Iceland. Information regarding context and date for much of the collection is poor. To overcome this problem we used information concerning burial practices to divide the burials into pre-Christian and Christian cohorts. The evangelisation of the population of Iceland is traditionally thought to have been a relatively rapid process that took place sometime around 1000 AD. Even allowing for some degree of licence in the historical account of this process, the pre-Christian sample (N=121) should date to the few centuries immediately following the settlement of the island. Only the data derived from this latter material were used to generate the results given below.

Written records dating from the twelfth and thirteenth centuries dominate the history of the settlement of Iceland. According to *Íslendingabók* (The Book of Icelanders), Irish hermits were the only people present on the island prior to its discovery by Norwegian Vikings in AD 870 and these clerics left after the arrival of the latter (Kristjánsson 1998). In the subsequent sixty years, immigrants from the Westfjords region of Norway settled the habitable areas of the island. The early Icelandic accounts imply that these Norse settlers were accompanied by a large number of slaves who were principally of Irish origin (Hjálmarsson 1993; Kristjánsson 1998). A significant slave component in the pioneering population of Iceland is possible given the evidence that the taking of slaves was an integral part of Viking warfare from the ninth century (Holm 1986). According to the *Landnámabók* (The Book of Settlements), significant immigration to the island had ceased by AD 930 and historians have suggested that the population could have reached 60,000 by that time (Hjálmarsson 1993).

This traditional account was accepted at face value until recent decades when some dissenting views emerged, particularly among archaeologists (for example Hermanns-Auðardóttir 1992; Vilhjálmsson 1990). Revisionist views of the skaldic literature maintain that the principal aim of their authors may have been to legitimise the landholding claims of the twelfth- and thirteenth-century élite in accordance with Germanic legal tradition by demonstrating their descent from the original settlers of particular territories on the island. Vilhjálmsson (ibid.) has argued that the *Landnámabók* may also have been used by this élite group as a device to distance Iceland from the control of the kings of Norway. Furthermore, he has argued that the traditional account of the settlement has become deeply embedded in modern nationalist discourse in Iceland. This has served to encourage a literal interpretation of these early texts and has impeded any significant reassessment of the traditional settlement account.

Seen in this context, the resilience of the skaldic account is perhaps understandable but it is also clear that an examination of sources of evidence other than the medieval literature could make a significant contribution to the reassessment of the traditional paradigm. To date, biological approaches have focused on the modern population of Iceland. Our survey of the collection of archaeologically retrieved human remains is the first to interrogate the remains of the early settlers themselves (Hallgrímsson et al., in prep.). For the purposes of the current study, we compared nonmetric trait variability in the settlement-period population of Iceland with the Irish samples mentioned above. While the primary reason for using the Icelandic data was to provide a control for the comparisons between the Irish samples, we also wanted to compare the genetic makeup of two groups that may have had similar histories. The Hiberno-Norse and the founding population of Iceland have been characterised in the archaeological literature and in traditional historiography as consisting of a Scandinavian-Irish mix, albeit in different proportions. If these groups were drawn from similar biological populations, their genetic makeup might reasonably be expected to parallel each other.

MORPHOLOGICAL VARIABILITY: DEFINING DIFFERENCE

A biological population consists of a group that is characterised by a relatively high level of consanguinity. This implies that members of the group tend to find breeding partners within its culturally perceived borders. Physical boundaries may favour this situation or, as often occurs among and between human groups, social boundaries based on concepts such as class and ethnicity are erected and maintained to promote endogamy. Human remains may be used to distinguish between biological populations by means of the analysis of the normal variability that occurs in the architecture of the skeleton. The use of morphology to investigate patterns of population variability has a long history (Buikstra et al. 1990). In this study, normal variations in cranial architecture that are usually referred to as nonmetric traits were used. It is thought that the expression of the variable bony features is primarily governed by genetic factors though the degree of genetic control seems to vary between traits. The heritability of particular traits also varies between populations. To minimise the effect of potentially confounding factors such as these, a constellation of skeletal features is scored for each individual. A reasonably large sample of each group, preferably of roughly contemporary skeletons from a particular historical context, is considered necessary in order to characterise each population. A group that is composed of individuals with a high degree of genetic affinity will show similar patterning in the distribution of skeletal traits. As the maintenance of culturally defined boundaries such as linguistic and ethnic differences tends only to impede rather than completely prevent interbreeding, there is a tendency for geographically adjacent populations to blend into one another in genetic terms. As a result, it is not possible to draw genetic boundaries around groups of people, rather, the normal distribution is that of the cline: a gradation from one constellation of traits to another across space. The corollary of this is that groups which are spatially separated in a significant way are likely to show less similarity in the patterning of normal variations in skeletal morphology. Morphological variability can be measured both within a single group and between a series of groups. Estimation of the degree of genetic affinity between groups, biological distance, can be used to rank groups in terms of relatedness. Within–group variability can also be measured and expressed in terms of the degree of homogeneity of trait distribution. A high degree of homogeneity within a representative sample is suggestive of a population with a long history of local continuity whereas low homogeneity may be suggestive of a group that lives in circumstances that promote mating with members of other biological populations. If these circumstances change and the interbreeding or gene flow is halted, the result will be a gradual return to a pattern of increased homogeneity through time. The characterisation of homogeneity is therefore time dependent and further emphasises the importance of contextualising data that are used in this way.

Statistical methods

For the purposes of this study, we used the traits described in the *Standards for data collection from human skeletal remains* (Buikstra and Ubelaker 1994). The traits that were observed are listed in Table 1. Traits were scored bilaterally for each individual as either present, absent or not available for inspection. The calculation of a measure of biodistance or between group variability involves characterising the frequencies of each trait per population being compared. The distance between samples is the mean difference across all traits. The trait frequency per trait within each sample was calculated using the formula

$$F = P/(P+A)$$

where F = frequency, P = number of traits scored as present and A = number of traits scored as absent. The statistical significance of the distance between each sample is obtained by means of a bootstrap method. In the latter, the observed distance is compared to a sample of randomised distances that are generated by repeatedly sampling the combined samples in such a way that individuals are randomly assigned to either group. This is a direct method of obtaining the probability that the distance between a pair of samples could have been obtained by chance. The final result of this statistical device is a p-value for each distance for each sample to be compared.

Calculating within-group variability involves making the assumption that genetic and morphological variability are correlated. Each trait in each individual is compared with the same trait in every other individual in the group. A measure of the degree of variability per trait within the sample could have been achieved by recoding the data as zero (for absent) and one (for present) and comparing the resulting variances using an F-test or Levene's test. This statistic was not used in this case because when traits expressions are dependent on one another, as occurs with some nonmetric traits, this creates a non-random trait distribution that cannot be controlled for. This makes it very difficult to combine the results of such comparisons across traits. To avoid this problem, we devised an index that measures similarity among individuals within groups. In this index, every possible pair of individuals within each group is compared. In this comparison, one is assigned each time the same value appears for a trait and minus one each time the trait values are different. The sum across traits is then obtained for each individual and this value is then summed for all possible pairs of individuals in each group. So this index of homogeneity measures the extent to which individuals within groups resemble each other in terms of their configuration of nonmetric traits. Confidence intervals for this statistic were calculated by means of a randomisation method.

Our data set included a large percentage of fragmentary remains where not all traits could be scored for each individual. Existing methods for the analysis of nonmetric trait data do not deal adequately with such datasets that contain a large number of missing values. The randomisation method developed by Konigsberg (1988) as well as the Mean Measure of Divergence statistic (Sjøvold 1977) both require the assumption that the variables are independent and have identical null distributions. In Konigsberg's study, for example, this assumption was met by eliminating all traits with high numbers of missing values.

In our research, the degree of fragmentation, and hence proportion of missing values, differs among the groups to be compared. For this reason, we sought to develop a statistical method that is not affected by between-group variation in the numbers of missing values. This methodological approach is explained more fully in a companion paper (Hallgrímsson et al., in prep.). In this method, biodistance is calculated as the mean difference in frequency across traits between all possible pairs of samples. Biodistance (D) was thus calculated as:

$$D = \frac{\sum_{i=1}^{n} \left| f_{1i} - f_{2i} \right|}{n}$$

Where D is biodistance, f_{1i} and f_{2i} are frequencies of the ith trait for populations one and two, and n is the number of traits.

Dendrograms were constructed to visualize the pattern of affinity among samples. The Fitch-Margoliash least squares routine for distance matrices was used to obtain the most parsimonious dendrogram. The Fitch programme in the Phylip package (Felsenstein, 1986–1993) was used to run this routine.

RESULTS

Trait frequencies for all of the skeletal samples that were scored are presented in Table 1. A biodistance matrix that charts between-group variability for the samples included in the analysis is shown in Table 2 while a least-squares dendrogram based on the distance matrix in the latter table is shown in Figure 1. The sample recovered from the Hiberno–Norse levels of the Dublin excavations is not significantly different from either of the two samples, Cabinteely and Temple Lane, that bracket it temporally. If, as seems likely, the skeletons uncovered during the Dublin excavations are representative of the Viking-age population of the settlement, this implies that local, pre-contact communities made a significant contribution to that population and were at least partially ancestral to it. In turn, the Viking-age population was at least partially ancestral to the group who buried their dead in the high-medieval cemetery uncovered at Temple Lane. There was a significant difference between the

Cabinteely and Temple Lane samples. While the caveat entered above regarding the size of the latter sample must be remembered, this suggests that a significant amount of gene flow may have affected the population of the Dublin area over the course of the centuries that separate these groups. This is consistent with the history and archaeology of the region.

All of the Irish samples were significantly different from the Icelandic outgroup. The absence of any degree of similarity between the latter and the sample recovered from the Hiberno-Norse levels of Dublin was particularly interesting and was contrary to expectations. These results suggest that Ireland did not contribute a significant component to the founding population of Iceland. This latter finding is discussed at greater length in a more detailed study of the Icelandic data (Hallgrímsson et al., in prep.).

The results of the within-group variation analysis are summarised in Figure 2 which shows indices of homogeneity for all of the samples. The series from Temple Lane and that from the Hiberno-Norse levels of Dublin both have very low coefficients of homogeneity, a scenario that is to be expected in populations of mixed origins. In contrast, the Cabinteely sample has a very high index of homogeneity, which is consistent with a population with a long history of local continuity. The possibility that the later phases of burial there overlap with the period of Viking settlement in the Dublin region was mentioned above with the implication that the later phases of burial could contain a cohort derived from the Scandinavian populations that settled in the region. To test for such a situation, we divided the Cabinteely sample in two, and compared the later two phases of burial, which coincided with a marked increase in burial activity, with the four earlier phases. This produced a biodistance value of 0.066 (p=0.982) which indicates that there is not a significant difference between the earlier and later phases of burial at the site and that a significant level of gene flow did not occur during the later phases.

Curiously, the Icelandic outgroup also produced a relatively high index of homogeneity. These results are not consistent with the diversity of origins that is implied in the skaldic literature. Rather, they imply that the pioneering population of that island was drawn from a relatively homogenous source group.

DISCUSSION

For this study, phenotypic data were used to characterise the genetic makeup of a sample of 93 individuals whose remains were recovered during the Dublin excavations from levels dated to between the tenth and twelfth centuries. This group was then compared with two groups from the Dublin region that bracket it temporally and, as a control, with an outgroup from Iceland. Analyses of patterns of between- and within-population variability in non-metric trait frequencies were used to characterise each sample and to compare the groups. The analysis of inter-population variability, or biodistance, revealed that the Hiberno-Norse sample was closely related to the local, pre-Norse inhabitants of the region as represented by the burials at Cabinteely. Analysis of intra-population variability revealed that the Hiberno-Norse sample was also significantly less homogenous than that from Cabinteely. This is possibly a function of context in that the Hiberno-Norse sample consists of material that has been pooled from a number of different sites. However, it seems unlikely that this explains the heterogeneity noted in the sample: while the remains were recovered from five sites, all but one of these were contiguous and covered a relatively concise space. The remains were also deposited over a time period that was likely to have been shorter than that represented in the highly homogenous sample from nearby Cabinteely. A population of mixed geographic origins is the more likely explanation of the heterogeneity observed in the Dublin sample. This does not conflict with the suggestion of a relatively high level of affinity with the local pre-contact population: it indicates rather that the latter was only partially ancestral to the Hiberno-Norse group. These results combine to suggest that the skeletal sample recovered from the Hiberno-Norse levels of the Dublin excavations was descended from both immigrant and local populations.

The comparison between the Hiberno-Norse sample and that of high-medieval date from Temple Lane also has interesting implications. The latter group was the most heterogeneous of all those analysed. This is consistent with a colonial population made up of peoples of diverse geographic origins. By the time the cemetery at Temple Lane was established, Dublin had been subjected to a significant influx of personnel from England and other possessions of the crown for at least a century. Despite the traditional historical narrative of the expulsion of the Hiberno-Norse population from the city in the aftermath of the Anglo-Norman invasion and the genetic diversity of the subsequent high-medieval colonial population, the biodistance data confirm the continued presence of the pre-Norman population of Dublin. While it could be argued that this finding may reflect the shared Scandinavian heritage of the Hiberno-Norse and at least some of the Anglo-Norman population, the results of the biodistance comparison with the founding population of Iceland militates against such a position. The Hiberno-Norse sample was not closely related to this latter group, so the logical explanation of the similarity between the Hiberno-Norse and high-medieval groups is that the former was partially ancestral to the latter.

The comparison of the Hiberno-Norse sample with the Icelandic data has interesting implications regarding the origins of the Scandinavians who settled in Dublin. The Icelandic data presented here suggest that Iceland was peopled as a result of a migration stream that drew primarily on a relatively homogenous population with a long history of continuity in the region of origin.

Traditionally, the westfjords region of Norway has been identified as the most likely point of origin. This is the same region that has produced the densest concentration of 'insular' metalwork that is presumed to have been looted during the piratical phase of Viking expansion (Wamers 1983; 1998) and might thereby be expected to have provided the colonists of the Dublin region. However, there is considerable evidence to suggest that at least some of the Viking groups responsible for the re-establishment of Dublin in the early tenth century had a long history of settlement in Britain and continental Europe where the lessons of urbanism were probably learned (Wallace 1988) and where significant biological admixture could have occurred with indigenous populations as well as with other peoples of Scandinavian origin. Contemporary Irish sources noted the heterogeneity of the 'foreigners' and reflected this in such contrastive terms such as *finngall* 'fair foreigner' and *dubhgall* 'dark foreigner'. The heterogeneity of the Hiberno-Norse sample from Dublin and its relative distance from the Icelandic group is consistent with a colonising population that is itself already relatively heterogeneous prior to any inter-actions with local Irish groups. These results provide further confirmation that the use of hold-all terms such as 'Irish' and 'Viking' can serve to mask the diversity of the peoples so described.

Anthony (1990) examined the demographic profiles and motivating forces that obtain in migrant societies. He noted that entire populations do not migrate except in exceptional circumstances that usually involve an element of coercion. Instead, 'it is often only a very narrowly defined, goal oriented sub-group that migrates' (ibid., 908). Pioneering parties tend to be dominated by young males such as in the traditional image of the piratical phase of Viking expansion in much of Europe. In his survey of the grave goods associated with early Viking-age burials in the Dublin region, Ó Floinn (1998) noted a ratio of 10:1 between what he termed male and female graves and interpreted this as indicating the presence of a sizeable proportion of women of Scandinavian birth in ninth and tenth-century Dublin. Notwithstanding the dangers inherent in determining the sex and birthplace of individuals based on grave goods buried with them, this pattern tallies with Anthony's model of the skewed demographics of migrant groups, a situation that would encourage hybridisation with indigenous peoples. The results detailed above for the composition of the sample of Hiberno-Norse date are consistent with such a scenario. The process of hybridisation, in Ireland as elsewhere, could have taken many forms and explanations could range from coercive models to changes in self-definition by cohorts of the local population. The latter process could have been encouraged by the opportunities offered by a gateway community (Hodges 1982) such as Viking-age Dublin. The urban setting, a novel and experimental entity in tenth-century Ireland, may have presented opportunities to some segments of the local population that would not have been attainable in the world described in the early medieval Irish law texts (Kelly 1988) which, on a conservative reading of the latter, could be interpreted as being almost petrified in social terms.

In the title of this paper, we paraphrase that of an article published by Patrick Wallace in 1992 in which he examined the physical traits of late Viking-age urban settlements in Ireland. Wallace argued that a distinctive identity could be discerned in the Irish settlements when these sites were compared with contemporary urban sites in the Baltic and in Britain (Wallace 1986; 1992a). This distinctive identity reflects an adaptation to the particular set of social and political contexts that were encountered by the Norse in Ireland (Ó Floinn 1998). These conclusions were based on the analysis of material culture items and their distribution and organisation in the landscape. In the analyses reported in this paper, our results conform to the acculturation and assimilation models that have been used to explain the patterning seen in the material culture data. We contend that the flow of cultural items between the immigrant and local populations in Ireland during the centuries on either side of AD 1000 was matched by a flow of genes through mating across the cultural divide and that this flow was not confined to the social élite.

Despite this history of integration and interbreeding, as well as the curtail-ment of direct contacts with Scandinavia from the eleventh century, Dublin maintained a distinct political and, judging from the artifactual evidence, cultural identity up until the Anglo-Norman invasion of 1170. This may be a reflection of the dynamic, opportunistic and pragmatic nature of ethnic affiliations. In the context of a cellular and fragmented political scene such as obtained in pre-Norman Ireland, the privileging of a particular set of roots of the family tree at the expense of other kinship ties could have been an effective device in the maintenance of political and economic autonomy. In a context of increasing cultural assimilation, the mythologising of the Viking past in Ireland by eleventh and twelfth-century scribes (Ní Mhaonaigh 1998) on both sides of the perceived divide would have served to reinforce the notion of difference while further legitimising the political realities of the day.

We began this paper by noting that Dublin began as a Viking enclave, something it shared with other Norse settlements along the Irish coast and retained until the Anglo-Norman conquest of 1170. It was located on the physical margins of a society that, despite its political fragmentation, appears to have resisted attempts at more intensive colonisation such as occurred in the Frankish empire and in England. To draw on a modern analogy, as a colonial enterprise the Viking presence in Dublin had more in common with the nineteenth- and twentieth-century situations of Hong Kong and Macau than with European expansion in the New World that was characterised by large-scale rural and urban settlement at the expense of indigenous peoples. The analogy with Hong Kong and Macau is a useful one: in biological terms, local indigenous peoples dominated the populations of those colonial outposts. Their co-operation with the maintenance of the enclaves was initially assured by coercion and subsequently by a process of identification with the economic goals and ideological values of the colonial power. The biological data presented here for the relationship between immigrant and local populations in Viking Dublin can be interpreted as being consistent with the operation of a similar process between the tenth and twelfth centuries.

After 1170, the absorption of Dublin and its population into a relatively centralised and powerful state system such as the Anglo-Norman Lordship of Ireland must have necessitated an adaptation to new political and social realities. The traditional narrative of the expulsion of the Hiberno-Norse population from Dublin is suggestive of the active discouraging of assimilation in the aftermath of the conquest. To draw on another modern analogy, this narrative implies the operation of a form of cultural apartheid with the establishment of a township for the Ostmen of Dublin at Oxmanstown. While there is little direct evidence from Dublin of the maintenance of a distinct Hiberno-Norse identity after 1170, the persistence of such a perceived difference is suggested by early fourteenth-century legal documents relating to Waterford that imply the Ostmen there were still recognised as a distinctive community, albeit one that had the same privileges as the English burgesses of the town (Bradley and Halpin 1992). The biological data presented here suggest that any mating barriers that might have been placed between the descendants of the Hiberno-Norse population of Dublin and the Anglo-Norman community were not maintained in the long term.

The data presented in this paper indicate that gene flow occurred between some of the groups under scrutiny but they reveal little about the culturally-determined management of this exchange. While, for example, assumptions that the immigrant population was predominantly male have significant implications for the dynamics of the acculturation process, gender differences in the vectors of gene flow are not easily elucidated using the type of phenotypic data that are described above. As a means of progressing the research reported here, we hope to study genotypic data through the analysis of ancient DNA. This will provide an opportunity to further test the results presented above while also providing greater resolution in terms of the dynamics of the interactions between local and immigrant populations in Viking-Age Dublin and beyond.

ACKNOWLEDGEMENTS

We would like to thank Daníel Gudbjartsson and Bragi Gudmundsson for their input to research reported here. We also wish to thank John Sheehan, Andy Halpin and Maurice Hurley for their useful comments on drafts of the paper. Finally, we are grateful to deCODE genetics Inc., Reykjavík, for funding the data collection in Iceland.

Trait	Pre-Christian Iceland (N=121)	Hiberno-Norse (N=93)	Cabinteely (N=101)	Temple Lane (N=33)
Metopic suture	72%	77%	83%	70%
Supraorbital notch	70%	66%	75%	70%
Supraorbital foramen	70%	67%	75%	70%
Infraorbital suture	39%	30%	41%	33%
Multiple infraorbital foramina	40%	28%	43%	36%
Zygomatico facial foramen	43%	72%	68%	67%
Parietal foramen	48%	9%	25%	45%
Epipteric bone	69%	63%	58%	24%
Coronal ossicle	53%	46%	64%	67%
Bregmatic bone	60%	45%	65%	39%
Sagittal ossicle	53%	59%	64%	52%
Apical bone	59%	53%	61%	48%
Lamboid ossicle	57%	64%	68%	52%
Asterionic bone	56%	54%	61%	55%
Ossicle in occipito-mastoid suture	59%	50%	58%	55%
Parietal notch bone	57%	60%	64%	58%
Inca bone	64%	89%	81%	58%
Condylar canal	58%	66%	49%	64%
Divided hypoglossal	68%	87%	67%	45%
Flexure of superior sagittal sulcus	67%	82%	81%	61%
Foramen ovale incomplete	62%	56%	43%	58%
Foramen spinosum incomplete	62%	52%	51%	67%
Pteryo-spinous bridge	55%	57%	52%	76%
Pteryo-alar bridge	58%	62%	49%	70%
Tympanic Dihiscence	79%	88%	83%	70%
Auditory exostosis	81%	69%	80%	70%
Mastoid foramen-location	62%	80%	72%	58%
Mastoid foramen-number	64%	77%	72%	58%
Mental foramen	81%	93%	87%	58%
Mandibular torus	72%	85%	67%	73%
Mylohoid bridge-location	71%	86%	65%	70%
Mylohyoid bridge-number	71%	86%	65%	79%
Supratrochlear notch	62%	56%	68%	82%
Supratrochlear foramen	61%	56%	68%	76%
Accessory lesser palatine foramina	54%	44%	49%	85%
Palatine torus	61%	18%	62%	70%
Maxillary torus	58%	0%	0%	45%
Rocker mandible	55%	57%	61%	0%
Suprameatal pit	76%	88%	86%	45%
Average across traits	62%	61%	62%	58%

Table 1 Observable traits by sample expressed as a percentage of the total.

	Hiberno-Norse	Cabinteely	Temple Lane	Pre-Christian Iceland
Hiberno-Norse	–	p= 0.078	p=0.067	p<0.01
Cabinteely	0.072	–	p<0.01	p<0.01
Temple Lane	0.0720.	084	–	p<0.01
Pre-Christian Iceland	0.125	0.118	0.122	–

Table 2 Matrix of Euclidean frequency distances among samples. The lower left of the table contains the distance values while the upper right contains the associated p-values obtained by bootstrapping (see text). Significant values (a = 0.05) are indicated in bold.

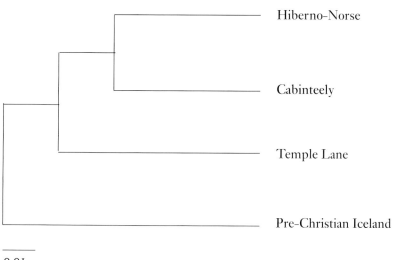

0.01
Frequency Distance

Figure 1 Least squares best-fit dendrogram for the groups mentioned in this study. The Fitch–Margoliash method (Phylip, ©Felsenstein, 1986–93) was used to obtain the dendrogram from the matrix of biodistances shown in Table 2. The scale shows Euclidian frequency distance.

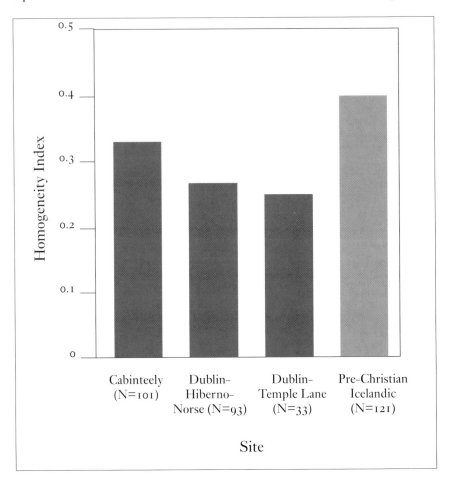

Figure 2   Indices of homogeneity for the samples mentioned in the text. A higher
homogeneity index signifies a higher degree of resemblance among individuals
within a sample. Error bars indicate 95% confidence intervals.

REFERENCES

Ambrosiani, B. 1998 Ireland and Scandinavia in the early Viking age: an archaeological
     response. In H.B. Clarke, M. Ní Mhaonaigh and R. Ó Floinn (eds.), *Ireland and
     Scandinavia in the early Viking age*, Dublin. 405–20.
Anthony, D.W. 1990 Migration in archaeology: the baby and the bathwater. *American
     Anthropologist* 92, 895–914.
Barth, F. 1969 Introduction. In F. Barth (ed.), *Ethnic Groups and Boundaries: the social
     organisation of culture difference*. Oslo, 9–38.

Bradley, J. 1988 The interpretation of Scandinavian settlement in Ireland. In J. Bradley (ed.), *Settlement and society in medieval Ireland*. Kilkenny, 49–78.

—— and Halpin, A. 1992 The topographical development of Scandinavian and Anglo-Norman Waterford. In W. Nolan and T.P. Power (eds.), *Waterford history and society*. Dublin, 105–29.

Buikstra, J.E., Frankenburg, S.R., and Konigsberg, L.W. 1990 Skeletal biological distance studies in American physical anthropology: recent trends. *American Journal of Physical Anthropology* 82, 1–7.

—— and Ubelaker D.H. 1994 *Standards for data collection from human skeletal remains*. In D. Aftandilian (ed.), Arkansas Archeological Survey Research Series No. 44. Fayetteville, Arkansas.

Burke, N. 1990 Dublin's north-eastern city wall: early reclamation and development at the Poddle-Liffey confluence. In H. Clarke (ed.), *Medieval Dublin: the making of a metropolis*. Dublin, 142–161.

Chapman, M. 1992 *The Celts: the construction of a myth*. New York.

Conway, M. 1999 Director's First Findings from Excavations in Cabinteely. Dublin: Margaret Gowen and Company Transactions 1.

—— 2000 Mount Offaly, Cabinteely: early medieval enclosed cemetery. In I. Bennett (ed.), *Excavations 1998: summary accounts of archaeological excavations in Ireland*. Bray, 36–7.

Fanning, T. 1994 *Viking Age ringed pins from Dublin*. Dublin: Royal Irish Academy.

Hallgrímsson, B., Ó Donnabháin B., Gudmundsson B., Gudbjartsson D., and Stefánsson K. (in prep.) *A tale of two islands: biological distance and morphological variability in Iceland and Ireland in the early historic period*.

Heckett, E.W. 1986 A group of Hiberno-Norse silk and wool headcoverings from Fishamble St/St John's Lane, Dublin. Unpublished thesis submitted for MA degree, Department of Archaeology, University College, Cork.

Hermanns-Audardóttir, M. 1992 The beginning of settlement in Iceland from an archaeological point of view. *Acta Borealia*, 2, 85–135.

Hjálmarsson, J.R. 1993 *History of Iceland: from the Settlement to the present day*. Reykjavík: Iceland Review.

Hodges, R. 1982 The evolution of gateway communities: their socio-economic implications. In C. Renfrew and S. Shennan (eds.), *Ranking, resource and exchange: aspects of the archaeology of early European society*. Cambridge, 117–23.

Holm, P. 1986 The slave trade of Dublin, ninth to twelfth centuries. *Peritia*, 5, 317–45.

Hooton, E.A., and Dupertuis C.A. 1955 *The physical anthropology of Ireland*. Papers of the Peabody Museum of Archaeology and Ethnology 30.

Hurley, M.F., Scully O.M.B., and McCutcheon S.W.J. 1997 *Late Viking age and medieval Waterford: excavations 1986–1992*. Waterford.

Kelly, F. 1988 *A guide to early Irish law*. Dublin.

Konigsberg, L.W. 1988 Migration models of prehistoric postmarital residence. *American Journal of Physical Anthropology* 77, 471–82.

Kristjánsson, J. 1998, Ireland and the Irish in Icelandic tradition. In H.B. Clarke, M. Ní Mhaonaigh and R. Ó Floinn (eds.), *Ireland and Scandinavia in the Viking age*. Dublin, 259–276.

Martin, C.P. 1935 *Prehistoric man in Ireland*. London.

Martin, F.X. 1988 Murder in a Dublin monastery. In G. MacNiocaill and P.F. Wallace (eds.), *Keimelia: studies in medieval archaeology and history in memory of Tom Delaney*. Galway, 468–98.

Mitchell, G.F. 1987 *Archaeology and the environment in early Dublin*. Dublin: Royal Irish Academy.

Morant, G.M. 1936 The craniology of Ireland. *Journal of the Royal Anthropological Institute*
    66, 43–55.

Ní Mhaonaigh, M. 1998 Friend and foe: Vikings in ninth- and tenth-century Irish literature.
    In H.B. Clarke, M. Ní Mhaonaigh and R. Ó Floinn (eds.), *Ireland and Scandinavia in
    the early Viking age*. Dublin, 381–402.

O'Brien, E. 1995 A tale of two cemeteries. *Archaeology Ireland* 9, 13–15.

—— 1998 The location and context of Viking-age burials at Kilmainham and Islandbridge,
    Dublin. In H.B Clarke, M. Ní Mhaonaigh and R. Ó Floinn (eds.), *Ireland and
    Scandinavia in the early Viking age*. Dublin, 203–221.

Ó Donnabháin, B. 1995a The human remains. In L. Simpson (ed.), *Excavations at Essex
    Street West, Dublin*. Temple Bar Archaeological Reports 2, 117–20.

Ó Donnabháin, B. 1995b Monuments of shame: some probable trophy heads from medieval
    Dublin. *Archaeology Ireland*, 9, 12–15.

—— (in prep.) *Life and death in Viking age Dublin: the human remains from the Dublin
    excavations 1974–1981*.

—— and Cosgrave U. 1994 The bioarchaeology of the cemetery at Temple Lane, Dublin.
    Unpublished MS submitted to Margaret Gowen and Co Ltd: April 1994.

Ó Floinn, R. 1998 The archaeology of the early Viking age in Ireland. In H.B. Clarke, M. Ní
    Mhaonaigh and R. Ó Floinn (eds.), *Ireland and Scandinavia in the early Viking age*.
    Dublin, 131–165.

Ó Néill, J. 1999 A Norse settlement in rural County Dublin. *Archaeology Ireland* 13, 8–10.

O'Rourke, D. 1988 Leather footwear from Viking Dublin. Unpublished thesis submitted for
    MA degree, Department of Archaeology, University College, Dublin.

Reid, M. 1994 Temple Lane, Dublin. In I. Bennett (ed.), *Excavations 1993: summary accounts
    of archaeological excavations in Ireland*. Bray, p. 29.

Sawyer, P.H. 1982 The Vikings and Ireland. In D. Whitelock, R. McKitterick and
    D. Dumville (eds.), *Ireland in early medieval Europe: studies in memory of
    Kathleen Hughes*. Cambridge, 345–61.

Simpson, L. 1997 5–6 Cecilia Street West, Dublin. In I. Bennett (ed.), *Excavations 1996:
    summary accounts of archaeological excavations in Ireland*. Bray, 20–21.

—— 1999 *Director's findings: Temple Bar West. Dublin:* Temple Bar Archaeological Report
    5. Dublin.

—— 2000 Forty years a-digging: a preliminary synthesis of archaeological investigations in
    medieval Dublin. In S. Duffy (ed.), *Medieval Dublin I: proceedings of the Friends of
    Medieval Dublin symposium 1999*. Dublin, 11–68.

Sjøvold, T. 1977 The occurence of minor non-metrical variants in the skeleton and their
    quantitative treatment for population comparison. *Homo* 24, 204–33.

Vilhjálmsson, V.Ö. 1990 Archaeological restrospect on physical anthropology in Iceland. In
    E. Iregren and R. Liljekvist (eds.), *Populations of the Nordic countries human population
    biology from the present to the Mesolithic: proceedings of the second seminar of Nordic
    physical anthropology*. Lund: University of Lund, Institute of Archaeology Report
    Series No. 46, 198–214.

Wallace, P.F.. 1986 The English presence in Viking Dublin. In M.A.S. Blackburn (ed.),
    Anglo-Saxon monetary history: essays in memory of Michael Dolley. Leicester, 201–21.

—— 1987 The economy and commerce of Viking Age Dublin. In K. Düwel, H. Jankhun,
    H.. Siems and D. Timpe (eds.), *Untersuchungen zu Handel und Verkehr der vor- und
    frühgeschichtlichen Zeit in Mittel-und Nordeuropa iv: der Handel der Karolinger- und
    Wikingerzeit*. Gottingen, 200–45.

—— 1988 Archaeology and the emergence of Dublin as the principal town of Ireland. In
    J Bradley (ed.), *Settlement and society in medieval Ireland*. Kilkenny, 123–60.

—— 1992a The archaeological identity of the Hiberno-Norse town. *R.S.A.I. Jn.* 122, 35–66.

—— 1992b *The Viking age buildings of Dublin.* Dublin, Royal Irish Academy.

Wamers, E. 1983 Some ecclesiastical and secular insular metalwork found in Norwegian Viking graves. *Peritia* 2, 277–306.

—— 1998 Insular finds in Viking Age Scandinavia and the state formation of Norway. In H.B. Clarke, M. Ní Mhaonaigh and R. Ó Floinn (eds.), *Ireland and Scandinavia in the early Viking age.* Dublin, 37–72.

Dublin's southern town defences, tenth to fourteenth centuries: the evidence from Ross Road

CLAIRE WALSH

INTRODUCTION

The sequence of earthen fortifications excavated at Christ Church Place/Ross Road in Dublin is probably the most complex and complete to be recorded from any town in north-west Europe. Several stretches of these Hiberno-Norse defences have been archaeologically excavated, at Fishamble Street (Wallace 1981, 1992); beneath the Powder Tower at Dublin Castle (Lynch and Manning, 1990 and Chapter 2 above), at Parliament Street (Gowen with Scally, 1996); more recently, the southern tail of a bank uncovered at Essex Street West (Simpson 1999) may also be part of the circuit (fig. 1). This article describes the defensive development of part of the southern circuit, excavated at Ross Road in 1993 (figs. 1,2,3).

While the sequence of fortifications is well recorded in the southern, eastern and northern part of medieval Dublin, there is scant evidence for the Hiberno-Norse defences at the western side of the town, and the embankment uncovered at Lamb Alley (Coughlan 2000) is more likely to relate to early twelfth-century expansion at this side of the town. Those defences excavated in both Waterford (Hurley et al., 1997) and Limerick (Wallace 1992) are later than the Dublin series, dating to the eleventh century, rather than to the true Viking phase of these towns. The banks in both Waterford and Limerick appear also to have been of single-phase construction, replaced in both instances by stone walls, unlike the continuously rebuilt embankments of Hiberno-Norse Dublin.

THE EARLIEST DEFENCES: THE *LONGPHORT* PHASE

The establishment of a *longphort*, or ship-camp, at Dubhlinn in AD 841 is documented in contemporary sources and the nature and location of this settlement is discussed by several authors (Wallace 1985, 1992, 2000; O'Brien 1998; Ó Floinn 1998; Clarke 1998; Simpson 1999, 2000). However, much of what was published in and before 1998 has been rendered obsolete by the firm evidence for ninth-century (and possibly earlier) occupation uncovered from excavations at Temple Bar West (Simpson 1999, fig. 1). This site, with established ninth-century habitation towards the Liffey shore in the form of a series of sunken houses with strong Anglo-Saxon affinities, strongly suggests that the longphort, or a related settlement, was located nearby. No earthworks which could relate to this longphort were uncovered in that excavation, but an inlet of the Liffey at the north end of the site may have been used for drawing up and securing the boats which were essential to the livelihood of the settlement. A bank, identified as a 'flood-bank', of which only the base of the south side extended into the excavated area, was uncovered along the line of the inlet. We could posit that the settlement expanded from this area, as a mid-to-late ninth-century settlement of conventional post-and-wattle structures, laid out in plots, has been uncovered at Temple Bar West.

There are several possibilities as to the form of the settlement in early Dublin: the ninth-century settlement may itself have been undefended, but with a fort of some kind perhaps where Dublin Castle was later constructed. If this was the case, we should expect ninth-century settlement in the immediate vicinity of the castle site, such as at the extensive Castle Street excavations, where, however, no such evidence appears to have been uncovered (Simpson 2000, 32). Wallace (2000), in a revision of earlier thought (1992), views Dublin in the mainstream of mid-ninth-century urbanisation, where settlement developed in plots around a fortress.

Despite the strong evidence for an established ninth-century settlement, the known defences in the area of Essex Street West at Parliament St (Gowen with Scally 1996) date to the tenth century. At Fishamble Street, occupation horizons predate the construction of the embankments (Wallace 1992, 44). There is some evidence for an embankment at Christ Church Place, which appears to pre-date the early tenth-century bank (see below, the National Museum of Ireland excavations, figs. 3 and 7); however this discovery finds no parallels at other excavated Dublin sites.

In both the location and development of towns of the early middle ages, 'defensibility seems to have been a secondary consideration' (Clarke and Ambrosiani 1995, 128), being subordinate to other concerns, such as the concept of the property plot (Wallace 2000, 263). The Dublin evidence is paralleled in most other settlements throughout the western Viking world, where ramparts and other defensive features are secondary to the settlement, and evidence uncovered to date for ninth-century urban defences is confined to a few exceptional sites, such as Hereford (Shoesmith 1982), and possibly in part at York. The evidence from towns of the Burghal Hidage, such as Winchester, suggests that the streets and defences were 'a single operation designed to provide a large defended enclosure' (Biddle 1975, 27). These towns are exceptional to those which experienced a more organic growth such as occurred

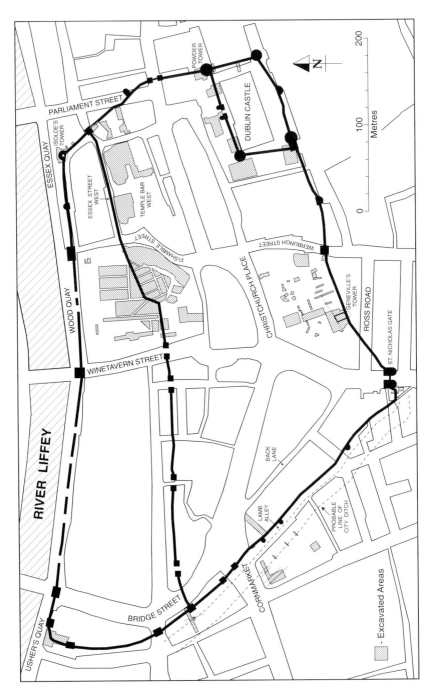

1 Medieval walled Dublin, showing excavations mentioned in text.

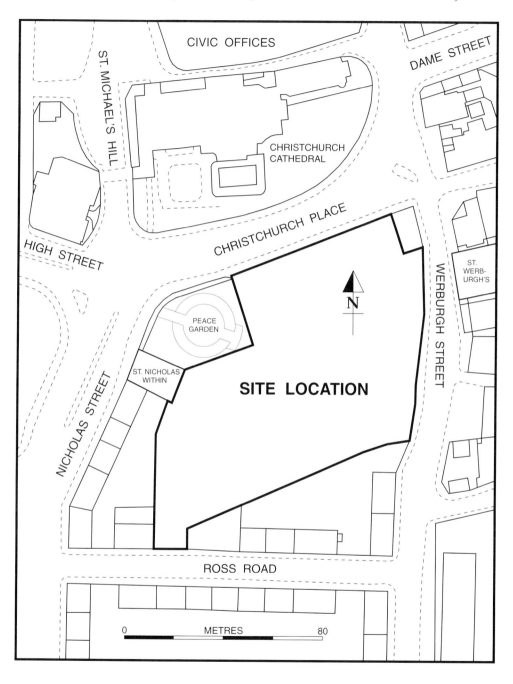

2 Site location.

at Dublin. In most cases it appears that the construction of urban defences was a late ninth- to early tenth-century mainstream development throughout England (Clarke and Ambrosiani 1995, 32), a development which appears also to be reflected in Dublin. Likewise, northern settlements of the Viking homelands first appear to have been defended in this period.

CHRIST CHURCH PLACE/ROSS ROAD

The Liffey formed the northern limit of the early settlement at Dublin, while the river Poddle provided considerable natural advantages to the east and south sides of the town. The ground at the south of the town sloped steeply down to the channel and flood plain of the Poddle (fig. 1).

The site at Ross Road was excavated over the course of twelve weeks in early 1993. Earlier work within the large development site had been undertaken by Margaret Gowen in 1992, who also carried out test excavation on the site. A link trench, to the south of the excavation, undertaken in the 1970s by Breandán Ó Ríordáin for the National Museum of Ireland (NMI) was also cut (fig. 3). When the excavation was concluded, a further area of work on the south of the site (Geneville's Tower) was undertaken by Margaret Gowen. In 1994, an excavation was undertaken on Werburgh Street over a ten-week period under the direction of Alan Hayden, where considerable evidence for habitation and also a section of the early town defences was uncovered (fig. 3).

The 1993 excavation discussed here uncovered the remains of earthen defences at the south side of the town. Over time, these rose from a simple, low earthen bank, less than 0.75m in height, to a raised earthen mound almost 4m in height. In the early twelfth century a stone structure was built to the south of the banks, and some short time later a stone wall was built adjoining this structure which appears to be just a localised stone-built feature at a vulnerable position on the defence; there is no evidence that it continued the circuit. Dumping of organic refuse to the south of this wall continued into the early thirteenth century, when a large stone building, thought to be part of Geneville's Tower, was constructed. Internal floor levels within this building continued in an unbroken sequence into the post-medieval period. The site therefore encompasses a section of the town defences with a date range from the late ninth-early tenth century to the seventeenth century.

The earlier levels, Phase 1, describe the sequence of activity generally relating to the northern part of the site, concerning the Hiberno-Norse defence horizons. In general, the preservation of organic material was quite poor, with most of the excavated material consisting of deliberately deposited and compacted mineral clays. Fences and other timber structures within the clays were poorly preserved, unless carbonised. A small area of stratified organic

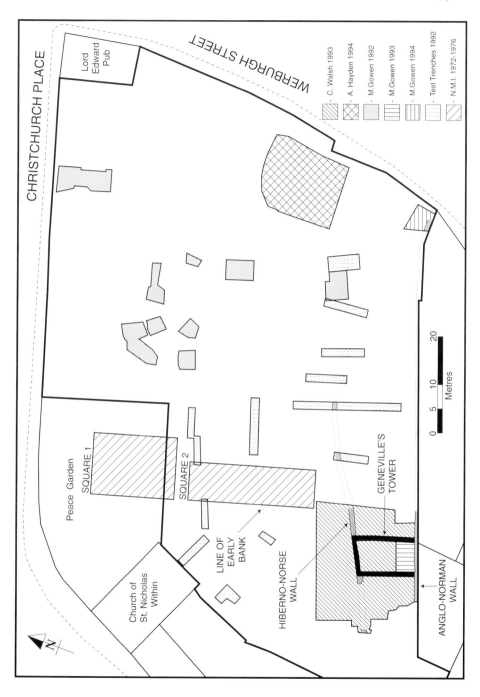

3 Excavation trenches, Christ Church Place/ Ross Road/ Werburgh Street.

occupation levels, comparable with those uncovered in the NMI excavations, was uncovered in the extreme north-east corner of the site. These are referred to below as the 'habitation layers'. In the discussion below, the NMI excavation is, for convenience, referred to as Christchurch Place, and the 1993 excavation is termed Ross Road.

THE NMI EXCAVATION

The earlier excavations at Christ Church Place, undertaken by the National Museum under the direction of Breandán Ó Ríordáin, have not been published. Access to the site archives was granted, on completion of the later excavation, whereupon the stratigraphical sequence of the later site was collated. A section measuring 6.80m north-south, along the western side of Square 2 of the NMI excavation, was mechanically re-excavated in 1993, and then cleaned and drawn. Unfortunately, the southern 4m–5m of the western section of Square 2 was never drawn from the earlier excavation, so the overlap of layers and stratigraphy is localised. Since the publication of Murray's (1983) work on the Viking buildings of Dublin, no further work has been undertaken on the plans from Square 2, and there is no collation to Ordnance Datum on the section drawings. The compilation of information from the two sites therefore awaits full analysis, in the event of a detailed report being forthcoming on the earlier excavation.

A useful account of the development of the site is provided by Murray (1983). The phasing and dating of the structures at Christ Church Place is buttressed by a series of coin finds, and a few dendrochronological dates. Murray's evidence illustrates that for the tenth century there were no recognisable structures close to the line of the embankments. This changed in the later tenth–early eleventh century, with a building at the south end of Square 1, but from the mid-eleventh century this part of the site was disturbed by later buildings, and the fairly securely-dated stratigraphy of the northern part of Square 1 did not extend to the southern part of the trench.

The site archive of Christ Church Place is difficult to interpret. The sequence of horizons of Square 2, relevant to the earlier part of the embankments, is listed below, with several evident anomalies. The major anomaly is the apparent presence of an earthen bank, which measures approximately 3.60m in width, with a height of 0.80m (fig. 7). This bank is truncated by the stone foundations of a fourteenth-century building to both north and south, and does not feature in the excavation records of the site. The ground to the south of the bank does not appear to have been excavated to subsoil, and there may have existed a ditch or gully to the south of the embankment. There is no stratigraphic link therefore with the embankments excavated in 1993, which lie *c*.10m further south, but it could be suggested that the bank in the NMI section, by virtue of its location to the north, is the earliest in the sequence of embankments at the south side of the Hiberno–Norse town.

Possibly related to the period of activity represented by this bank is a layer of redeposited boulder clay, to the north of the embankment, which is described in the site archive as akin to a 'nicely cobbled yard'. This could in fact have been an extensive roadway, related to the embankment. Several pits and postholes were sealed beneath the redeposited clay and cobbles, but no finds were recorded from the features. There do not appear to have been any pits or early features in the southern 6m of the NMI excavation, the area in close proximity to the Ross Road excavations. This suggests that the earliest level of occupation in the area was contained or bounded to the south by the earthen bank.

A deposit of featureless soil, *c*.0.20m in depth, termed 'the penultimate layer' was spread over most of the southern part of the NMI site. The site notes indicate that this is tenth century in date. The extensive burnt horizon of phase 1, level 2, Ross Road can be traced over the southern part of Square 2. Several scrappy fences and screens were constructed on this level. These can be collated with the fences and screens of Phase 3 uncovered to the north-east of the 1993 excavation (fig. 6). While Murray (1983, 51–54) indicates that there were no buildings in Square 2 until the late tenth century, the plans indicate that some form of structure with a defined hearth was constructed close to the line of the defences (fig. 6).

The finds registers for Square 2 were checked, in the hope that concentrations of artefacts – specifically, perforated antler or bone plates – could link a site or workshop with the extensive dumps of these objects uncovered in the 1993 excavations further south. While there was considerable evidence for bone and antler working from Square 2, the objects did not concentrate in specific areas, and it seems likely that the workshop from which these objects derived lay a short distance west of the NMI excavation.

Other layers were recognised in both excavations, such as a deposit of fabric recovered from the south-west corner of the NMI excavation, which connects with the 1993 excavation. Overall, however, attempts to link the well-stratified material from 1993 with the coin-dated sequence from Square 2 have not been very successful. The indications are however that much of the material from the 1993 excavation dates to the earlier part of the tenth century, a period for which there was little or no structural evidence from the southern part of Square 2.

DATING OF THE STRUCTURES AT ROSS ROAD

The sequence of Hiberno–Norse embankments excavated in 1993 at Ross Road is dated by radiocarbon. Samples of short-lived wood, that is, stakes from four fences within the banks, were submitted for carbon 14 dating. The dates were recalibrated by Dr Christopher Ramsey of the University of Oxford, using the stratigraphic sequence as excavated. Where relevant, linked material from the NMI's earlier excavations is introduced to corroborate dating. In general, the finds from Ross Road are not particularly diagnostic. The most interesting find from the earliest levels is a fragment of a glass bangle, which has a production date from the late seventh to the ninth century (Judith Carroll, pers. comm.).

Earliest activity

The earliest evidence for defences at the 1993 excavation at Ross Road, bank 1, is dated by C14 to the early tenth century. The extensive occupation deposits recorded in the NMI excavations in Square 2 immediately north of the 1993 excavations were not dated by C14, and the earliest levels at that site have not been dated. The first buildings on that site are dated by coin-association to the late tenth-early eleventh century, with larger buildings constructed in the early eleventh century (Murray 1983).

The bank in the composite section from Square 2 of the NMI excavations, about 10m north of the 1993 excavation, may be of primary defensive origin. This structure, which measures approximately 3.60m in width, and 0.80m in height, lies approx. 10m north of the primary banks uncovered at Ross Road, and can therefore be assumed to be earlier in date. A possible cobbled road which lies inside (to the north) of the bank in Square 2 sealed a series of shallow charcoal-filled pits and postholes, which formed no apparent pattern. This indicates that an earthwork, probably pre-dating the early tenth century, existed on the south side of the Hiberno-Norse town, on the crest of the steep slope overlooking the Poddle. Whether these features relate to a westward expansion from an early fort, located perhaps at the site of Dublin Castle, or the remnants of an earlier abandoned earthwork, is inconclusive.

BANK 1, ROSS ROAD (FIGS 4, 7)

Bank 1, Ross Road, survived as a low mound of redeposited boulder clay, 0.45m high and over 2.50m in width (fig. 4). It extended east-west across the entire northern part of the excavated area. The low bank may have had a pathway along its top, as areas of metalling (308) formed of small rounded stones were noted at the north-western and eastern ends of the excavation. The mound was higher on the outer side due to the steep slope southwards and the presence of a series of parallel gullies on the down slope (fig. 7). The redeposited boulder clay may have derived in part from these gullies, which lay immediately down-slope of the embanked material. All may have been open contemporaneously, but were originally excavated in sequence.

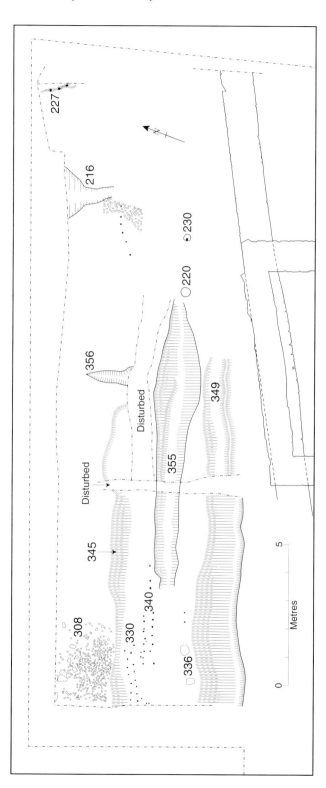

4 Banks: phase I, level I.

Gully 349 extended for over 7m east-west, with a width of *c.*1m, and a depth of 0.65m. This appears to have remained open for some time, as a distinct lens of sod or turf had accumulated in its base. The gullies may have parallels in those excavated along the line of the earlier Roman defences at York (Coll 1991, 262), one of four of which was shown to have held timbers, and was interpreted as a possible palisade trench. The other three were interpreted as replacement boundary-trenches. There was no evidence that any of the gullies at Ross Road had formerly held timbers.

Several unsubstantial fences (330, 340) and larger posts (220, 230 and 336) were driven into subsoil. All maintained a general east-west alignment, but none were continuous across the area of excavation. Only the bases of the fences survived. Two were charred and 352, a carbonised fence, was submitted for C14 dating (GrN–20246, AD 890–AD 980). At the north-east end of the site several organic layers were deposited: these extended into the NMI area, where they equate to what is termed the 'penultimate layer' in that site archive. A slight fence was constructed, but there is no evidence for buildings within the bank from the NMI excavations at this level.

Low banks, classified as flood banks, were excavated at Fishamble Street, which have been dated to the early tenth century (Wallace 1981, 110). Pits, gullies, and three burials at Fishamble Street all date to these early levels (Geraghty 1996, 9). These features are likely to be contemporary with Bank 1, Ross Road, and serve to illustrate that the north-south parameter of the Hiberno-Norse town was laid out from an early period. A similar structure at Parliament Street (Gowen with Scally 1996) has also been identified as a flood bank: however, at Ross Road, no flood banks were necessary because of its high elevation above the Poddle, and the function of the structure must be considered, if not primarily defensive, a town boundary. It is possible that the burning of the fences resulted from one of the burnings of the town, several of which are documented throughout the tenth century (Duffy 1996).

BANK 2, ROSS ROAD (FIG. 5)

This level encompasses the construction of an earthen bank on top of bank 1, and of several lines of gullies and associated fences. There is a succession of activities, resulting in one overall structure, which appears to have been consumed by fire. This episode of activity dates probably to the mid-tenth century (fig. 5). An extension of Bank 2, Ross Road, appears to be the structure uncovered and part-excavated at the south end of Werburgh Street in 1994 by Alan Hayden (fig. 1). Three trenches were excavated through the Werburgh Street bank, and it too stood to a height of 0.75m (A. Hayden, pers. comm.). Earlier gullies and slot trenches, similar to those of Phase 1, level 1, Ross Road,

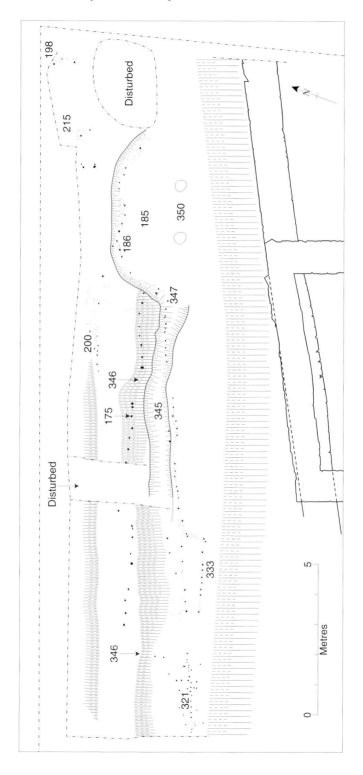

5 Banks: phase 1, level 2.

were exposed in part beneath this bank at Werburgh Street. The structure may also be that termed Bank 2 at Exchange Street Upper/Parliament Street, which is dated to the mid- to late tenth century (Gowen with Scally 1996, 15). Bank 2 (Parliament Street) measured up to 3.70m in width and achieved a height of 0.70m. It is described as non-defensive. The structure may also be recognised as Fishamble Street Bank 2, which was stabilised at the core with a post-and-wattle fence, which may be a response to the wetter materials from which the bank was formed.

The stratigraphic sequence of construction of Bank 2 is as follows. Further gullies were dug to the south of Bank 1, Ross Road. Gully 345 deepened towards the eastern end of the site. It measured 0.80m in width, and a maximum of 0.45m in depth, with a gently sloping northern edge. Two postholes (350) cut through the soils associated with the gully.

Several further deposits of clays, silts and burnt wattle strands, with an overall height of 0.75m, were added to the level 1 bank to form Bank 2. Discrete layers of grey/brown sod were evident, and it is possible that layers of sods or turves were laid down within the earthen mass, to 'knit' the material and form a more cohesive embankment. There was no evidence for timber lacing within the bank, which at this level measured a total of 1.15m in height (with a higher external aspect of 1.70m) and over 2.50m in width. Consolidating layers of turves or sods were noted in the upper layers of the eleventh century defensive bank at Bakehouse Lane, Waterford, where timber lacing in the bank structure was absent (Hurley et al. 1997, 24, 25). Clay and turves are intrinsic to the construction of contemporary English ramparts (Richards 1991, 53) and formed the rampart of period 5a (late ninth-early tenth century) at Hereford (Shoesmith 1982, 34).

The layers which ultimately formed the level 2 bank do not appear to have been deposited in one planned episode: several horizontal layers at the northern limit of the site, incorporated in the structure, represent the tail end of occupation deposits from plots to the north of the site, indicating that the bank was raised in height over some time. These organic layers also contained a range of artefacts, including polished bone pins and a fragment of a jet or lignite bracelet that might perhaps characterise them as 'occupation' levels.

Another gully (346) cut through the backfill of gully 345. It appears that this is a recut of an earlier gully along this alignment, as it lay immediately to the south of bank 1, and served effectively to raise its level at the southern side to a height of 0.80m. No evidence for an earlier cut remained, however. Gully 346 extended east/west across most of the site, and like the earlier gullies, did not extend to the western end of the site. It measured 0.65m in width, with a steeply sloping northern edge. The base of the gully lay at a depth of 1.70m below the crest of the bank. There is no evidence that it had held timbers, or had any structural function. The ground beyond the gully sloped steeply southwards.

Several fences were contemporary with gully 346 and bank 2, and some formed an intrinsic part of the defensive complex. Fence 175 was constructed on the southern slope of the bank. Several of the posts of fence 347, built along the line of gully 346 were carbonised. Fences 321 and 333 were constructed down-slope of the bank. Both extended for a considerable distance east/west, along the line of the (infilled) gully 346. At the eastern limit of the fences, a semi-circular feature (185) was cut through the underlying clays. The cut measured 5.50m east/west by 1.70m north/south, with a depth of 0.42m. The side of the cut was vertical, due to the construction of a post-and-wattle fence (186) around the base. The tops of the fence posts were charred. The southern edge of the feature was cut away by later activity, but there was no indication that the fence formed an enclosure. A fragment of a crucible recovered from within the enclosure suggests that it may have been a sheltered hearth for metalworking. The base of the cut was level, and was covered by a layer of car-bonised grass or straw. The fire which charred this material was not responsible for charring the posts of fence 186, however. Organic soil accumulated over the carbonised layer within the feature and was overlain by further layers of charcoal and silt. Burnt posts and wattle from fence 186 lay on the surface of the silt. This appears to have resulted from an episode of widespread burning. An extensive layer comprising charcoal, ash, mottles of burnt and oxidised clay (161, fig. 7)) up to 0.35m in depth, was present over the entire site. There was a concentration of burnt posts and wattles over much of the southern slope of the bank. The fences and slight structures within the defences at this level were also carbonised, and the contemporary organic soils were sealed by the widespread layer of burning.

The widespread layer 161 appears to represent the destruction of bank 2 by fire, and is contemporary with the deposition of several male skulls and cranium fragments over the banks. One mandible fragment had a cut on the inferior surface which is best explained as a result of a beheading (report by Laureen Buckley). One could speculate that the burnt horizon represents an attack on the town. The settlement was plundered and burnt in 936, and may have been refortified by 938. The settlement, then referred to as the *dún* suffered another onslaught in 944, with serious consequences. Howard Clarke suggests that Bank 2 at Fishamble Street was constructed in the aftermath of Dublin's 944 destruction by the army of the king of Tara, when 'its houses, fences, ships and all other structures were burned; its womenfolk, young men and commoners were carried off into bondage'. However the description of the settlement as a *dún* does indicate that defensive embankments were in place, and banks 1 and 2 at Ross Road were certainly in existence by 944. The reconstruction of Bank 2, Ross Road into Bank 3 may have happened as early as 938, or resulted from the 944 attack.

The site archives of the NMI excavations describe a burnt screen and general layer of burning which overlay the 'penultimate dark organic soil', which appears to relate to the level of burning recorded at the Ross Road site. Another burnt horizon at this site mentioned by Murray (1983, 204–5) in which several of the houses, specifically in Square 1, were burnt down, is dated to *c*.AD 1000. While the dating of the early levels of the NMI site is admittedly crude, and could conceivably be earlier, the earliest house in Square 2, which was built 'just above the boulder clay' and which is dated to the late tenth–early eleventh century, is not burnt. As this house is closer to the defences, it is unlikely that it would have escaped the general fire while those further north were burnt. A widespread level of burning was also evident at Werburgh Street (94E25) when all the houses of level 5a (dated by coin-association to the early eleventh century) were destroyed by fire. This well-dated episode at Werburgh Street is without doubt, as appears the case with the NMI excavation, later than the burnt horizon of Bank 2, Ross Road.

BANK 3, ROSS ROAD (FIG. 6)

Following the burning of an area of the town, some time may have elapsed before further construction was undertaken in this area. Mixed deposits of clay, silt, small stones and patches of sods, which may represent clearance from the town, were deposited over the burnt horizon. A fence (145) was erected on the northern side of the site. For most of its length, it followed the line of the crest of the level 2 bank, whose profile remained apparent (fig. 6). The purpose of the fence does not appear to have been defensive, and it determined the southern boundary of the town plots within the bank. The fence extended across the entire site, and stood to a maximum height of *c*.0.40m.

This boundary function of fence 145 was also evident from the differing nature of the deposits which were amassed to either side of it. Several thick layers of clays and inorganic silts were deposited on the southern side of fence 145. A second fence (155) was constructed, close to the line of 145, on its southern side. The two fences diverged, with 155 continuing eastwards following more closely the line of the earlier bank. It may be significant that fence 155 maintained more or less the same western limit as the earlier gullies. Fence 155 appears to have functioned primarily to stabilise a series of thick clay/marl layers, which were deposited to either side of it. Organic soils and compacted grey clays and silts, to a height of up to 0.70m, accumulated in the area between the two fences. These deposits do not appear to represent a deliberate construction of a bank; rather, they represent dumped deposits from within the town. Part of an amber ring was found in the silts.

Clays 141, with a total height of 0.60m, were deposited to the south of fence 155 (fig. 7). These clays do represent a deliberate attempt to create an embankment, which extended the face of the level 2 bank for a further 2.50m

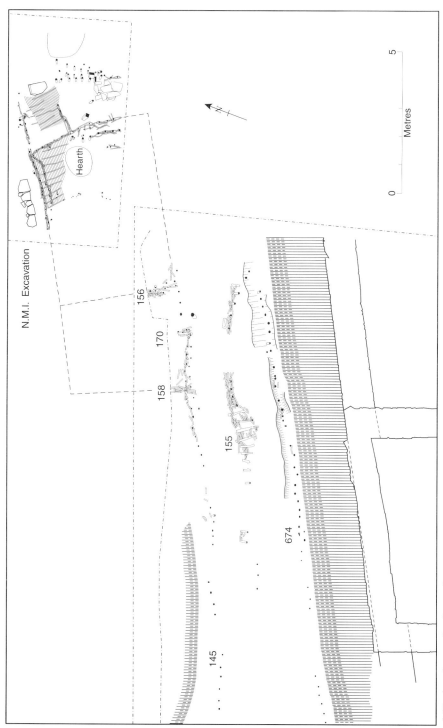

6 Banks: phase 1, levels 3 and 4.

southwards but did not raise the height to any significant degree (fig. 7). These deposits were quite clean, quarried boulder-clay, and sticky pure clay, which may have been brought from close to the original Poddle river-bed to the south. It is probable that the slope to the south of the bank had been deliberately scarped, to create a greater fall than that which existed due to the presence of the Poddle river-bed at the base of the slope. Any evidence for this deliberate scarping would, however, have been removed by the construction of the early twelfth-century wall (Phase 2, fig. 7).

Fence 145 delimited the southern boundary of occupation activity within the town. Several short lengths of fences and screens can be linked with features excavated by the NMI (fig. 6), though unfortunately not readily dateable by the site archives, and not included in Murray's (1983) stratigraphy. Localised spreads of organic silts containing moss, hair and pieces of fabric were contemporary with these fences. Significant quantities of bone plates, used as button or bead blanks, were recovered from a fairly wide area across the site, indicating debris from a workshop. Several ring-pins and a motif-piece were also recovered.

Two discrete groups of features are represented by these fences, and an enclosed hearth, which may have been a structure, is represented (fig. 6). Several wattle screens may indicate a path and entrance to a small structure in the north-east side (Murray's property 5). In the NMI excavations at Christ Church Place the alignment of properties was off a path which extended north-west/south-east across the site, and fence 145 runs on an alignment roughly perpendicular to this path. The plot appears to have been only *c.*3m in width, significantly narrower than the other plots in this part of the town. The area may have been used in the main for housing animals in small pens, or as a dumping area for human cess and debris, but the evidence also shows that a small structure was squeezed in here. The fences and plot lines indicate a fairly well-regulated area of the town, where all available ground was in use.

The establishment of properties and houses at the southern end of square 2 has been dated to the late tenth–early eleventh century (Murray 1983, 52); however evidence from the Ross Road excavation would suggest that this happened earlier. Fence 145 was dated by C14, yielding quite a wide range, with a date between AD 920–1050. However, when taken with the date for the fence from bank 4 (see below, it is likely that the date of construction is towards the earlier part of the date-range, and a date in the mid to late tenth century is reasonable for this phase. The construction of bank 3 may have been a response to the attack on the town, as witnessed in bank 2 (see above).

BANK 4, ROSS ROAD

Bank 3 was raised and extended southwards to become Bank 4, by further deposits of fairly sterile clay/marl which measured up to 0.80m in depth (figs.

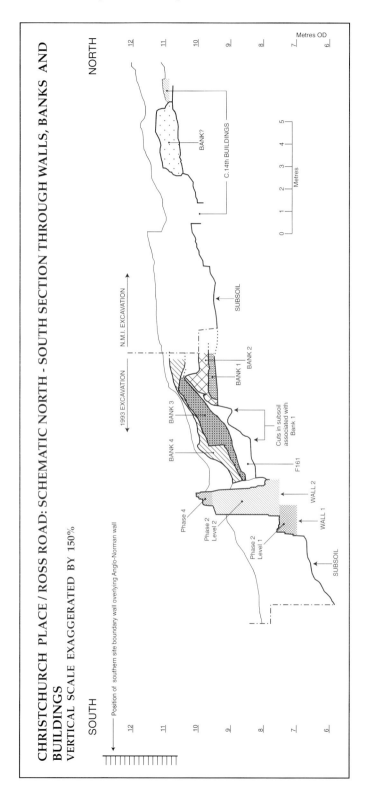

7 Schematic north–south section across site.

6, 7). This appears to have happened by the late tenth century. A fence (674, fig. 6) was constructed on these clays. At its eastern end, the fence was set in a palisade trench, which measured up to 0.44m in width and 0.50m in depth and here the posts were bigger – up to 0.15m in diameter. Slight traces of wattle remained in the fill of the trench, but in general the timbers were extremely decayed, particularly towards the western end of the site, where the fence was represented by postholes and stakeholes alone.

Several decayed timbers, which may be the remnants of boards laid on the surface of the clays, survived in a band roughly along the line of the palisade trench. The timbers were too decayed to identify, and the longest measured less than 0.70m in length, with a width of between 0.20 to 0.28m. There was no evidence for a baseplate or other associated timber substructure, and it is possible that the boards may have fallen from the fence, or that they may have been pegged to the surface of the clay bank, as was the case with a section of the embankments at Wood Quay (Wallace 1981, 111). This feature was present on the mid-tenth century bank 2 at Wood Quay, and was re-used to stabilise the outer face of bank 3, Wood Quay, built AD *c.*1000. This could provide a parallel for bank 4 at Ross Road. The line of the boards at Ross Road demarcated the southern limit of a deposit of silt and stones which extended as far north as fence 145 and had a maximum depth of 0.65m. Further deposits of fairly uniform grey clay/silt, over 0.40m in height, were laid down over the earlier levels. These layers occurred in relatively horizontal bands, but may have been subsequently levelled to form a surface (see phase 2). The artefacts recovered from the clay indicate that material from within the town was mixed with sterile deposits to form the bank. The bank finally measured approximately 6m in width, and rose to a height of over 4m above the edge of the Poddle river-bed (fig. 7).

A post from the palisade trench submitted for C14 dating yielded a date-range from AD 900 to 990. This date indicates that the overall form of the banks was completed by the end of the tenth century, and remained thus until probably the beginning of the twelfth century. This story is paralleled at Fishamble Street, where the substantial bank 3 is dated to AD *c.*1000 . The bank at Fishamble Street was enlarged 'especially by the addition of layers of estuarine mud in the eleventh century' (Wallace 1992, 44), while estuarine mud and marl composed much of the material of the tenth-century banks 3 and 4 at Ross Road. At Fishamble Street, boards of Bank 2 were used to consolidate the structure, which was crowned with a post-and-wattle fence, and later by a stave palisade. At Ross Road, rotted boards, whose prime position in the bank is uncertain due to their advanced state of decay, were uncovered along a length of bank 4. Overall, evidence for timber revetments and bracing on the earthen embankments at Ross Road is poor, in contrast to the evidence from contemporary English sites (Radford 1970, 92), where timber revetments were invariably placed both to front and rear of the earthen ramparts.

All in all, the sequence of embankments at Ross Road tallies surprisingly well with those from Fishamble Street. The second defensive embankment at Fishamble Street is dated to sometime around AD 1000 (Wallace 1992, 44). This was built in at least four different stages. At one point, it was crowned with a palisade fence. At a later stage, a stave wall with rear braces was placed on top of the bank. Bank 2 is equated with the Parliament Street Bank 3. However, the distinctive features of Fishamble Street Bank 2, the post-and-wattle palisade and the stave wall, are absent from the Parliament Street bank. The post-and-wattle palisade is present in Bank 4, Ross Road. The final level of Bank 2, Fishamble Street, saw the bank covered with estuarine mud, which dried out to form a firm surface. This form of the bank was recognised at Dublin Castle and at Parliament Street. The bank beneath the Powder Tower at Dublin Castle was faced with stone (Lynch and Manning 1990, and Chapter 2 above), but this has not been encountered elsewhere on the circuit of the bank.

The final deposit over the bank at Ross Road, at the southernmost limit of the clay banks was a peaty silt and sod deposit (131) which contained elder branches, presumably derived from trees growing on the exterior of the bank. The deposit from which the branches were retrieved represents erosion of the top and face of the bank. A sample of one branch sent for C14 (Grn-20244) yielded a date between 1020 and AD 1170.

TOWN DEFENCES AND PLOT LAYOUT

It is worthwhile to contrast the land use and plot layout within the town adjacent to the defences. At Fishamble Street, the 'only major change in … plot divisions seems to be related to the construction of a large defensive embankment' (Wallace 1992, 40). The plots there backed up to the embankment, with intensive settlement and dwellings in this area by the late tenth century. At Parliament Street, the first plots were laid out by the early tenth century, although an earlier structure on a different orientation was uncovered (Gowen with Scally 1996, 11). The indications from Simpson's excavation at Exchange Street Lower are that the narrow ends of the plots fronted onto the line of the embankment, as at Fishamble Street. This was replaced by the use of the area within the defences for widespread industrial activity, which is indicated by open hearths, fences and a kerbed clay platform (Simpson 1999, 30).

The earliest levels at Werburgh Street (fig. 3) were not fully archaeologically excavated, but a plot layout which persisted to the early twelfth century was apparent from the earliest level. The ground close by the defences was open, with evidence for small enclosures, probably animal pens, and the relationship of the plots to the embankment mirrors that at Christ Church Place/Ross Road. As at Christ Church Place, plots were oriented side-on to the defences, with a narrow plot squeezed into the space between a wider plot and the bank by the late tenth century. The Werburgh Street and Christ Church Place plots were accessed by paths which extended diagonally down-slope, presumably to the embankments. This is further confirmation that plot layout tends to follow the natural topography at Dublin (Wallace 1985, 112).

Only in the twelfth century, when the banks were replaced with a stone wall (see below), did the town encroach on the banks at Ross Road, the ground being dug through by many cess pits. These were generally confined to the eastern part of the site, suggesting that access to the defences may have been maintained at the west side of the Ross Road excavation.

THE FIRST STONE WALL AT ROSS ROAD (FIGS 8, 9)

There is evidence for the construction of two stone walls of late Hiberno-Norse date at Ross Road. The earlier wall (839) which measured 0.80m in height and at least 1.20m in width, has been cut away largely by the construction of the later, and survives for a short stretch beneath the later tower. There is no evidence that the structure 839 extended further east-west to either side, and it appears to represent a 'facing' (or defensive feature) on the river at this point. This is corroborated by the presence of several, earlier post-and-wattle fences to its south in the river bed which occurred only in this area. It is interesting that the sole evidence for stone facing on the earthen banks was recovered from beneath later towers, as at Ross Road and beneath the Powder tower at Dublin Castle. It may be significant that the wall appears to have stood only where there existed an earlier stake-lined revetment on the river channel, in an area later used for a mural tower. This construction may parallel the type of stone facing found on the Hiberno-Norse bank at Dublin Castle (Lynch and Manning 1990, and Chapter 2 above).

The second wall (788) was constructed in a trench which cut into the southern flank of the earlier banks. The foundation trench for the wall contained sherds of Ham Green 'A ware' and a single sherd of North French ware, which places the construction of this wall probably in the second quarter of the twelfth century.

Wall 788 is paralleled in some aspects of its construction in the wall uncovered at Wood Quay (Wallace 1981), being of fine limestone construction, with an external footing. However, a series of putlog holes for scaffolding evident in the Ross Road wall was not found in its Wood Quay equivalent. Also the vertical joints evident in the construction of the wall at Wood Quay were not apparent at Ross Road, although a later build of the wall at the extreme eastern end of the excavated area was apparent. The stone wall at Ross Road was standing to a height of 2.60m, and measured 1m in width at the top, with a

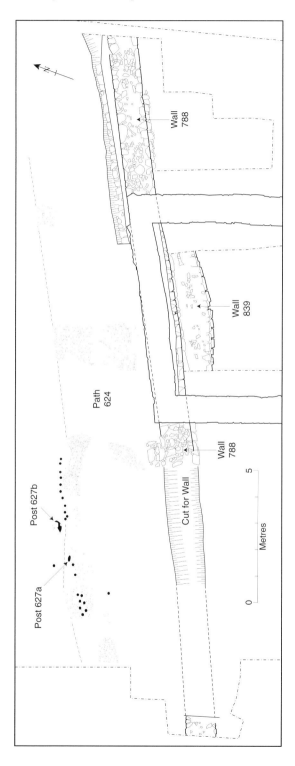

8 Hiberno–Norse walls.

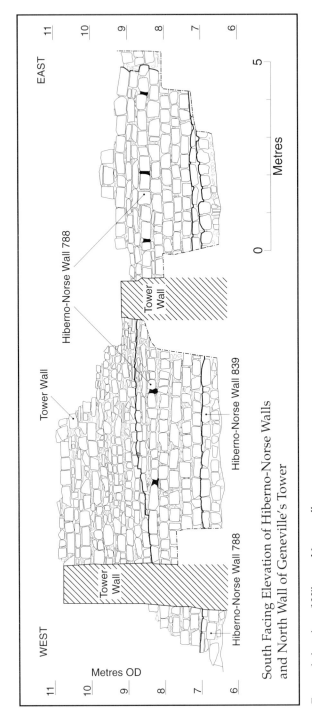

9 External elevation of Hiberno-Norse walls.

batter towards its base, where it matches the recorded 1.60m width of the lower courses of the Winetavern Street wall (fig. 7; Walsh 1997). It had a plinth both within and without: the inner one was sealed with clay in the construction cut. The facing masonry to both sides was of rectangular blocks, laid in regular courses and bonded with lime mortar, as was the rubble core. The wall was never totally free-standing, as it was cut into the earlier banks on the southern side, and retained the outer face of the earthen ramparts at both Ross Road and Wood Quay. The wall had been demolished to ground level in the later twelfth century, and to the west of the excavation had been completely removed in a massive 'robber' trench. Good stone was taken for re-use elsewhere, and poor stone and spalls littered the ground at this level. There is no evidence for the presence of a ditch of the Hiberno-Norse phase outside the wall at Ross Road, but the Poddle would have functioned as a natural moat.

A well-laid metalled pathway (624) extended along the inside of the wall (fig. 8): a fence extended along the north edge of the path, and two posts may indicate the position of a gate from the banks onto the path. The path appears to have been allowed to lapse in usage throughout the period when the wall stood, becoming covered in sods and soils, and its line was not maintained into later levels. No evidence for a wall street, allowing access to the wall for defensive purposes, is mentioned in relation to the wall at Winetavern Street (Wallace 1981). Timbers recovered from the eleventh-century ditch at Bakehouse Lane, Waterford, may have formed a walkway structure on the top of the bank, while a metalled track was laid outside the early twelfth-century wall there, between the wall and the (partly infilled) wide defensive ditch (Hurley et al. 1997, 30). The construction of the ramparts at Waterford in the late eleventh century may have been spurred by the warfare recorded as having occurred in 1088; however, the impetus for the construction of stone walls in the early twelfth century in both Dublin and Waterford may also be attributed to other factors such as prestige.

The evidence suggests that the wall at Wood Quay may have been built before the wall at Ross Road, as it is dated to AD *c.*1100 (Wallace 1981), while the wall at Ross Road is dated to the second quarter of the twelfth century. However the southern side of the town at Ross Road was refortified with a new wall and tower in the period immediately following the Anglo-Norman invasion, whereas the wall at Wood Quay was repaired and evidently maintained into the thirteenth century. At Wood Quay, the line and structure of the early twelfth-century town wall appeared to have continued in use following the Anglo-Norman invasion (see below). A small section of this wall was excavated beneath Winetavern Street (Walsh 1997) but no independent dating evidence was uncovered at that site. The line of the wall continues westwards into Cook Street, but here it is not possible to know without excavation how much of this structure is later.

A section of the inside of this pre-Norman wall was also uncovered in 1998 at a site in Exchange Street (Georgina Scally, pers. comm.) but no independent dating for its construction was uncovered at this site. A later wall, probably thirteenth century in date, was built immediately outside the earlier wall at that site.

ANGLO-NORMAN WALL

The construction of new walls to the east of the town along the Poddle estuary and the southern side of the town at Ross Road is likely to have been initiated as part of the Anglo-Norman refortifications at Dublin Castle, begun in 1204, and completed over the following twenty years. The demolition of the Hiberno-Norse wall at Ross Road dates to the late twelfth-early thirteenth century, and it is unlikely to have been razed unless there was an alternative wall some distance further south. The profile of the rapid dump layers at the southern side of the site, following the demolition of the Hiberno-Norse wall, indicates that these layers built up against a wall to the south, which is the new Anglo-Norman wall. Evidence for this southern wall was uncovered in a machine trench at Ross Road (fig. 7, 10).

GENEVILLE'S TOWER

The twelve metres of ground taken in to the town by the construction of the new wall was spanned by the interior of a mural tower known as 'Geneville's Tower' (fig. 10). The construction of this tower dates also to the first part of the thirteenth century. The tower is named after Sir Geoffrey de Geneville (or Joinville), who became justiciar of Ireland in 1273, and was famed for his castle-building. Though primarily lords of Trim, Co. Meath, the family evidently held land and property in Dublin. The tower lies almost midway between St Nicholas's Gate and the Pole Gate on the town wall (fig. 1). The large mortar-bonded structure measures 6.40m by 11.80m. It has several distinctive features, including the east doorway at a height of over 1.50m above the contemporary ground level. This must have been accessed by a wooden ladder or stairs, a common feature in castles of the thirteenth century.

The second floor level, and probably also roof beams, were supported by large wooden posts held on stone piers: this feature is also paralleled at other late twelfth-early thirteenth century castles, such as Trim, Maynooth and Athenry. No windows or internal features other than two doorways dating to the thirteenth century survived in the tower. The foundations of the tower, except where they rest on the underlying Hiberno-Norse wall, were placed in

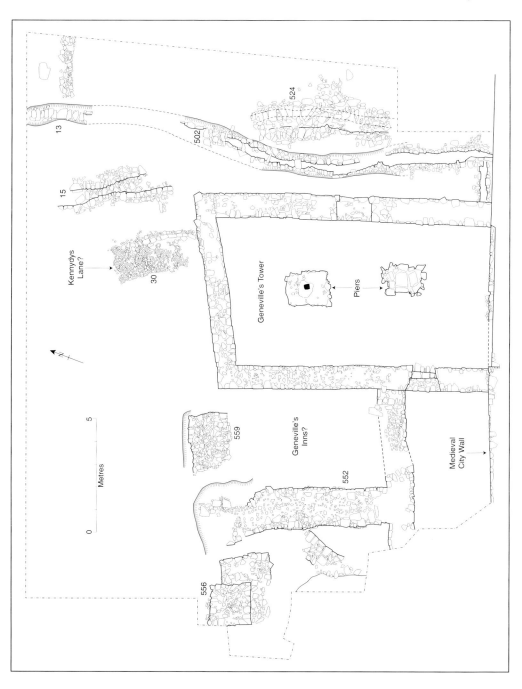

10 Medieval stone buildings.

construction trenches which cut to subsoil. In contrast, a contemporary building on the west side (possibly Geneville's Inns) was built on a series of piers, connected by relieving arches, which were built over the soft organic silts (fig. 10).

The two distinct building practices may reflect the differing functions of the structures, and the fact that Geneville's Tower was three storeys high. Sir John Perrot's survey of 1585 describes it thus: round without the wall and square within, three storeys high with two timber lofts. The evidence for the D-shaped tower at the front of the town wall is an opening in the town wall, which suggests that the tower at this location was open-gorged at the rear, which is consistent with a very early thirteenth-century date. Parallels can be seen in the work of Walter de Lacy at Trim Castle where the curtain walls, defended by similar open-gorged semi-circular towers, were completed between 1201 and 1207. There are many parallels for the construction of a sub-rectangular building at the rear of an open-gorged semi-circular tower, where extra accommodation is required.

The possibility exists, therefore, that the two parts of the tower were built in two distinct episodes, and that the rectangular back to Geneville's Tower was built somewhat later than the front part. Vessels such as Ham Green knight jugs are dated to 1175–1225 and the bulk of these sherds from Ross Road belong to the level of the construction of the tower. This suggests that the tower was built by the first quarter of the thirteenth century.

The ancillary structure mentioned above abutted the west wall of the tower, and appears to have been built shortly after the construction of the tower. This may be the building, first mentioned in 1339 as lying to the east of Nicholas Street, and referred to in various leases as 'Geneville's Inns'. In 1588 a laneway adjoining St Nicholas's Church led to 'Jenevals Innes' (Gilbert 1889–1944, ii, 214): this is the precursor of Kennedy's Lane, indicated on John Rocque's (1756) map (fig. 10, 11). It is also possible that the rear of the tower was the building known as Geneville's Inns, accommodation for the garrison.

The projected line of the Anglo-Norman ditch, dated to *c.*1186 at Nicholas Street (Walsh 1997) lay south of the excavation at Ross Road. The ditch contained the Poddle river where it occurred to the south of the excavated area at Ross Road.

KENNEDY'S LANE (FIGS 10, 11)

The tower passed into the possession of a Mr Parkins in 1585, and by 1603 was held by Richard Durning. By the mid-seventeenth century, Souter Lane, a medieval street, was being called Kennedy's Lane. Kennedy got the tower 'at the lower end of Kennedy's Lane' in 1682 (Gilbert 1889–1944, v, 285). The

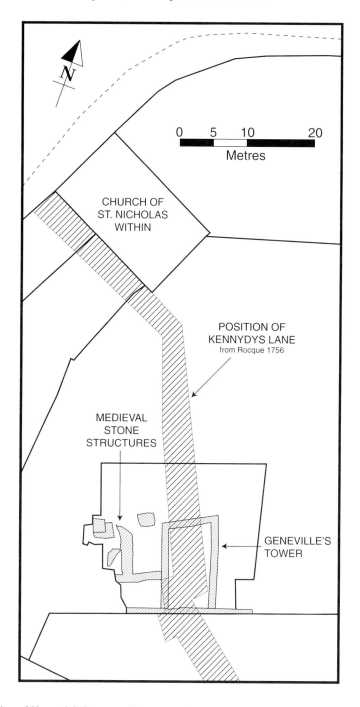

11 Position of Kennedy's Lane, per Rocque 1756.

tower may have continued in occupancy into the 1720s, but had been submerged by development by the time Rocque produced his map in 1756. An overlay of Kennedy's Lane, as depicted on Rocque (fig. 11) shows that the kink towards the south end of the lane results from the north wall of the tower, where the lane passed within the former building. It is apparent also that several of the new eighteenth-century plots used the line of the earlier medieval buildings.

Scant evidence of Kennedy's Lane was recovered from the excavation. Part of a truncated cobbled path, of late-medieval date, on the north of the tower, may be the sole physical remains of the lane (fig. 10).

CONCLUSION

The first embankment excavated at Ross Road is dated to the early tenth century. However there is evidence from the NMI excavations of the 1970s for an earlier embankment with associated pits and other features to the north of this bank. This may be an earlier earthwork on the site, and could be related to a fortress, but the evidence is scant and inconclusive.

The series of embankments uncovered at Ross Road parallels those excavated at both Fishamble Street and Parliament Street. At Ross Road, however, there was no need for flood banks, and it is suggested that these early banks represent if not defences, a town boundary. However, they developed rapidly into a defensive rampart, with evidence for at least one battle on the site, (suggested by a fire which consumed the defences and several fragments of human cranium, one of which bore signs of a beheading) which is dated to the first half of the tenth century. The radiocarbon dates from the structures indicate that the form of the earthen defences was largely completed by the end of the tenth century, with four main episodes of construction represented, and remained more or less so until the construction of a stone wall in the early twelfth century.

ACKNOWLEDGEMENTS

The excavation and post-excavation was funded by the developers, Pierse Contracting/Jury's Hotels. Excavation of the tower and deposits outside the twelfth-century wall was undertaken by Alan Hayden, co-director, and director of the Werburgh Street site. I am grateful for his comments on castles. I would particularly like to thank Dr Christopher Ramsey for his contribution on the radiocarbon dates, Franc Myles for the later history of the site, and the staff of the National Museum of Ireland for access to the Christ Church Place archive. All the plans are the magnificent work of Conor Mc Hale.

BIBLIOGRAPHY

Addyman, P.V. and Hall, R.A. 1991 *Urban structures and defences*. The Archaeology of York, vol. 8, fasc. 3. York.

Biddle, M. 1975 The evolution of towns: planned towns before 1066. In *Towns in England and Wales*. CBA Research Report 14. London.

Clarke, H. and Ambrosiani, B. 1995 *Towns in the Viking age*. Leicester.

Clarke, H.B. 1998 Proto-towns and towns in Ireland and Britain in the ninth and tenth centuries. In *Ireland and Scandinavia in the early Viking age* (eds) H.B. Clarke et al. Dublin.

Coll, S. 1991 Anglo-Scandinavian features in Lendal. In P.V. Addyman and R.A. Hall (eds) *Urban structures and defences*. The Archaeology of York, vol. 8, fasc. 3., 258– 63. York.

Coughlan, T. 2000 The Anglo-Norman houses of Dublin: evidence from Back Lane. In *Medieval Dublin I. Proceedings of the Friends of Medieval Dublin symposium 1999*. Ed. S. Duffy. Dublin.

Duffy, S. 1996 Historical background. In M. Gowen with G. Scally *A summary report on excavations at Exchange Street Upper/Parliament Street, Dublin*. Temple Bar Archaeological report no. 4. Dublin

Geraghty, S. 1996 *Viking Dublin: botanical evidence from Fishamble Street*. Royal Irish Academy Ser. C, vol. 2. Dublin.

Hurley, M.F., Scully, O.M.B., and S.W.J. Mc Cutcheon 1997 *Late Viking age and medieval Waterford. Excavations 1986–1992*. Waterford.

Murray, H. 1983 *Viking and early medieval buildings in Dublin*. BAR British Series 119. Oxford.

O'Brien, E. 1998 The location and context of Viking burials at Kilmainham and Islandbridge, Dublin. In *Ireland and Scandinavia in the early Viking age* (eds) H.B. Clarke et al. Dublin.

Ó Floinn, R. 1998 The archaeology of the early Viking Age in Ireland. In *Ireland and Scandinavia in the early Viking age* (eds) H.B. Clarke et al. Dublin.

Radford, C.A.R. 1970 The later pre-Conquest boroughs and their defences. *Medieval Archaeology* 14, 83–103.

Richards, J.D. 1991 *Viking age England*. London.

Shoesmith, R. 1982 *Hereford City excavations 2. Excavations on or close to the defences*. CBA Research Report 46. Oxford.

Simpson, L. 1999 *Director's findings: Temple Bar West*. Temple Bar Archaeological Report 5. Dublin.

—— 2000 'Forty years a-digging: a preliminary synthesis of archaeological investigations in medieval Dublin', in *Medieval Dublin I. Proceedings of the Friends of Medieval Dublin symposium 1999*. Ed. S. Duffy. Dublin.

Wallace, P.F. 1981. Dublin's waterfront at Wood Quay. In Milne and Hobley (eds) *Waterfront archaeology in Britain and Northern Europe*. CBA Research Report 41. Oxford

—— 1985 The archaeology of Viking Dublin. In H.B Clarke and A. Simms (eds) *The comparative history of urban origins in non-Roman Europe*. BAR Int. series 255, 103–145. Oxford.

—— 1992 The archaeological identity of the Hiberno-Norse town. *R.S.A.I. Jn.* 122, 35–66.

—— 2000 Garrda and airbeada: the plot thickens in Viking Dublin. In *Seanchas: studies in early and medieval Irish archaeology, history and literature in honour of Francis J. Byrne*. Ed. A.P. Smyth. 261–274. Dublin.

Walsh, C. 1997 *Archaeological excavations at Patrick, Nicholas and Winetavern Streets, Dublin*. Dingle.

Plate 1 Overview of the site from the east.

Plate 2 Overview of the site from the south-west.

Plate 3 The Viking walls (839 over 788) from the south.

Plate 4 North side of Level 3 bank, looking west.

Plate 5 Robbed 'stump' of Hiberno–Norse wall, west of Geneville's Tower.

Plate 6 The east wall of Geneville's Tower.

Plate 7 Late twelfth-century layers abutting the Hiberno–Norse wall.

Plate 8 Bank 3 from the north-west.

Plate 9 Anglo-Norman clay floor within Geneville's Tower, from the south.

Plate 10 Ancillary structure on the west side of the tower, possibly 'Geneville's Inns'.

Dublin in transition: from Ostman town to English borough

JAMES LYDON

In the winter of 1171–2 King Henry II kept his court at Dublin. He entertained the Irish in style in a great hall ('a royal palace of wattles' as one English chronicler called it) specially constructed for the occasion outside the walls of the city near the church of St Andrew and the site of the Ostman Thing.[1] This would have been a post-and-wattle building of the kind revealed in the Dublin excavations, a style that was to survive in Dublin into the thirteenth century.[2] Henry's hall is a useful reminder to us that post-and-wattle buildings do not necessarily have to be mean and drab: the chroniclers dwell on the splendours of the 'great hall' where he entertained his noble Irish guests and introduced them to the gourmet delights of crane flesh.[3]

That King Henry was prepared to cut a figure and impress his new subjects in Ireland is plain from some of the preparations made in England for his expedition: 2 skins of mountain cats; 25 ells of scarlet and 25 ells of green cloth; special 'dress' boots; 12 pieces of silk cloth; gold and silver to adorn his swords for ceremonial occasions – these were among the items supplied by different sheriffs in England. But there was also 1,000 lbs. of wax supplied from Winchester, an astonishing quantity which suggests that the king expected to seal many documents while in Ireland, not only those letters which he would have to send in the normal course of events, but charters which related to Irish business as well.[4] This he did, though not very many have survived. While he was in Dublin, he put his seal to what is undoubtedly the most famous of these charters, that in which he gave what he specifically calls 'my city' to the men of Bristol:

1 William Stubbs, *Chronicles of the reigns of Henry II and Richard I* (London, 1867), i, 28–9. 'After the manner of that country' is how another work by the same English chronicler puts it: William Stubbs (ed.), *Chronica Rogeri de Hovedene* (London, 1868–71), ii, 32. See Marie Therese Flanagan, *Irish society, Anglo-Norman settlers, Angevin kingship* (Oxford, 1989), pp 201–7. 2 See Tim Coughlan, 'The Anglo-Norman houses of Dublin: evidence from Back Lane' in Seán Duffy (ed.), *Medieval Dublin I. Proceedings of the Friends of Medieval Dublin symposium 1999* (Dublin, 2000), p. 232. 3 Gerald of Wales (Giraldus Cambrensis) tells us that they 'greatly admired the sumptuous and plentiful fare of the English table and most elegant service by the royal domestics' and that 'throughout the great hall, in obedience to the king's wishes they began to eat the flesh of the crane, which they had hitherto loathed': *Expugnatio Hibernica: The conquest of Ireland*, ed. and trans. A.B. Scott and F.X. Martin (Dublin, 1978), p. 97. 4 H.S. Sweetman (ed.), *Calendar of documents relating to Ireland,*

Henry King of the English, Duke of Normandy and Aquitaine, and Count of Anjou to the archbishops, bishops, abbots, earls, barons, justices, sheriffs, ministers and all other his faithful, French and English and Irish of all his land, greeting. Know that I have given and granted and by this present charter confirmed to my men of Bristol my city of Dublin to be inhabited. Wherefore I wish and firmly command that they inhabit it and hold it of me and my heirs, well and in peace, freely and quietly and honourably, with all liberties and free customs which the men of Bristol have at Bristol, and throughout all my land. Witnessed by William de Braosa, Reginald de Curtenai, Hugh de Gundevilla, William fitz Aldelm, Ranulph de Glanvilla, Hugh de Cressei, Reginald de Pavilli. At Dublin.

The original is a small strip of parchment, still preserved among the muniments of Dublin Corporation.[5] But it measures a mere 6.5 by 5.5 inches and has no seal attached. Indeed were it not so important historically it would hardly be worth a second glance. It is hard to believe that such a mean looking charter could be the origin of Dublin's existence as a municipality, the original royal grant from which all later extensions of the liberties of Dublin were to derive. It is not just the small dimensions of the charter that raise doubts – many of Henry II's other charters are just as small, or even smaller. It is its peculiar character that raises questions. To give Dublin to his men of Bristol to be inhabited is not very meaningful, when he retained it for himself as part of the new royal demesne in Ireland. What is important is that they were to have there 'all liberties and free customs' which they have at Bristol. These were not further clarified, which is not too unusual. We know, for example, that other lords later founding towns in Leinster commonly granted to the burgesses the liberties of Breteuil, a small town in Normandy, and these were never spelt out in the original charters.[6] The Bristol men who came to live in Dublin knew well what these liberties were and we may be sure that it was they who persuaded the king, possibly on his way to Ireland, to extend their liberties to Dublin. What *is* missing from this original charter is any indication of the territorial limits within which these liberties were to apply. It is possible that there was another charter in which the king set out the territorial limits of the city's jurisdiction and put his seal, as it were, on the right of the municipality to exist within those limits. In doing this Henry would be to some extent confirming a situation

---

1171–1307, 5 vols (London, 1875–86), i, nos 29, 37.　**5** A facsimile of the charter can most conveniently be found in J.T. Gilbert (ed.), *Calendar of ancient records of Dublin*, 19 vols (Dublin, 1889–1944), i, frontispiece; the text in idem (ed.), *Historic and municipal documents of Ireland, 1172–1320* (London, 1870), p. 1, or Gearóid Mac Niocaill, *Na buirgéisí XII–XV aois* (Dublin, 1964), pp 75–6. For a discussion of the context in which this charter should be viewed see Howard B. Clarke, 'The 1192 charter of liberties and the beginnings of Dublin's municipal life', *Dublin Hist. Rec.*, xlvi, no. 1 (1993), 5–14.　**6** Mac Niocaill, *Na buirgéisí*, ii,

which already existed, just as he did with religious corporations, like Holy
Trinity at Christ Church or St Mary's abbey, when he confirmed them in
possession of lands which they held before the English came to Ireland.[7] In
other words, when the king came to Dublin he found a municipality of sorts
already in existence. His care was to confirm this, while at the same time
protecting his own rights in Dublin. He needed a *caput* or capital and Dublin
had to be his choice. That is why he reserved it for himself when he gave back
Leinster to Strongbow in fee.[8]

If it is true that King Henry on his arrival in Dublin found a municipality of
sorts already in existence, then neither his famous charter, nor for that matter
the arrival of Strongbow and other invaders in Dublin, marked such a turning-
point in the history of the city that it somehow blots out the significance of pre-
invasion institutional developments. Archaeologists have said much the same
thing when surveying the revelations of excavations over recent years. A
balanced perspective would see a continuity in the material culture of Dublin,
for all the novelties that were introduced as a result of the twelfth-century
invasion and occupation of the city by foreigners.[9] Equally important is the
continuity of institutional life that formed the base on which the post-invasion
municipality was built.

The clearest evidence for continuity is, of course, in the church. It has been
clearly demonstrated, for example, that 'the intramural pattern of churches' in
Dublin had been established before the arrival of the English.[10] When Henry II
issued new charters in Dublin confirming the lands held by different religious
houses he explicitly recognised the grants made by pre-conquest benefactors,
Irish as well as Ostmen. The royal charter to Holy Trinity, for example, lists
lands granted to the priory by Donnchad, king of Leinster (who died in 1089),
Énna Mac Murchada, also king of Leinster (who died in 1126), and the latter's
more famous brother, Diarmait Mac Murchada, as well as many lesser lords in
Leinster.[11] Even as late as the end of the fourteenth century, when records had
become lost, it was still boasted that the church of Holy Trinity had 'been
founded and endowed by divers Irishmen, whose names are unknown, time out
of mind and long before the conquest of Ireland'.[12] Of the Ostmen the most

327–8.   7 M.J. McEnery (ed.), 'Calendar to Christ Church deeds', in *Reports of the deputy keeper of the public records in Ireland*, 20, 23, 24, 27 (1888–96); 20, no. 364; J.T. Gilbert (ed.), *Chartularies of St Mary's abbey, Dublin*, 2 vols (London, 1884–6), i, 88, 138.   8 Cambrensis, *Expug. Hib.*, p. 89; G.H. Orpen, *Ireland under the Normans*, 4 vols (Oxford, 1911–20), i, 250–1.   9 In general see the survey by Linzi Simpson, 'Forty years a-digging: a preliminary synthesis of archaeological investigations in medieval Dublin', in Duffy (ed.), *Medieval Dublin I*, 11–68.   10 Howard B. Clarke, 'Conversion, church and cathedral: the diocese of Dublin to 1152' in James Kelly and Dáire Keogh (eds), *History of the Catholic diocese of Dublin* (Dublin, 2000), p. 47.   11 McEnery (ed.), 'Cal. Christ Church deeds', no. 364 (c); see also King John's confirmation in 1202 in Charles McNeill (ed.), *Calendar of Archbishop Alen's register c.1172–1534* (Dublin, 1950), pp 28–9.   12 Walter Harris, *The history and antiquities*

famous was King Sitric Silkbeard who gave the valuable site of the church of Holy Trinity as well as lands at Baldoyle and Portrane. But many other Ostmen, such as the sons of Thorkill, also endowed the new cathedral.[13] What were called 'ancient tenures' had to be protected under the new law that was now in operation. Such tenures also included fishing rights on the river Liffey. This led to conflict between the pre-invasion corporations like St Mary's abbey and the new municipality, which developed in the late twelfth and thirteenth century.[14] When King John in August 1215 was faced with yet another conflict over riverine rights, this time arising out of claims made by Holy Trinity, he ordered his justiciar to conduct an inquiry into what he termed 'the ancient right to have a boat on the Anna Liffey'. Significantly he instructed that Ostmen as well as English should be among the jurors presenting the evidence, clearly accepting that pre-conquest rights were involved.[15]

Holy Trinity itself provides a very good example of continuity between Ostman and post-invasion Dublin. Like the other pre-conquest religious houses, it does not show the invasion as having any immediate fundamental impact. Indeed the great event, the occupation of Dublin, is not even mentioned in the annals in the so-called 'Black Book'.[16] In the annals associated with St Mary's abbey there are just three entries for the year 1170: the death of Thomas Beckett; the founding of the abbey of Fermoy; and, in between, this short entry: 'In the same year Dublin was taken by Earl Richard' – not an event of earth-shattering importance.[17] Holy Trinity retained the Augustinian character that Archbishop Laurence O'Toole had introduced before the invasion and there was no attempt to turn the cathedral chapter into a secular college after the current English fashion. Indeed the priory remained substantially Irish and it was only gradually anglicised.[18] Not only was the founder, Bishop Dúnán, commemorated each year with a special festival of nine lessons, all the well-known Irish saints were also remembered – St Patrick, of course, styled even then as the apostle of Ireland; St Brigit, St Colmcille, St Enda, St Brendan, St Aidan, St Malachy, and many more too numerous to be listed here. But lesser known Irish saints were also commemorated – such as *Laserianus*, who is Mo Laisse, the first bishop of Leighlin; St Dulech; St Beccán. Indeed it is a fact worth remem-

of the city of Dublin (Dublin, 1766; repr. Ballynahinch, 1994), p. 372.   **13** For a survey of grants see Clarke, 'Conversion, church and cathedral', pp 35–6.   **14** In general see A.E.J. Went, 'Fisheries of the river Liffey' in Howard Clarke (ed.), *Medieval Dublin: the living city* (Dublin, 1990), 182–91.   **15** Sweetman (ed.), *Cal. Docs. Ire., 1171–1251*, no. 641. **16** Aubrey Gwynn, 'Some unpublished texts from the Black Book of Christ Church, Dublin', *Analecta Hibernica*, no. 16 (1946), p. 329.   **17** Gilbert (ed.), *Chartul. St Mary's, Dublin*, ii, 269.   **18** Because of the intimate connection with Worcester cathedral it is possible that when Bishop Patrick introduced Benedictine monks into Holy Trinity they were Englishmen from Worcester; see Aubrey Gwynn (ed.), *The writings of Bishop Patrick* (Dublin, 1955), p. 7; for the Worcester connection see also Denis Bethell, 'English monks and Irish reform in the eleventh and twelfth centuries' in T. Desmond Williams (ed.), *Historical Studies*, viii (1971),

bering that the cults of Irish saints were not only preserved in Anglo-Norman Dublin, but that later some were extended throughout the metropolitan see, to be solemnly celebrated on their feast days with special services.[19]

Like other medieval churches Holy Trinity possessed its own famous collection of relics, deposited there by Dúnán and later by Bishop Gregory or Gréne (1121–61).[20] Among them were portions of the true cross and of the cross of St Peter, of the vest of Our Lady, a fragment of the manger in which lay the baby Jesus after His birth and even some of the milk from Her breast which She fed to Him, and very many more. All of these relics continued to be venerated after the invasion and throughout the middle ages brought many pilgrims to the church. If they were pre-invasion in origin they were no less treasured or venerated for that.

Chief among them were two of great renown. One was the famous crucifix that spoke at times and was responsible for many miracles. Giraldus Cambrensis tells us that when the citizens of Dublin saw Strongbow approach the city with his army they tried to carry the cross to safety across the sea. But, he wrote, despite having tried 'every resource and industry' to remove the cross from the cathedral, it could not be budged. Later, after the city was captured, an archer offered a penny to the cross. But when the archer tried to leave, he was hit in the back by the offering flung back at him. The same thing happened a second time. Then he confessed to the people standing by that on that very day he had plundered the residence of the archbishop. He therefore did penance and made restitution to the archbishop. Then, writes Giraldus, he 'brought back the penny in great fear and awe for the third time to the cross. This time finally it remained and did not move'. After relating another miracle, Giraldus concludes: 'With these and other manifestations and evidences of its power, shown during the time of our arrival in that country, the cross had earned everywhere respect and veneration'.[21]

But the prize relic was undoubtedly the Bachall Íosa, believed to be the staff or crosier that an angel had brought to St Patrick which, down to the end of the middle ages, continued to bring pilgrims to Dublin. Indeed a fifteenth century parliament enacted that even 'Irish enemies' were to have safe conduct in and out of the city so that they might come to venerate the famous relic.[22] In 1461 the Black Book recorded its miraculous preservation when a great tempest smashed in the east window of the cathedral during the night. The falling masonry broke screens and chests and much was destroyed, including many valuable charters. The writer in particular bemoaned the damage to the charter

pp 116–17.   **19** John C. Crosthwaite (ed.), *The book of obits and martyrology of the cathedral church of Holy Trinity* (Dublin, 1844), pp xliii–xlix.   **20** The best account is still that by James Todd contained in the introduction to Crosthwaite (ed.), *Book of obits*, pp vi–xxiii. **21** John J. O'Meara (trans.), *Gerald of Wales: the history and topography of Ireland* (Dundalk, 1951), pp 86–7.   **22** Crosthwaite (ed.), *Book of obits*, p. xxix.

of Henry II. But at the same time, he wrote, there occurred a great miracle. The falling stones destroyed the screed on which the Bachall and other relics were placed. All were lost, except for the Bachall – 'which thing, in all the circumstances, is to be taken for a miracle'.[23]

Holy Trinity, then, serves as a good example of continuity between Ostman and Anglo-Norman Dublin. The invasion marks no great divide. That is not to say that there were no changes, or that the new situation did not create problems. It did. When the priory of All Hallows or the monks of St Mary's abbey, like Holy Trinity, sought confirmation from Henry II of their lands and possessions, they were safeguarding themselves against the inevitable changes which a new ruler, with new laws and customs, could bring.[24] We have already seen that the simple matter of boating and fishing rights on the Liffey brought problems as early as the thirteenth century. Holy Trinity can be used to illustrate a more fundamental change that the extension of feudal custom brought to Ireland, when the king's rights to temporalities during a vacancy, arising from the death of a bishop or abbot, meant that income from property passed as an escheat, through the escheator, to the royal exchequer.[25] To have ancient right (or 'ancient tenure', as it was called, that is, from pre-conquest times) recognised in law was vital since it would mean that the king would not claim such lands as escheats. They were held in frankelmoign, as the king accepted when he confirmed All Hallows in possession of their pre-conquest lands.

This was accepted for long after the English invasion. But suddenly in 1326 the escheator took possession of all temporalities following the death of the prior. An inquisition demanded by the canons revealed that 'the church of Holy Trinity Dublin was founded by various Irishmen, and its granges, lands and tenements given by Irishmen unknown, before the conquest, in free alms to God and the said church and the canons serving there, [so] that there should be no *custodiam* [that is, seizure of temporalities] by reason of vacancy in the office of prior, and that none of their lands are held by the king in *capite* [in chief]'.[26] It could not be clearer. The lands granted to Holy Trinity before the arrival of the English were held in frankelmoign. The intervention of the conquest made no difference in law. Despite that, subsequent escheators seized the temporalities during vacancy. Finally the king himself had to intervene and a royal inquisition, taken significantly on 4 November, the feast of St Laurence O'Toole, found that 'from time immemorial' the canons held their property 'in

---

23 Ibid., pp xix–xx.   **24** Gilbert (ed.), *Chartul. St Mary's, Dublin*, i, 81,138: 'the lands had been given to them in frankelmoign before Earl Richard of Strigoil came to Ireland'. In the charter to All Hallows the king confirmed them in possession of their lands 'as best held before my coming to Ireland' and in particular that the lands were to be held 'in perpetuity and in frankelmoign': Richard Butler (ed.), *Registrum prioratus Omnium Sanctorum iuxta Dublin* (Dublin, 1845), p. 11.   **25** A.J. Otway-Ruthven, *A history of medieval Ireland* (London, 1968), p. 132.   **26** McEnery (ed.), 'Cal. Christ Church deeds', no. 220.

free alms' and could elect their prior 'without licence from the king', as had been their right in pre-conquest times.[27] So, ancient rights were recognised and the conquest was not allowed to overthrow ancient tenures or to impose new feudal custom on pre-conquest lands. Like so much else, it illustrates the essential continuity between Ostman Dublin and the Anglo–Norman city.

Within the city itself the same kind of continuity can be seen. It has often been said, and for long seemed to be taken for granted as an established fact, that after the new English settlement of Dublin the indigenous Ostman population was swept violently aside to make way for new settlers. They formed a new Ostman community on the northern bank of the Liffey, the *Villa Ostmannorum* or Ostmantown.[28] But Oxmantown had been established long before the conquest. The building of a new bridge across the Liffey in the very early twelfth century almost certainly was because of a new expansion across the river.[29] Around the same time the church of St Michan was built to serve the needs of the inhabitants.[30] It may even be that the migration of Bishop Samuel to the same church of St Michan, following the dispute over his claim to metropolitan authority, provided the impulse for another expansion of this new settlement.[31] The foundation of the abbey of St Mary, practically next door on the northern bank, certainly helped to make the new villa a more important centre. The point is that even before Strongbow took possession of Dublin the Ostmen had already created the *Villa Ostmannorum*.

There is plenty of evidence to show that Ostmen continued to live in Dublin. In 1174 when Strongbow attacked Munster he sent to Dublin for reinforcements and Cambrensis tells us that he was joined at Cashel by a large force of Dublin Ostmen, four hundred of whom were killed in a subsequent ambush.[32] In 1212, as we saw earlier, King John asked that Ostmen should join English in presenting evidence about Liffey fishing and boating rights which certainly indicates an Ostman population at that date. In the mid-thirteenth century a 'Macdual de Rathmichel' who was called an Ostman ('*Estman*') was on a charge in the archbishop's court.[33] In 1224 land near St Olaf's church was held 'de Arfinon Meardor, Ostmanno'.[34] In 1249 a certain Richard Olaf made a grant of

27 Ibid., no 231. See James Lydon, 'Christ Church in the later medieval Irish world, 1300–1500', in Kenneth Milne (ed.), *Christ Church cathedral, Dublin: a history* (Dublin, 2000), 82, n.44; James Mills (ed.), *Account roll of the priory of Holy Trinity 1337–1346* (Dublin, 1892, repr. 1996), pp 156–57, 160.   28 'With the arrival of Henry II … the inhabitants were compelled to settle outside the walls in what came to be known as Oxmantown': R. Dudley Edwards, 'The beginnings of municipal government in Dublin', in Clarke (ed.), *The living city*, p. 145. See also Edmund Curtis, 'Norse Dublin' in Howard Clarke (ed.), *Medieval Dublin: the making of a metropolis* (Dublin, 1990) p. 107.   29 See John Bradley, 'The topographical development of Scandinavian Dublin', in F.H. Aalen and Kevin Whelan (eds), *Dublin city and county: from prehistory to present* (Dublin, 1992), pp 50–1.   30 Clarke, 'Conversion, church and cathedral', p. 39.   31 Aubrey Gwynn, 'The first bishops of Dublin' in Clarke (ed.), *The living city*, p. 55.   32 Cambrensis, *Expug. Hib.*, p. 139. 33 Gilbert (ed.), *Hist. & mun. docs. Ire.*, p. 147.   34 Ibid., p. 480.

land which he owned in a Dublin street and shortly afterwards, in another deed, he was called a citizen of Dublin.[35]

There are not many obvious Ostman names on surviving lists of names of those admitted to the Dublin guild merchant. But there are some and there may be more hiding under names that describe a craft or trade.[36] Even more interesting is the name 'Padin piscator (the fisherman)' admitted in the early 1220s.[37] Almost certainly an Irishman Páidín, he was not the only Irishman admitted to the thirteenth-century guild.[38] This raises the even more interesting question of the extent to which there was a continuing Irish population in the city after the invasion.[39] That there was an Irish colony in Ostman Dublin is undoubted, when it was in effect a symbol of the authority claimed by successive high-kings.[40] This Irish population left its mark, not least upon the place names associated with the town and the kingdom of which it was the capital. It is an extraordinary fact that the place names listed in John's 1192 charter as the boundaries of the city were all (except for St Kevin's and St Patrick's) Irish.[41] Students of Scandinavian place names have pointed out how remarkably few there are in the vicinity of Dublin. Those that do exist, such as Howth (Irish Beann Eadair), show a common characteristic of passing straight from Old Norse into English. One implication is that Norse survived as a spoken language.[42] Irish, too, survived as a spoken language in Dublin after the conquest and it was to be some

---

35 McEnery (ed.), 'Cal. Christ Church deeds', nos 493, 502. In 1236–37 a Richard Olaf was admitted as a 'free citizen' of Dublin: Philomena Connolly and Geoffrey Martin (eds.), *The Dublin guild merchant roll, c.1190–1265* (Dublin, 1992), p. 115. See also p. 118, n.19. A Robert Thurgod was called a 'citizen' of Dublin *c*.1264: McEnery (ed.), 'Cal. Christ Church deeds', no. 94. **36** P.F. Wallace has supported the old view of Curtis that 'the old Scandinavian element was the basis of the later population of Dublin and the other Norman towns ... at least as far as the crafts are concerned': 'Anglo-Norman Dublin: continuity and change' in Donnchadh Ó Corráin (ed.), *Irish antiquity* (Cork, 1981), p. 262. If we accept the suggestion of Geoffrey Martin that the Dublin guild merchant actually originated in Dublin before the invasion, then the absence of many Ostman names on the post-invasion roll would not be surprising: *Guild merchant roll*, p. xviii. **37** Ibid., p. 47. Later in 1238–39 a 'Padinus Hibernicus Sutor' was admitted to free citizenship: ibid., p. 116. **38** For example, Johannes Hiberniensis recorded on the earliest membrane of the roll: ibid., p. 3, Gillemuri O Loan (p. 29), Hildemer, Athelward and Martinus Obreine (p. 31), Willelmus Hibernicus (p. 58). **39** For some evidence of continuity of occupation in the city and its hinterland, before and after the invasion, by the Welsh descendants of Gruffudd ap Cynan, see Seán Duffy, 'The 1169 invasion as a turning-point in Irish-Welsh relations' in Brendan Smith (ed.), *Britain and Ireland, 900–1300* (Cambridge, 1999), p. 105; 'Ostmen, Irish and Welsh in the eleventh century', *Peritia*, 9 (1996), pp 378–96. **40** For an excellent review of the importance of Dublin in the post-Clontarf period as a 'capital' of sorts to those aspiring to the kingship of Ireland see Seán Duffy, 'Pre-Norman Dublin, the capital of Ireland', *History Ireland*, no. 4 (1993), pp 13–18. **41** Mac Niocaill, *Na buirgéisi*, i, 78. **42** D. Greene, 'The influence of Scandinavian on Irish' in B. Almquist and D. Greene (eds), *Proceedings of the seventh Viking congress* (Dublin, 1971), p. 81: 'Norse must have survived as a spoken language in Dublin and some other settlements up to the time of the English invasion in 1169 at least', because so many place names 'were received directly from Norse into English'.

time before English took over. The fact that latimers, professional interpreters, continued to be employed is important, not least that it was considered a trade worthy of representation in the Dublin guild merchant.[43] The continuity of Irish place names is significant, best summed up in the regular use, even in official records, of the Irish form of the name for the Liffey.[44]

There is other evidence of continuity. The number of earlier churches that remained dedicated to Irish saints does not necessarily mean that Irish worshippers remained. But the fact that Irish carpentry techniques survived into the thirteenth century, in the new waterfront for example, is surely significant. Another interesting hint of an Irish population bridging the gap between pre- and post-invasion is the long tradition of Irish *mirabilia* or 'wonders' which survived there, some of which were recorded by Cambrensis in his *Topography*. Most startling of all is the Norse version of similar *mirabilia* derived from an Irish original, different to that used by Cambrensis. The Irish original was a thirteenth-century Dublin oral version, proof of the continued existence in Dublin of an Irish-speaking population preserving these *mirabilia* and passing them on orally.[45]

If all this seems a bit far-fetched, there is one final piece of evidence that is even stronger. In 1275–6 the city was in the king's hands. The account of the bailiffs and two others was enrolled on pipe roll 4 Edward I and contained details not normally accounted for when the city was still held at farm. The original roll was destroyed in 1922, but fortunately Walter Harris had made a transcript of this entry in the eighteenth century.[46] The accountants are charged with £4. 15*s*. 4*d*. 'of the issues of the guild merchant of the English' (*de exitibus gilde mercature Anglicorum*); 34*s*. 'of the issues of the guild merchant of those coming from overseas' (*de exitibus gilde mercature veniencium ultra mare*); and 25*s*. 4*d*. 'of the issues of the guild merchant of the Irish' (*de exitibus gilde mercature Hibernicorum*). We can only conclude that either there were three guild merchants in Dublin, for the English, the Irish, and merchants from overseas; or, more likely, that the Dublin guild merchant had three sections. Either way it clearly shows Irish being accepted into a Dublin guild merchant in the late thirteenth century.

All of this indicates a continuing Irish presence in Dublin long after the English occupation of the city. It seems that to some extent at least Ostman Dublin was perpetuated in the new Dublin. Physically this was certainly the

---

43 Connolly & Martin (eds), *Guild merchant roll*, p. 64: Andrew le latimer was admitted 1232–33.   **44** See Sweetman (ed.), *Cal. Docs. Ire., 1171–1251*, nos 138, 854, 974, 1129, 1299, 1980; Maurice P. Sheehy, 'The Registrum Novum: a manuscript of Holy Trinity cathedral: the medieval charters', *Reportorium Novum*, iii, no 2 (1964), p. 109; see index to McEnery (ed.), 'Cal. Christ Church deeds', under 'Liffey' for some examples.   **45** Kuno Meyer, 'The Irish mirabilia in the Norse "Speculum Regale"', *Ériu*, iv (1910), pp 14–16.   **46** It is printed in Mac Niocaill, *Na buirgéisí*, ii, 472–73, n. 95.

case. The newcomers took over an existing set of fortifications, including a fine stone wall, gates, a castle, a bridge, as well as a city already laid out in streets, open spaces, and plots with houses.[47] But did they also take over a city which had already developed some at least of the institutions which we associate with the later English municipality? Or did Henry II's charter and the subsequent confirmations and extensions initiate a definite break with the past and the beginning of a new era in the history of Dublin?

The first thing that needs to be emphasised is that the existence of a large city wall, with gates, a fosse, a bridge, a castle, not to mention earlier defensive earthworks, in itself argues for some kind of municipal organisation, capable of finding the necessary resources (the money, the materials, the skilled craftsmen, and a labour force) which were essential for the works. Is there any evidence one way or the other? An immediate problem is that Ostman Dublin has left no records, indeed no written sources apart from some scattered ecclesiastical records. We have to depend on what can be gleaned from outside or later post-conquest sources. But there are hints. First of all, the existence of the Thingmote implies that Ostman Dublin had its Thing, or assembly of citizens, which in some sense represented the city.[48] When Cambrensis related how Dermot Mac Murrough's father was killed by the Dubliners and was buried with a dog in unconsecrated ground, he added that 'it was their custom to sit as if before the *rostra* in the *forum*' in 'a large building'.[49] Whatever exactly that may mean, it does imply that the Ostmen sat in some sort of assembly in a public building. They clearly seem capable of taking corporate decisions. So, did Dublin have any real corporate sense?

It certainly had ecclesiastically. In 1074 its clergy called Dublin 'the metropolis of Ireland' (*Hiberniae insulae metropolis*).[50] After the death of Bishop Samuel, in about 1121, Ralph archbishop of Canterbury received a letter from 'all the burgesses (*omnes burgenses*) of the city of Dublin together with the assembly of the clergy'.[51] If one were to take that literally, it means that Dublin in 1121 already had burgesses, and presumably the burgages that gave them their status. But it might be reckless to go that far. The term *populus* was also used – the *populus* of Dublin with the clergy presented Samuel to Canterbury for consecration.[52] So, even if he does not refer to burgesses as such, he does accept that corporate decisions were being taken. Consistently the people of

47 For an overview, see Simpson, 'Forty years a-digging' and the sources cited.   48 For the Thingmote see Charles Haliday, *The Scandinavian kingdom of Dublin* (Dublin, 1884, repr. 1969), pp 162–6.   49 Cambrensis, *Expug. Hib.*, p. 67.   50 Clarke, 'Conversion, church and cathedral', p. 50.   51 Martin Rule (ed.), *Eadmeri historia novorum in Anglia* (London, 1884), p. 297; translation of the full letter in Aubrey Gwynn, 'First bishops of Dublin' in Clarke (ed.), *The living city*, pp 56–57. Henry I wrote a letter to Archbishop Ralph concerning a letter which he had received from the king of Ireland (Tairdelbach Ó Conchobair) that the *burgenses* of Dublin had elected Gregory as bishop: Flanagan, Irish society, p. 30n.   52 Rule (ed.), *Eadmeri historia novorum*, p. 73.

Dublin presented candidates to Canterbury for consecration as bishops. There is no way that we can escape the conclusion that the people of Ostman Dublin did have a corporate sense and that they did have some way of representing this.[53] It may be significant that by the early twelfth century a new term appears in the annals when dealing with the person they would earlier have called the *rí* or king of Dublin. In 1146 and again in 1148 Mac Torcaill and Mac Ottir were both called *mórmaor*. We need not go as far as John Ryan did and translate the term as 'Lord Mayor'.[54] But it does suggest that a new office had emerged in the Ostman city.

Shortly after Henry II departed from Dublin Strongbow, acting on behalf of the king, granted a burgage to a settler from Exeter. This implies that burgages were there already, ready-made as it were, to be granted away. But even more interesting, the record says that this was done 'on behalf of the king of the English and with the consent and assent of the citizens of Dublin' (*cum consensu et assensu civium Dublin*).[55] Where and how could the citizens give their consent? It can only be that this refers to an assembly already in existence when the English came. If we remember the close connection with Chester and especially Bristol, in both of which there was a developed borough and borough institutions, why should it be surprising to find something similar in pre-conquest Dublin? It may even have been organised into burgages on the English model, and our 'burgesses' of 1121 may not be too far-fetched after all!

The problem is to find some evidence of those earlier burgages. It is a fact that Ostman Dublin was divided into what would later be called messuages, that is small plots of land, usually with a house or building. For example, annals record the high-king Máel Sechnaill in 989 imposing a famous levy of one ounce of gold on each *gardha* or garth in Dublin.[56] The continuous existence of such house-sites and lots along Fishamble Street, over a long period of time, is a well-established fact.[57] These may well represent the burgage plots of pre-

---

53 For a good survey of 'urbanisation' in tenth-century Dublin, see H.B. Clarke in idem et al. (eds.), *Ireland and Scandinavia in the early Viking age* (Dublin, 1998), pp 353ff. Ostman Dublin had levied and collected taxes of a kind on many parts of the midlands, suggesting that 'some kind of urban administration, necessary to collect and account for the tax, was already in existence': Charles Doherty, 'The Vikings in Ireland: a review' in ibid., pp 298, 302. In 1023 Dublin had its own *airecht* or assembly: Katharine Simms, *From kings to warlords* (Woodbridge, 1987), p. 54.   54 John Ryan, 'Pre-Norman Dublin' in Clarke (ed.), *The making of a metropolis*, pp 121–2.   55 J.T. Gilbert (ed.), *Register of the abbey of St Thomas, Dublin* (London, 1889), pp 369–70.   56 John O'Donovan (ed.), *Annals of the kingdom of Ireland by the Four Masters*, 7 vols (Dublin, 1851), ii, 722–3; W.M. Hennessy (ed.), *Chronicum Scotorum* (London, 1866), pp 222–3, 254–5.   57 Patrick F. Wallace, '*Garrda* and *airbeada*: the plot thickens in Viking Dublin' in Alfred P. Smyth (ed.), *Seanchas: studies in early and medieval Irish archaeology, history and literature in honour of Francis J. Byrne* (Dublin, 1999), pp. 261–74; 'The archaeological identity of the Hiberno-Norse town', *R.S.A.I. Jn.*, 122 (1992), p. 43. A frontage of thirty feet was common for such plots and the continuity of such frontages is demonstrated by grants subsequent to the invasion, as in the grant of John

conquest Dublin and have formed the basis of burgages after the arrival of the English. Wherever the English settled in Ireland they used the land divisions that already existed, from the *tuath* (which they latinised *theodum*) down to the townland and below. Even small grants of land used existing divisions.[58] It would be surprising if in Dublin they did not also use existing land divisions. Indeed, short of knocking down streets of houses and starting to build from scratch, they had little choice in the matter.

When Henry II issued a charter confirming the pre-conquest lands of St Mary's abbey, the charter called them 'their burgages (*burgagia sua*)'.[59] The records of Holy Trinity also tell us that before the conquest the canons received from 'Seger the aged' his burgage, and half a burgage from another Ostman.[60] There are many more examples, in confirmation of pre-conquest land holdings in Dublin, of plots being called burgages.[61] It has to be accepted that in such instances the confirmations are naturally applying post-conquest terminology, *burgagium*, to what might have been called something else in Ostman records had they survived. But it should also be noted that references to a 30-foot frontage in such burgages might also suggest a pre-conquest origin.

There the matter must end for the present. But all the evidence does suggest the existence of some kind of municipal organisation in Ostman Dublin. It might also help to explain some of the puzzles connected with the early history of the English municipality. For example, it was not until 1215 that Dublin was officially granted the *firma burgi*, or farm of the borough, paying an annual rent of 200 marks to the king for the privilege.[62] But in 1212 the bailiffs had already accounted for the privilege at the exchequer and their account had been recorded on the pipe roll for that year.[63] There is evidence that even much earlier the city was paying an annual rent to the lord of Ireland. In a charter to the abbey of St Thomas, the lord John in 1185 granted to the abbey 'a tenth of my rent of the city of Dublin', which is the same as the farm.[64]

It seems, then, that Dublin was held at farm from the very beginning and that this was not formally recognised in a charter until 1215. If it seems ridiculous that such a long time should be allowed to lapse before giving formal legal recognition, then it should be remembered that it was not until 1485 that Dublin was legally incorporated, even though the city had for centuries before that been acting as a corporation. It had its own common seal and was making grants with the common consent and assent of its citizens, as well as exercising

Cumin (1181–1212): McNeill (ed.), *Cal. Alen's register*, pp 32–3.   **58** James Mills, 'The Norman settlement in Leinster-the cantreds near Dublin', *R.S.A.I. Jn*, 24 (1894), p. 174. **59** 'burgagia sua': *Chartul. St Mary's, Dublin*, i, 81.   **60** McEnery (ed.), 'Cal. Christ Church deeds', no. 364(c).   **61** McNeill (ed.), *Cal. Alen's register*, p. 29.   **62** Mac Niocaill, *Na buirgéisí*, i, 86–8.   **63** *The Irish pipe roll of 14 John, 1211–12*, ed. Oliver Davies and D.B. Quinn (Belfast, 1941; *U.J.A.*, 3rd ser., iv, suplement), p. 12; H.G. Richardson, 'Norman Ireland in 1212', *I.H.S.*, iii (1942–3), p. 150.   **64** Gilbert (ed.), *Reg. St Thomas, Dublin*, p. 281.

its own laws in an independent court. We saw that even as early as the year
Henry II had been in Ireland Strongbow granted a burgage plot to a citizen of
Exeter 'with the consent of the citizens'.

It can be strongly argued, therefore, that Henry II found in Dublin at least
the rudiments of municipal organisation. His charter to the men of Bristol was
not literally to give them his city – he had retained it as part of his royal
demesne in Ireland – but rather to protect the Bristol merchants already
resident in Dublin. Indeed it is probable that when Henry stopped at Bristol on
his way to Ireland, it was put to him by those who had interests in Dublin that
they needed to be protected in what was for them now a potentially dangerous
situation. They had long been trading with Ostman Dublin and had established
safeguards there under Ostman rule. Now they needed protection from the new
lord of Ireland. It is interesting that *c*.1175 the king confirmed to the men of
Chester the right they had to buy and sell in Dublin in the time of his
grandfather Henry I and the privileges that they enjoyed there.[65] His 1172
charter was primarily designed therefore to defend the rights of the men of
Bristol to buy and sell in Dublin and to carry there for their protection the
rights that they enjoyed in Bristol. It was only slowly that those rights, liberties
and customs were spelled out and defined in the Dublin context by successive
lords of Ireland. But they were implicit in the charter of Henry II. Within a few
months of leaving Ireland he issued another charter at St Lo in Normandy, in
which he gave 'my burgesses of Dublin' freedom to trade without molestation
throughout all his lands.[66] When John on 15 May 1192 issued a charter defining
the territorial limits of the jurisdiction of the city of Dublin, he said that the
citizens were to have their boundaries 'as perambulated on oath by the good
men of the city under precept from King Henry, my father', and then those
boundaries were set out in detail.[67] There is no evidence that this was actually
done while Henry II was in Dublin during the winter of 1171–72; but it is
reasonable to suppose that it was then, during his long sojourn in the city, that
those boundaries were first perambulated. If so, they must be the same
boundaries of the Ostman city, implying that certain rights were to be exercised
by the city within those limits.

There can be little doubt that the new municipality that emerged as a result
of the English conquest presents many features that date back to Ostman
Dublin. The lay-out of the town and its system of fortifications, the corporate

65 J.H. Round, *Feudal England* (London, 1895), p. 465. The enjoyment of 'privileges'
(*consuetudines*) implies some kind of borough organisation in Dublin. It may be relevant to
notice that in *c*.1158 Mac Murrough granted to the Augustinians 'a certain measure called
Scaith, out of every measure called a lagen, or gallon, in the brewing of beer made in the
town of Ferns', which clearly implies some kind of borough organisation: Herbert Francis
Hore, *History of the town and county of Wexford* (London, 1900–11), vol vi, p. 180).   66 Mac
Niocaill, *Na buirgéisí*, i, 76–77. He dates it *c*.1174, but 1172 seems preferable.   67 Ibid., p. 78.

sense that enabled the citizens to give common consent to grants, perhaps even the very burgages that conferred burgess status and all that went with it – these imply some degree of continuity. So do the religious corporations, their property and lands. And so too does the population of Dublin, Ostman and Irish, that survived the conquest and continued, at least for a time, to play a part in the future development of Dublin under the new lords of Ireland. It is not always possible to speak with authority about this transitional period in Dublin's history, given the scarcity of documentary evidence and the difficulty of interpreting what does survive. But there seems no doubt that the transition from Ostman Dublin to the English borough was neither as dramatic, nor traumatic, as has often been supposed.[68]

68 'The Norman conquest under Strongbow and Henry II swept whatever civic institutions may have existed before 1170 into oblivion': Aubrey Gwynn, 'Medieval Bristol and Dublin', *I.H.S.*, no 20 (1947), p. 277.

The Dominican annals of Dublin

BERNADETTE WILLIAMS

St Mary's Cistercian abbey, situated on the north bank of the Liffey, just across the river from the medieval city of Dublin, was an abbey of vast wealth and prestige of which, sadly, only the chapter house (*c*.1200) remains today. St Mary's was the wealthiest Cistercian house in Ireland and as such would have had a vast archive relating to its history and possessions.[1] Fortunately, some of the archive has survived and, in 1884, John T. Gilbert edited two volumes, which he entitled *Chartularies of St Mary's abbey, Dublin: with the register of its house at Dunbrody, and annals of Ireland*.[2] The first volume consists of two chartularies of the Dublin abbey and the second contains the register of St Mary's, Dunbrody, Co. Wexford, together with accounts of lands, possessions and revenues of both houses. Additionally, in the second volume, Gilbert included four sets of annals, all with a Dublin connection. These four annals, often erroneously referred to as 'the annals of St Mary's', are in fact four separate and distinct works. Each has its own individual purpose and bias and, therefore, the historical value of each needs to be correctly assessed.

The main object of this paper is to identify, conclusively, it is to be hoped, that the fourth annal is Dominican rather than Cistercian in origin and further to identify the scribe as John de Pembridge, prior of the Dominican house in Dublin in the mid-fourteenth century. It is difficult to analyse this annal without discussing the early Christian entries which it does certainly contain, and this in turn leads inevitably to an examination of the source, or sources, of the early Anglo-Irish annals in general, as follows.

PART ONE: THE SOURCES OF THE ANGLO-IRISH ANNALS

Ireland had, from early times, a well-established annalistic tradition. However, either before the Anglo-Norman invasion or in its aftermath, a new source of annalistic data arrived in Ireland, probably from England and Scotland.

---

1 St Mary's was originally founded as a daughter house of Savigny in 1139. In 1147, when the Savigny order united with the Cistercians, St Mary's became subject to Combermere and later in 1156 to Buildwas. Its benefactors included the Irish, the Dublin Ostmen and the Anglo-Normans. 2 *Chartularies of St Mary's Abbey, Dublin: with the register of its house at Dunbrody, and annals of Ireland*, ed. J.T. Gilbert, 2 vols (R.S., London, 1884).

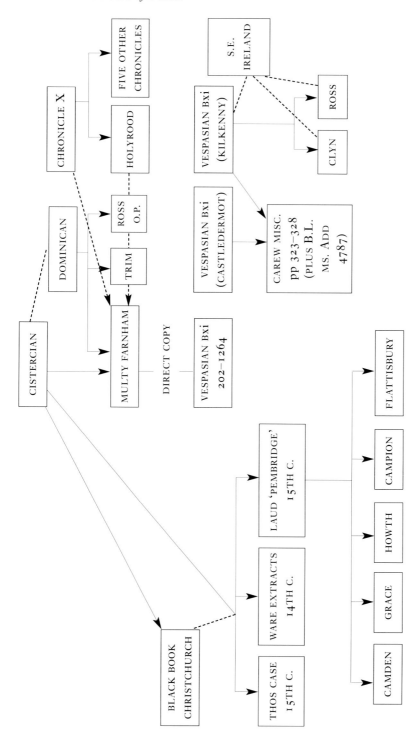

1 An attempted reconstruction of the 'family tree' of the Anglo-Irish annals.

Scholars, particularly Robin Flower[3] and Aubrey Gwynn,[4] have attempted to identify this external source. This is never an easy task as, ideally, the chronicle under consideration should be compared with all extant chronicles belonging to a contemporary period or earlier. The task of tracing a source is simplified if the chronicle being studied has long and detailed entries which contain rumour, gossip and unusual comments. Unfortunately, that is a rare occurrence and therefore, failing that, a sequence of similar, preferably unusual, entries must be sought. An added bonus in this situation is when two chronicles share the same incorrect date for an entry or, even more significantly, when marginalia from one chronicle is incorporated into the text of a later chronicle.

There are two well-known early Anglo-Irish annals of the thirteenth century. The first are the 'Annals of Multyfarnham' (AD 45 to 1272), assembled and written in 1272 by the Franciscan friar, Stephen de Exonia, which survive in a late thirteenth-century manuscript volume in the library of Trinity College, Dublin.[5] However, for the period 1215 to 1260, it is the Dominican order or Friars Preachers rather than the Franciscans or Friars Minor which takes priority: clearly Stephen de Exonia had access to some Dominican source. The second are the Dublin 'Annals of Christ Church' (birth of Christ to 1168), extant in a fourteenth-century hand in the Black Book of Christ Church, Dublin.[6] These annals consist of only one folio divided into two columns having the annalistic entries on both sides of the folio, the last entry being for the year 1168. There was probably at least a second folio of entries as one letter on what was probably a conjoint folio appears to have a single identifiable letter in a similar hand.

Aubrey Gwynn suggested that these Christ Church annals were used as a source for the annals of Multyfarnham.[7] This assumption was based on the belief that the extant annals of Multyfarnham were in a fifteenth-century manuscript and that therefore the annals in the Black Book of Christ Church were the earlier.[8] However, Multyfarnham, as extant, was compiled and written, as already remarked, in 1272,[9] the last date entered; the Christ Church annals, as extant, were written in an early fourteenth-century hand and end in 1168.[10] There is indeed a close relationship between both sets but Multyfarnham are a

3 Robin Flower, 'Manuscripts of Irish interest in the British Museum', in *Analecta Hibernica*, no. 2 (1931), pp 292–340 (hereafter, Flower, 'Manuscripts – British Museum').   4 Aubrey Gwynn, 'Some unpublished texts from the Black Book of Christ Church, Dublin', in *Analecta Hibernica*, no. 16 (1946), pp 281–377 (hereafter Gwynn, 'Black Book').   5 TCD MS 347. See M. L. Colker, *Trinity College Library, Dublin: descriptive catalogue of the mediaeval and renaissance Latin manuscripts* (Aldershot, 1991), pp 710, 738–9. For the Latin edition of the annals, see *Annales de Monte Fernandi*, ed. A. Smith, in *Tracts relating to Ireland* 2 (Dublin, 1842), no. II.   6 Representative Church Body Library, MS C 6 I.I (Black Book of Christ Church) fol. 213 r, v. The text is written in two columns on each side of the folio. For the Latin edition of the annals see Gwynn, 'Black Book', pp 324–9.   7 Gwynn, 'Black Book', p. 315.   8 Gwynn's mistake may have arisen from erroneous information in T.K. Abbott, *Catalogue of the manuscripts in Trinity College, Dublin* (Dublin, 1900), p. 53, which mistakenly attributes the manuscript to the fifteenth century.   9 See Colker, *Trinity College Library: descriptive catalogue*, pp 710, 738–9.   10 Gwynn, 'Black Book', pp 303, 329.

far more complex production and any attempt to unravel the threads of these two annals will, of necessity, be full of conjecture and open to error. Unfortunately, in both cases the entries are short and terse, often consisting of a few words to a year and a varying number of years to the century. The contents of these entries also constitute a problem as they are usually mere notices referring to very well-known and frequently-reported events such as the naming of a new pope or king, notices of the early saints, or references to well-documented political developments. Clearly, there is not enough information in such entries to give much assistance in tracing the chronicler's source. If two chronicles have a similar sequence of entries this can be useful, unless the entries are of a very general nature: from the beginning of the Christ Church annals to 1066 the entries are very similar, but not totally identical, to the entries in Multyfarnham, but whereas the entries in the latter expand considerably after 1066 the entries in the Christ Church annals continue to be short notes.

If the entries in an annal are not sufficiently individual to make for ready verification of the source then any unusual entries become very important. With the annals of Multyfarnham these can be narrowed down to just a handful. The first such entry is the one noted by Robin Flower when he was considering the source of the early Anglo-Irish annal; the entry states that, in the year 797, the abbey of Winchcombe in Gloucestershire was founded.[11] Flower postulated the theory that, because the annals of Multyfarnham and the annals of Christ Church both record the foundation date of this Benedictine abbey, then the annals of Winchcombe itself must be the source for the Anglo-Irish annals.[12] Aubrey Gwynn supported Robin Flower's theory and suggested as further proof the fact that the foundation date of Winchcombe was incorrectly given as 797, instead of the correct but later date of 972:[13] this false early date would imply an interest in making the abbey appear more ancient and worthy and thus more important. Flower could not test his theory as he believed that the annals of Winchcombe had not survived.[14] Unfortunately, he was in error both in his belief that the Winchcombe annals had not survived and in his theory that they were the source for the Anglo-Irish annals. The annals of Winchcombe are in fact present in the British Library in a Cotton manuscript,[15] and, when examined, no evidence for their use as a source for the Anglo-Irish annals is apparent.

There are, as one might expect, some entries common to both Winchcombe and Multyfarnham but this is inevitable, especially considering the brevity of

---

11 'Anno 797 Fundator abbacia de Wycumbe', *Annals of Multyfarnham*, p. 4; 'dcclxxxxvii Fundator abbatia de Wincheguine', Gwynn, 'Black Book', p. 327.   **12** Flower, 'Manuscripts – British Museum', p. 319.   **13** Gwynn, 'Black Book', p. 313.   **14** Flower, 'Manuscripts – British Museum', p. 319.   **15** BL MS Cotton Tiberius E IV. F, fol. 1r – 28r. Some folios are partially damaged as a result of the Cotton fire in 1731, but otherwise the manuscript is in reasonable condition. See also R.R. Darlington, 'Winchcombe annals 1049–1181', in *An early medieval miscellany for Doris Mary Stenton*, ed. P.M. Barnes and C.F. Slade (Pipe Roll Soc., new ser., xxxvi, 1960) pp 111–37.

the early entries in the annals of Multyfarnham and the general content of those entries.[16] On the one hand, there are entries present in Multyfarnham which are not present in the annals of Winchcombe. On the other hand, an interesting feature of the annals of Multyfarnham is the absence of entries from 1043 until 1065 (the dates are entered but the line left blank); entries for those years are present in the Winchcombe annals.[17] Most significant however is a blank space beside the year 797 in the annals of Winchcombe;[18] this is the date given for the foundation of Winchcombe in Multyfarnham.[19] Even more important is an entry in Winchcombe, beside the year 811, which begins, 'Hoc anno dedicata ecclesia Wincelcombe … ', and continues for three full sides.[20] Moreover, these folios in the Winchcombe annals are the only ones to use double columns. It is difficult to imagine that some part of this most important entry would not have been copied by the scribe if the source he was using was the annals of Winchcombe.

Although the Winchcombe annals cannot be regarded as a source for the Anglo-Irish annals, the theory that the basis of the Anglo-Irish annals lies in England is indeed most logical. Gwynn, accepting Flower's theory of Winchcombe as the source of the Anglo-Irish annal, suggested that the annals of Winchcombe were brought to Dublin, probably during the incumbency of Bishop Gilla Pátraic (Patrick) of Dublin (1074–84).[21] Even though the Winchcombe annal is out of the question, the theory that some annal arrived in Dublin from England is certainly reasonable given the many connections in trade and religion between Dublin and England in this period.[22] For example, the annal could have been a gift from Lanfranc, archbishop of Canterbury; we know from a letter written by his successor, Anselm, to Bishop Samuel of Dublin, in 1096, that books had been brought to Ireland from England. Anselm reproached Samuel for giving away books, vestments and other ornaments which Archbishop Lanfranc had given to Samuel's predecessor, Bishop Dúnán (Donatus).[23] The movement in books was not all one way: Abbot Geoffrey of

---

16 One entry which might be of significance is the entry for A.D. 43 which reads 'obiit beata maria magdalena'; the word 'maria' is an additional word placed above the line. *Annals of Winchcombe* fol. iv. The annals of Multyfarnham have the same entry but this is too common an entry from which to draw any conclusion, *Annals of Multyfarnham*, p. 1. Both annals have the entry concerning Pope Alexander but Multyfarnham has the date as 'Anno centesimo xiiij', *Annals of Multyfarnham*, p. 1, whereas the annals of Winchcombe enters the information after 'xci', *Annals of Winchcombe*, fol. 2r. 17 *Annals of Multyfarnham*, pp 4–5; *Annals of Winchcombe*, fol. 19rv. 18 Ibid., fol. 13r. 19 *Annals of Multyfarnham*, p. 4. 20 *Annals of Winchcombe*, fol. 13v–14v. 21 Gwynn, 'Black Book', pp 313–14. For the Winchcombe-Dublin connection see A. Gwynn, 'Lanfranc and the Irish Church', *Irish Eccles.Rec.*, 57 (July, 1941) pp 1–9; 58 (August, 1941) p. 101. For Bishop Patrick see A. Gwynn, 'The first bishops of Dublin', *Reportorium Novum*, 1 (1955) pp 7–13, and A. Gwynn, *The writings of Bishop Patrick, 1074–1084* (Scriptores Latini Hiberiae, vol. i, Dublin, 1955). 22 See, for example, Benjamin T. Hudson, 'The changing economy of the Irish Sea province: AD 900–1300', in *Britain and Ireland 900–1300*, ed. Brendan Smith (Cambridge, 1999), pp 39–66. 23 For the background see A. Gwynn, 'Lanfranc and the Irish Church', *Irish*

Burton wrote to a bishop in Ireland *c*.1114 and obtained a book about St Modwenna.[24] A second possibility, though less likely, is transmission from York to Dublin.[25] If, during this period, King Sitric Silkbeard, founder of Holy Trinity (Christ Church),[26] had desired books or annals, it would have been natural to turn to York but, apart from an entry relating the capture of the city of York in 893,[27] there is no recognisable York connection.

The most significant element to be found in the early years of both the annals of Multyfarnham and of Christ Church is Cistercian. Robin Flower recognised the Cistercian element,[28] but, perhaps because of his Winchcombe theory, did not fully explore it, apart that is from suggesting St Mary's abbey, Dublin, as a possible origin. Aubrey Gwynn also noted the Cistercian element but he discounted the evidence as insufficient.[29] Apart from internal evidence, the format of both Multyfarnham and, most particularly, the annals of Christ Church[30] conforms with contemporary Cistercian practice regarding decoration, which has been described thus: 'Their decoration is generally sober; there are no large miniatures or historiated initials, and gold is very rarely used. But red and blue initials alternate with decorative effect',[31] and which is a good description of the decoration of both the annals of Multyfarnham and Christ Church.

Both annals list the foundation of the Cistercian order in 1098,[32] Malachy as archbishop of Armagh 1133,[33] the foundation of Mellifont 1142,[34] the death of Malachy at Clairvaux 1148,[35] the death of St Bernard of Clairvaux in 1153,[36] and, finally, the death of Donnchadh Ua Cerbaill ('Donatus Urgali'), the founder of Mellifont, in 1168.[37] The Christ Church annals add the dedication of the church at Mellifont in 1157.[38] Apart from these entries concerning

Eccles.Rec., 57 (1941) pp 481–500; 58 (1941) pp 1–15.   **24** Robert Bartlett, 'Irish, Scottish and Welsh saints', in *Britain and Ireland 900–1300*, ed. Smith, p. 69.   **25** It was the practice during the period 971 to 1069 for the bishop of Worcester to be both bishop of Worcester and York; annals could have reached Dublin from Worcester via York see, A.P. Smyth, *Scandinavian York and Dublin: the history and archaeology of two related Viking kingdoms*, 2 vols (Dublin, 1975, 1981). Malachy was also in York, see Bernard of Clairvaux, *The life and death of Saint Malachy the Irishman*, trans. R.T. Meyer (Kalamazoo, 1978), pp 52, 139, n. 107. Certain sections of the Thomas Case annals have been identified by Gilbert as emanating from the Life of Malachy: see *Chartul. St Mary's, Dublin*, ii, pp 259–60.   **26** A. Gwynn, 'The origins of the see of Dublin', *Irish Eccles.Rec.*, 57 (1941), 40–55, 97–112.   **27** *Annals of Multyfarnham*, p. 4.   **28** Flower, 'Manuscripts – British Museum', p. 319.   **29** Gwynn, 'Black Book ', p. 315.   **30** Representative Church Body Library, MS C 6 I.I (Black Book of Christ Church) fol. 213rv. The text is written in two columns and the capitals alternate in red and blue.   **31** C.R. Cheney, 'English Cistercian libraries: the first century', in *Medieval texts and studies* (Oxford, 1973), p. 331.   **32** *Annals of Multyfarnham*, p. 6; Gwynn 'Black Book', p. 328.   **33** *Annals of Multyfarnham*, p. 8; Gwynn 'Black Book', p. 328. In Gwynn's edition the entry states 'Malachias fit archidyaconus Armacanus' and this is indeed the entry in the manuscript, Representative Church Body Library, MS C 6 I.I (Black Book of Christ Church) fol. 213v.   **34** *Annals of Multyfarnham*, p. 8; Gwynn, 'Black Book', p. 328.   **35** *Annals of Multyfarnham*, p. 8; Gwynn, 'Black Book', p. 328.   **36** *Annals of Multyfarnham*, p. 9; Gwynn 'Black Book', p. 328.   **37** *Annals of Multyfarnham*, p. 9; Gwynn 'Black Book ', p. 329.   **38** Gwynn 'Black Book', p. 328.

Mellifont, the interest shown in John de Courcy,[39] and Hugh de Lacy,[40] in the annals of Multyfarnham (the annals of Christ Church are extant only to 1168) may not only reflect their high status but also their considerable patronage of the Cistercian order. The only other Anglo-Irish name mentioned in this early section of the annals, William Marshal, was the founder of the Cistercian abbeys of Graiguenamanagh and Tintern.[41] The importance of the Marshal family in general may well account for the entries concerning them in the annal but the entry, in 1211, reporting that Richard Tuyt died when a tower fell on him at Athlone,[42] is of less general significance and may be accounted for by the fact that he founded the Cistercian abbey of Abbeylara near his castle at Granard in County Longford.[43]

The fact of Cistercian involvement in the annals gives rise to the possibility of other sources of the Anglo-Irish annal. A link exists between the annals of Multyfarnham and the Scottish chronicle of Holyrood.[44] In Multyfarnham, following the report of the Norman conquest and the appearance of a comet, there is an entry, in 1069, which states, 'Bellum in Bledima'.[45] This entry was noted by M.O. Anderson when she suggested a relationship between these two annals of Multyfarnham and Holyrood.[46] She postulated the theory that the Holyrood, Multyfarnham and five other annals had, for the period 1065–1189, a common source, which she called X.[47] She proposed Winchester as one possibility.[48] Coincidentally, another unusual entry in the annals of Multyfarnham is the notice, in 1113, concerning Winchester, 'Wyncestria comburitur, multis monachis combustis'.[49] Of further interest is the fact that the source common to Holyrood and Multyfarnham had other entries in it besides those derived from X; for example, only these two record the establishment of the canons in Salisbury in 1089,[50] and also the date of the death of Malcolm III of Scotland as 1094 instead of 1093.[51] This relationship between the two annals was also essential in resolving a puzzling entry in the annals of Multyfarnham, in 1080, which states: 'Walter, the bishop of Durham, was killed by a strong wind'.[52]

---

39 *Annals of Multyfarnham*, pp 10, 11. **40** Ibid., pp 10, 13. **41** Ibid., pp 133–4, 142–3. **42** *Annals of Multyfarnham*, p. 11. **43** A. Gwynn and R.N. Hadcock (eds.), *Medieval religious houses: Ireland* (Dublin, 1970), p. 124. **44** *A Scottish chronicle known as the chronicle of Holyrood*, ed. M.O. Anderson, Scottish Historical Society, 3rd. ser., 30 (Edinburgh, 1938). **45** *Annals of Multyfarnham*, p. 5. For an identification of the battle see *Chronicle of Holyrood*, p. 108, n. 5. Irish pirates were involved in this battle, J. Beeler, *Warfare in England 1066–1189* (Cornell, 1966), p. 38. **46** *Chronicle of Holyrood*, p. 6 et seq. **47** Ibid., p. 21. **48** Ibid., p. 21. St Bernard of Clairvaux speaks of a Bishop Malchus of Lismore (ob. 1135) who was a monk at Winchester, see Bernard of Clairvaux *The life and death of Saint Malachy the Irishman* trans. and annotated R.T. Meyer (Kalamazoo, Michigan 1978), p. 24, 131n. 29. **49** *Annals of Multyfarnham*, p. 7. **50** 'Osmundus episcopus constituit canonicos xxxvi in ecclesia Salisberiensi', *Chronicle of Holyrood*, p. 110. 'Osmundus constituit canonicos Salisbyrie', *Annals of Multyfarnham*, p. 6. **51** *Annals of Multyfarnham*, p. 6; *Chronicle of Holyrood*, p. 111. **52** 'ventu valido Walterus Denelmensis episcopus occisus est', *Annals of Multyfarnham*, p. 6.

The chronicle of Holyrood has the correct entry for that year, ' … there was a strong wind at Christmas. Walter the bishop of Durham was killed', two events, which clearly got conflated in the Multyfarnham annal.[53] Anderson suggested that the section of the chronicle of Holyrood, which ended in 1189, probably reached its present form in the Cistercian abbey of Coupar Angus founded in 1164.[54]

This further Cistercian link bolsters the theory that both the annals of Multyfarnham and of Christ Church used a source, present in Ireland and containing Cistercian entries, up to and including the death of the founder of Mellifont in 1168. However, this early source does not include the entries common to both Multyfarnham and Holyrood.[55] The relationship between Holyrood and Multyfarnham only begins in 1065.[56] It is clear that an annalist in Ireland had access to a source, either directly or indirectly, which was not available to the Dublin annalist, but which was also used by the chronicle of Holyrood in the course of its probable composition in the Cistercian house of Coupar Angus in Scotland.

The early Cistercian source was used by later annalists. Aubrey Gwynn suggested that the annals of Christ Church were used by the so-called St Mary's annalist,[57] and it is indeed logical to assume that the Dublin annalist used the annals of Christ Church as a source. In fact they both have the same error in the year 1098 when they report the capture of Jerusalem instead of the capture of Antioch.[58] Gwynn also suggested that the annals of Christ Church were the basis for the early part of the 'Kilkenny Chronicle'.[59] This is in fact not so. It is the annals of Multyfarnham and not those of Christ Church, which were used directly as a source for a section of an Anglo-Irish chronicle which was written in Kilkenny before 1316.[60] Of the eighty years extant in the early section of this manuscript, only five are additional to those found in Multyfarnham. Furthermore, this chronicle provides an excellent example of a situation where marginalia, present in the original source, are copied directly into the text of the material copied. The words 'tunc erat tres reges de Britonibus et tres de Saxonibus' are added to the text of the annals of Multyfarnham in a different

---

53 'ventus validus in natale domini. Walcherus episcopus Dunelmensis occisus est', *Chronicle of Holyrood*, p. 110. **54** Ibid., p. 37, et seq. **55** The annals of Christ Church contain five entries which are also present in the chronicle of Holyrood but as these refer only to the king, the queen, Lanfranc and Anselm, they cannot be considered as emanating solely from that source. **56** *Chronicle of Holyrood*, p. 107; *Annals of Multyfarnham*, p. 5. **57** Gwynn, 'Black Book', p. 316. **58** *Chartul. St Mary's, Dublin*, vol. ii, p. 252. Gwynn, 'Black Book', p. 328. It is important to note that the annals of Multyfarnham do not have this entry. **59** Gwynn, 'Black Book', p. 320. **60** BL MS Vespasian B XI ff. 133v, 134v, 135v, 136v, 137v. Flower, 'Manuscripts – British Museum', p. 330–32. For the Kilkenny chronicle, see Flower, 'Manuscripts – British Museum', pp 330–340. For identification of a section of this chronicle as emanating from Castledermot see Bernadette Williams, 'The "Kilkenny" chronicle', in T.B. Barry et al. (eds.), *Colony and frontier in medieval Ireland* (London, 1995), 75–96.

hand,[61] and, in the Kilkenny chronicle, this is incorporated into the text.[62] Further proof is provided by an error, present in Multyfarnham (also in the same additional hand) which mistakenly applies the name of Strongbow to William the Conqueror.[63] This erroneous entry is repeated in the Kilkenny chronicle.[64] There can be no doubt that this portion of the manuscript was copied directly from the annals of Multyfarnham, and not from a common source.

It is clear that there is a close relationship between the more complex Multyfarnham annals and the Christ Church annals. Both used a source, present in Ireland and containing Cistercian entries, up to and including the death of the founder of Mellifont in 1168. But this early source does not contain the entries which are common to both Multyfarnham and Holyrood and which begin at 1065. Therefore it is logical to argue that an annalist in Ireland had access to a source, directly or indirectly, which was not available to the Dublin annalist, which was also used by the chronicle of Holyrood in the course of its probable composition at the Cistercian house of Coupar Angus in Scotland. The whole subject of the source of annals is fraught with problems which are made more difficult by the scarcity of surviving manuscripts. For example there are thirteen early entries, from 1124 to 1266, in the Multyfarnham annals which refer to Lincoln and for which, at present, there is no explanation, despite the fact that these entries cannot be mere coincidence.

Mention, at this point, must be made to two seventeenth-century transcripts of two Anglo-Irish Dominican annals which are no longer extant.[65] There is no indication of how complete the transcripts are and one might suspect that they are probably only brief extracts. The transcript of the 'Annals of Ross' has as its title merely 'Annales', but Ware appended the following note: 'Anonymi Hibernici forte ord. fratrum Praedicatorum Ross'.[66] The reason for assigning the annal to Ross is clearly the entry, in 1267, which states that the Dominicans or Friars Preachers entered Ross and which gives the date 20 October.[67] This identification is strengthened by an entry in 1293 concerning Thomastown in Ossory.[68] From the beginning of the annal in the year 184 to 1259, every entry present is, in the great majority of the cases, virtually identical with the entries in the annals of Multyfarnham. The similarity ceases in 1259.

The second transcript is of the 'Annals of Trim' and has as its title 'q. Annal Coenob. Dominic. Trim.' and 'Chron. cuiusdam fratris ord. Praedicatorum'.[69] Fortunately in this case the transcriber himself makes clear that the annals belong to Trim and therefore the notices of the establishment of eight different friaries cause no problem. The chronicle is preceded by a list of thirteenth-

61 TCD MS. 347, fol. 395r; *Annals of Multyfarnham*, p. 3.   62 BL MS Vespasian B XI fol. 134v; Flower, 'Manuscripts –British Museum', p. 330. 63 TCD MS 347 fol. 396v; *Annals of Multyfarnham*, p. 5.   64 BL MS Vespasian B XI fol. 134v; Flower, 'Manuscripts – British Museum', p. 330.   65 The 'chronicle of Trim', BL MS Add. 4789 ff. 206v–207v and the 'chronicle of Ross', Bodl. MS Rawl. B 479 ff. 68r–69r.   66 Ibid., fol. 68r.   67 Ibid., fol. 68v. 68 Ibid., fol. 68v.   69 BL MS Add. 4789 fol. 206r.

century Dominican foundation dates ending with Killmallock in 1291 and a list of Dominican provincial chapters ending in 1347.[70] The chronicle itself begins with the year 432 and there are entries for thirty three years up to and including 1260. Of those years, twenty five are virtually identical with the entries in Multyfarnham. As with the annals of Ross, the similarity of entries between the annals of Trim and the annals of Multyfarnham ceases after 1260.

It would appear, therefore, that the Dominicans of Ross (fd. 1267), the Dominicans of Trim (fd. 1263), and Stephen de Exonia all had access to a similar source and that that source was Dominican. Obviously, Stephen de Exonia could not have copied either the annals of Trim or the annals of Ross as both friaries were only founded after 1260. Moreover, Trim has information concerning the arrival of the Franciscans or Friars Minor in Ireland which was not available to Stephen de Exonia. It is interesting to note that some facts concerning the Friars Preachers are present in the annals of Multyfarnham but not in the annals of Trim and Ross. The solution to this might lie in the notes taken by the seventeenth-century transcriber; for example, the information concerning the confirmation of the two orders and the death of the two founders, Dominic and Francis, is so well known that the transcriber might have felt no need to include them in his notes, but the entry in the Trim annal concerning the arrival of the Friars Minor would clearly be of interest as it was a subject of speculation in the seventeenth century by the great Franciscan historians Luke Wadding and Donough Mooney.

It is interesting to speculate as to which Dominican priory, founded prior to 1260, possessed the source for these annals. Upon consideration, only two foundations appear to answer the requirements and those are Drogheda (fd. 1224) and Mullingar (fd. 1237). Either of these foundations could have supplied the later source for the Franciscan annals of Stephen de Exonia. A very interesting aspect of the survival of these two transcripts, however, is that they suggest that the Dublin Dominican annalist, Pembridge (to be discussed below), was not familiar with them: he does not include in his own annals the early Dominican information which they contain.

PART TWO: 'JOHN' DE PEMBRIDGE'S DUBLIN ANNALS

Virtually all historians of later medieval Ireland refer, at some time or other, in the course of their research, to the Dublin annals as edited in volume two of Gilbert's *Chartularies of St Mary's abbey*. Yet there is a crying need to examine them in depth in order for their provenance and historical value to be correctly assessed. The point to be stressed is that these annals are, in fact, four separate and distinct works and therefore differing emphasis should be placed on the

70 Ibid., fol. 206r.

material gleaned from each one as each, inevitably, has its own individual bias and 'agenda'.

The first set of annals

The first set of annals of the group of four, which Gilbert calls 'Annales Monasterii Beate Marie Virginis, juxta Dublin'[71] is taken from a fifteenth-century manuscript in Trinity College, Dublin.[72] Unfortunately the manuscript is without title or heading and is incomplete. The entries begin with the birth of Christ and in the early section there are large periods of time with no entries. However, the missing sections in the later part of these annals are far more crucial from the viewpoint of Irish historians; the years from 1179 to 1192 are absent and also a significantly large section between 1221 and 1308.[73] Missing parchment also accounts for a gap between 1309 and 1315. Another serious gap is that of thirty five years between 1316 and 1361. After that the annals then continue, with a number of years being either ignored or missing, to 1382. The latter year contains a notice of the death of James Butler, earl of Ormond, on 18 October, but is followed with a notice of the death of his son on 7 September 1405.

The final entry in these annals is for 25 May 1427 where we are informed that they were written by Thomas Case, clerk of the church of St Werburgh in Dublin[74] – not St Mary's abbey – who finished them on the Saturday before the feast of Saint Aldelm, bishop, in the latter year. From this we can determine that Thomas Case finished *copying* on that day. The fact that Thomas Case, writing this note in 1427, did not end his entries in 1427 but with the year 1405,[75] suggests that he merely copied an unnamed manuscript and did not in fact himself contribute to any part of it: otherwise the years between 1382 and 1427 would most certainly have been entered.

There is no problem with associating the early part of these annals with a Cistercian affiliation and, despite the fact that St Mary's abbey is only mentioned specifically four times,[76] there is also no problem with identifying the early section to 1221 with St Mary's. The Cistercian order is mentioned 28 times but the Cistercian entries cease in 1221.[77] The latter section 1308–1427, though undoubtedly a Dublin annal, cannot be safely said to show any affiliation to any specific order.

---

71 *Chartul. St Mary's, Dublin*, vol. ii, pp 241–86.   72 TCD MS 175 ff. 2v–13v; see also Colker, *Trinity College Library: descriptive catalogue*, i, pp 330–1.   73 Other examples of large gaps are to be found between 1221 and 1307. Missing parchment accounts for a lacuna between 1309 and 1316.   74 Thomas Case is not mentioned in H.F. Twiss, 'Some ancient deeds of the parish of St Werburgh, Dublin, 1243–1676', *R.I.A. Proc.*, xxxv (1918–20), 282–315; H.F. Berry, 'Ancient deeds of St Werburgh's 1243–1676', *R.S.A.I. Jn.*, xlv (1915), 32–44.   75 The year 1405 is not a separate year but included under the general heading of the year 1382, *Chartul. St Mary's, Dublin*, vol. ii, p. 286.   76 In 1139 as a Savigny monastery; in 1221 the death of Bernard superior of St Mary's; in 1209 the death of Abbot Leonard. Reference to Buildwas (p. 272) can also be taken as a reference to St Mary's.   77 *Chartul. St Mary's, Dublin*, vol. ii, p. 281 (there is one mention of St Mary's in 1370).

The second set of annals

The second set of annals are merely notes written by Sir James Ware.[78] The latter extracted these notes, he informs us, from annals of Irish interest which he identified, without any obvious reason, as 'Annales Monasterii Beatae Marie Virginis, Dublin'. These are very brief notes indeed, covering initially only the years 684, 1095, 1180 and 1186. After these entries there follow very brief, mostly one-line entries, from 1187 to 1319. There are three final additional entries for the years 1337, 1361, and 1434. Given the frequent references to Cistercian matters, there is no need to challenge his title. However Ware does not state – as Gilbert implies – that it was the Thomas Case manuscript to which he was referring. Ware had access to the Case manuscript but, as his notes cover the years that are substantially missing from Case, we cannot draw any safe conclusions as to his source. He may well have been using a manuscript emanating from St Mary's abbey but not necessarily the manuscript that Thomas Case was copying.

The third set of annals

The third set of annals in the collection consists of two fragments;[79] the first covers, in significant detail, the years 1308–1310 and the second, in equal detail, 1316–17. These folios are in a fourteenth-century hand and are very familiar to anyone working with the Bruces as they deal with information concerning Robert Bruce and his brother Edward during their time in Ireland. There is no reason for assigning these annals to St Mary's. Indeed St Mary's is only mentioned once – the imprisonment of the earl of Ulster in the abbey. The Dominicans are also only mentioned once; the Friars Minor are mentioned three times and, with four references, these annals in fact show a far greater interest in the affairs of the priory of Holy Trinity at Christ Church. There is a great similarity between these fragments, regarding the detail for the years 1316–17, and the following fourth annal, a subject which deserves to be explored.

The fourth set of annals

These annals, entitled 'Annales Hibernie ab anno Christi 1162 usque ad annum 1370' in the Laud manuscript, are by far the largest and the most important set of annals.[80] They are extant in two fifteenth-century manuscripts, Trinity College, Dublin, Ms 583 and Bodleian Laud Misc. 526.[81] Both of these manuscripts have the appearance of being copies of an original as neither seems to be

---

78 Ibid., pp 287–292; BL MS Add. 4787 ff. 30–34; TCD MS 804, pp 309–14.   79 *Chartul. St Mary's, Dublin*, vol. ii, pp 293–302; BL MS Add. 4792 (on three leaves of vellum). 80 *Chartul. St Mary's, Dublin*, vol. ii, pp 303–98.   81 Colker, *Trinity College Library: descriptive catalogue*, pp 1030–1041. For a 1607 edition see William Camden, *Britannia* (London, 1607), 794–832.

a working document; that is to say there are no marginalia, no corrected errors, no spaces left for names to be inserted, etc. These annals have been referred to as the Laud manuscript or Pembridge's annals. The importance of these annals cannot be overestimated; they are more than twice as long as the Thomas Case annals and are of great historical value.

The most frustrating aspect of Gilbert's edition of Pembridge, and consequently the major difficulty facing the reader, is his failure to give the entire text of this, the longest, annal. The reason for this failure is difficult to comprehend, but since that inadequacy is frequent for the early part of the annal, the reader is unable to read Pembridge's annal in its entirety without consulting the original manuscript. An example of this flaw, one of very many, is to be found on page 307 where Gilbert begins editing a Pembridge item with the words, 'Defuncto Ricardo Rege, Johannes etc. (ante p. 277)'. When the reader duly goes to page 277 he or she finds the sentence beginning 'Defuncto Ricardo Rege, Johannes', but there is no indication from Gilbert as to how much of the following fifteen lines is to be assumed to be present in the original Pembridge manuscript. For the researcher to experience a full uninterrupted examination of Pembridge it is necessary to consult the original manuscript.

Gilbert used the Bodleian Laud Manuscript Misc. 526 for his edition of the annals. This Laud manuscript carries no identification of the author. Had Gilbert consulted the mid-fifteenth century manuscript of the same annals in Trinity College, Dublin, he would have found, at the conclusion of 1347, the rubricated note, which states 'Hic finitur cronica Pembrigii'.[82] This claim is entirely credible because up to and including the year 1347 each year is only identified by the words Anno Domini followed by the year in Roman numerals. From the following year, 1348, the method of dating changes and, continuously to the end of the annals, the regnal year is added to the dating of each year.[83] These annals by Pembridge, and the anonymous continuator who was responsible for the years 1348–70, are important for many reasons not least of which is that they was used as a source by Philip Flattisbury, James Grace and William Camden and extracts from them are present in the 'Book of Howth'.

The questions that arise are: who was Pembridge, when were these annals written, andwho was the anonymous continuator? The clear answer is that, despite early entries of Cistercian interest, Pembridge was a Dominican friar in St Saviour's priory in Dublin, situated across the river Liffey from Holy Trinity. The multiple references to the Friars Preachers and their priory make this undeniably a Dominican annal. The name Christopher became associated with Pembridge at an early stage. In a letter to his uncle, Richard Stanihurst, James Ussher declared that he had not seen a copy of Christopher Pembridge's chronicle.[84] In 1746, Walter Harris, in his edition of the *Works of Sir James*

---

82 TCD MS 584 f 34v.   83 Chartul. *St Mary's, Dublin*, vol. ii, p. 390.   84 C.R. Elrington

Ware, names Pembridge as C. Pembridge, a native of Dublin, declaring that he wrote the larger part of those annals of Ireland which Camden published at the end of his *Britannia* in 1607 and he carried the annals down as far as the year 1347.[85] From this comment by Harris it became accepted that Pembridge's first name was Christopher. However, when one examines Ware's *De Scriptoribus Hiberniae*, written by Ware himself, the only one who knew and had seen and used the manuscript, nearly a hundred years earlier in 1639, there is no mention of a C. Pembridge. Ware only names the author as Pembridge.[86] An explanation may be that a note by Ware was misinterpreted by both Ussher and Harris, neither of whom had seen the manuscript. If Ware instead of writing in some note 'cronica Pembrigii' abbreviated it to 'C.' or perhaps 'Ch.' or even 'Chr. Pembrigii' then this could easily have been misinterpreted as Christopher.

Prior to the publication in 1998 by Dr Philomena Connolly of a calendared edition of the Issue Rolls of the period, the name Pembridge had not been found in any printed source. Here for the first time was the information that the prior of the Dublin Dominicans at exactly the correct time was a John de Pembridge. We can be certain that Pembridge was prior from 1329 to 1333; between 1333 and Easter 1335 John de Mora and Philip de Mora were priors and Pembridge was once again prior at some period between 1341 and 1343.[87] As no other evidence exists for a Pembridge in Ireland at that period, identification of the Dominican annalist as John de Pembridge seems indicated and indeed logical.

John de Pembridge ceased writing in 1347 and from internal evidence it can be determined that he was writing his annals after 1332. In an entry in 1308 Pembridge refers to the Dublin mayor, John le Decer, and mentions that he was subsequently buried with the Franciscans;[88] John le Decer died in 1332,[89] so Pembridge was obviously writing the entry for 1308 in or after 1332. In 1343,[90] when Pembridge reports the arrival in Ireland of Ralph Ufford on 13 July, he stated that the weather became bad on Ufford's arrival and did not improve until after the death of Ufford – which did not occur until 1346.[91] Therefore Pembridge was writing that entry in or after 1346. One interesting fact to note is that the year 1344 is not entered.[92] Perhaps Pembridge was absent from Ireland during that year; perhaps he was at a general chapter of the Friars Preachers. It is interesting to speculate that after he had ceased to be the head

---

and J.H. Todd (eds), *The whole works of the Most Rev. James Ussher, D.D.*, 17 vols (Dublin, 1847–64), xv, p. 4; this first letter of vol. xv of Ussher's *Works* is not dated but, as Richard Stanihurst died in 1618, it must have been before that date. **85** Walter Harris (ed.), *The whole works of Sir James Ware* (Dublin, 1746), p. 83–4. **86** James Ware, *De scriptoribus Hiberniae* (Dublin, 1639). **87** Philomena Connolly (ed.) *Irish Exchequer Payments 1270–1446* (Dublin, 1998), pp 337, 342, 345, 351, 357, 408. For Philip de Mora, see pp 364, 369, 373. I am most grateful to Dr Connolly for all her help and assistance in this matter. **88** *Chartul. St Mary's, Dublin*, vol. ii, p. 337. **89** Ibid., p. 377. **90** Ibid., p. 385. **91** Ibid., p. 388. **92** Ibid., p. 385; Laud MS fol. 36.

of the Dominican order he turned his attention to historical writing. He ceases writing after 2 April 1347/48.[93] Why? Here it is useful to turn to the annals of the Franciscan friar, John Clyn of Kilkenny, who tells us that in 1348 'the Black Death began near Dublin and Drogheda and that the cities of Dublin and Drogheda were almost destroyed and emptied of inhabitants so that in Dublin alone … 14,000 men died.'[94] He adds that in the Franciscan friary of Drogheda twenty five friars died and in Dublin in the same order twenty three friars died.[95] He later adds that in Kilkenny eight of the Dominicans died.[96] The friars were particularly susceptible to the plague as they lived in the towns and ministered to the people. Indeed Clyn tells us that in Kilkenny the confessor died with the confessed.[97] If Pembridge was in Dublin he was in great danger. However, Pembridge could also have been in Drogheda as in 1348 the chapter of the Friars Preachers was held there.[98] The odds against Pembridge surviving in either place were not good. Not unnaturally, considering the devastating effect of the Black Death, it appears that writing ceased.

After 1347, subsequent to the notice in the TCD Ms 'Hic finitur chronica Pembrigii', there is no question but that the annals remain in Dominican hands as burial notices and information about the Dominican priory in Dublin continue to predominate. The anonymous continuator therefore must also be a Dominican. When the anonymous continuator began his section of the annals, he began his entry for the year 1348 with the statement that the first plague occurred that year,[99] thereby implying that he knew that there were more to come. Similarly in 1361 he notes the second pestilence.[100] In 1370, the final year entered in the annal – as extant – the continuator notes what he calls the third and greatest plague.[101] The chronicle finishes there. Perhaps he also succumbed to the plague?

As the annal begins – as extant – with the year 1162 it is evident that Pembridge used for the early section sources available to him, one of which at least was Cistercian. It would be entirely logical to use the Cistercian chronicle already present in the city as the source for his early entries. The consensus of historical opinion is that the Cistercians were involved in the early establishment of the Friars Preachers in Dublin. In 1706 the Dominican historian John O'Heyne wrote: 'The abbey is situated on the banks of the river so that when the tide is in ships can come up to its walls. It belonged first to the monks of St Bernard who gave it to the Dominicans in the year 1223 [recte 1224] on condition that on Christmas Day every year they should offer a lighted candle to the abbot of St Mary's abbey, in acknowledgement of the gift.'[102] The detail

93 Ibid., p. 390.   94 'Annales Hiberniae ad annum 1349', in *The annals of Ireland, by Friar John Clyn and Thady Dowling*, ed. Richard Butler (Dublin, 1849), p. 35.   95 Ibid., p. 36. 96 Ibid., p. 37.   97 Ibid., p. 35.   98 BL MS Add. 4789, fol. 206r.   99 *Chartul. St Mary's, Dublin*, vol. ii, p. 390.   100 Ibid., p. 395.   101 Ibid., p. 397.   102 John O'Heyne, *Epilogus chronologicus exponens succinte conventus et fundationes sacri ordinis praedicatorum in regno*

of the candle at Christmas adds a sense of authenticity to O'Heyne's statement. Both Thomas de Burgo in 1762 and Coleman in his appendix to O'Heyne in 1902 agree with the latter.[103] Benedict O'Sullivan suggested that Henry of London, the then archbishop of Dublin, was instrumental in giving the site to the Friars Preachers either directly or indirectly but there is no documentary evidence for this theory.[104] Evidence from Pembridge indeed contradicts this theory. In Pembridge's annal for 1211 there is a lengthy scurrilous tale about Archbishop Henry. This is the entry (which, it should be noted, is not in the Thomas Case annal) which calls Henry of London 'Scorch-villein'. Pembridge tells us that when Henry of London was made archbishop of Dublin in 1212 he called all his tenants together and asked them by what tenure they held their lands of him. The tenants, we are told, then innocently produced their charters and deeds for Henry. Henry then ordered them to be burned and Pembridge tells us that the freeholders evermore called him Scorchvillan.[105] Bearing in mind the great praise bestowed in the annals upon all Dominican benefactors it is most unlikely that Henry of London was in any way an original benefactor of the Dominicans. The statements of O'Heyne, de Burgo and Coleman that the Cistercians gave the land, are far more plausible especially when one notes that a report in St Mary's chartulary states that the Cistercians of Dunbrody also gave land to the order of Dominicans.[106] This connection between the Cistercians and Friars Preachers adds force to the likelihood of a Dominican having access to a Cistercian annal.

There is both an element of assembling (using a Cistercian annal as one of his sources) and creation in Pembridge's work. At what stage Pembridge's own personal contribution began can only be conjecture but a date around 1308 must be seriously considered. In 1308 he tells us that the Dublin mayor John le Decer fed the friars once a week at his own table and here Pembridge adds the important information that this is what his elders have told him.[107] Also, it is in 1310 that Pembridge first begins to mention the price of goods. He tells us that there was a great shortage of food, a crannoc of wheat selling for 20 shillings and more; the Dublin bakers responded to the high price by giving false weight to their bread and were duly caught, and the punishment was that the bakers were drawn upon hurdles through the streets of the city at horse tails.[108] The entries now begin to take on a personal aspect and nowhere is this more clear than in the extremely long entries of 1315 to 1317.[109] Reading his account of the years of the Bruce upheaval it is evident that he has had a personal knowledge

---

Hyberniae (Louvain, 1760); edited and translated by Ambrose Coleman as *The Irish Dominicans of the seventeenth century*, together with Ambrose Coleman, *Ancient Dominican foundations in Ireland* (Dundalk, 1902), pp 25–7.   **103** Ibid., p. 23.   **104** Benedict O'Sullivan, 'The Dominicans in medieval Dublin', in *Medieval Dublin: the living city*, ed. Howard Clarke (Dublin, 1990), pp 83–99, 212.   **105** *Chartul. St Mary's, Dublin*, vol. ii, p. 312.   **106** Ibid., p. xciv.   **107** Ibid., p. 337.   **108** Ibid., p. 339.   **109** Ibid., pp 344–58.

of the events of that time. We find the detailed information that in 1315 the value of wheat which was 18 shillings at mid-Lent had dropped to 11 shillings by Easter.[110] In 1317 we are told that Nicholas de Balscot came from England with news.[111] In 1318, he tells us that 'three weeks after Easter, came news to Dublin that ... ',[112] and later, 'Sunday after the feast of St Michael, news came to Dublin that the lord Alexander Bicknor had landed in Youghal',[113] and again in 1318, 'news arrived from England to Ireland that the town of Berwick was captured by the Scots'.[114] The entries abound with phrases such as 'news came from Connacht', 'news arrived from England', 'rumour states', or 'rumour came to Dublin', and 'afterwards news came to Dublin'. Only a chronicler who had experienced that period firsthand could write in such manner.

Pembridge begins his Dominican entries with the foundation of the order in 1198.[115] It is evident that Pembridge was not familiar with the manuscript that Thomas Case subsequently used because that manuscript noted the arrival of the Friars Preachers in England in 1221,[116] nor could he have been familiar with the manuscript that Ware was using for his notes which tells us that the Friars Preachers entered Ireland in 1224.[117] Pembridge was also not familiar with the Dominican source, used by Stephen de Exonia, in the late thirteenth century. Pembridge records neither of these important Dominican events in his annals and he obviously would have done had he had that information. Pembridge does tell us, however, that in 1274 at the coronation of Edward I, the archbishop of Canterbury was Friar Robert Kilwarby of the order of Friars Preachers and the coronation oath is included in the entry.[118] It is also Pembridge who tells the diverting story in 1313 of Friar Roland Jorz, archbishop of Armagh, who arrived in Howth with his crozier and was then chased out of Leinster in, we are told, 'disgrace and confusion' by the men of the archbishop of Dublin.[119] This episode highlights the primatial controversy between the two archbishops, the archbishop of Armagh being forbidden from bearing his crozier in the province of Dublin. Presumably this entry is in Pembridge because the then archbishop of Armagh, Roland Jorz, was a Dominican friar.

Strong evidence for the Dominican claim comes from the numerous notices of burials in Dominican priories in these annals, usually accompanied by very precise dating. The first notice is in 1285 with the notice of the death in Arklow Castle on 26 September of Theobald Butler and his subsequent burial in the Dominican priory at Arklow which he himself had founded,[120] and there are another nineteen such specific notices of such burials. As one might expect from a Dominican annal, Geoffrey de Geneville, lord of Meath and founder of the Dominican friary of Trim, and his family, is featured prominently beginning with the announcement of Geoffrey's marriage,[121] his return from the Holy

---

110 Ibid., pp 349–50.   111 Ibid., p. 355.   112 Ibid., p. 358.   113 Ibid., p. 358.   114 Ibid., p. 358.   115 Ibid., p. 307.   116 Ibid., p. 281.   117 Ibid., p. 288.   118 Ibid., p. 317. 119 Ibid., p. 342.   120 Ibid., p. 319.   121 Ibid., p. 315.

Land,[122] his period as justiciar[123] and the death of his wife in 1304.[124] Geoffrey's subsequent entry into the order of Friars Preachers in Trim is recorded,[125] as is his death and burial in the priory in 1314.[126] The death in 1324 and subsequent burial among the Dominicans of Trim of Nicholas de Geneville, son and heir of Lord Simon de Geneville, is reported,[127] as is the burial in the convent of the Dominicans at Trim in 1347 of Joanna fitzLeones, wife of Simon de Geneville.[128] Among the de Geneville family notices can be included that of the arrival in Ireland of Roger Mortimer with his wife, Geoffrey's granddaughter, the heiress of Meath.[129]

Other Dominican benefactors also feature prominently in these annals, for example the de Berminghams. Their loyalty to the Friars Preachers is exemplified by Meiler de Bermingham who founded Athenry priory and it was his daughter Basilia who forced her husband Jordan de Exonia to oust the Friars Minor from Slade and replace them with the Friars Preachers.[130] In these annals Peter de Bermingham is pronounced the noble vanquisher of the Irish in 1308;[131] William de Bermingham's execution in 1332 was greeted with the sad lament *heu heu proh dolor*!. He was described by Pembridge as most renowned and excellent in arms and the annalist wonders aloud as to who, hearing of his death, would not cry. After such partisanship we are not surprised to learn that William de Bermingham was buried in Dublin among the Dominicans.[132] The death of Walter de Bermingham in 1349 is accompanied by the comment that he was the best justiciar Ireland ever had.[133] These annals also tell us that Margaret de Bermingham, wife of Robert Preston, was buried with the Friars Preachers in Drogheda in 1361.[134] She is one of the very few women whose burial is noted in the annals – two of the other women are de Genevilles.

Under the year 1316, Pembridge has a long tale about a butcher of Athenry, John Hussey, who while fighting for Richard de Bermingham was tempted to desert by O'Kelly who promised to make him a great lord in his country.[135] Why this story is included is not clear; it is either that it shows a de Bermingham rewarding loyal service or it may be that John Hussey was related to the Dublin Husseys and as such of interest to a Dublin chronicler. It is more likely however that he or his family were Dominican benefactors; in 1418 a Matthew Hussey, baron of Galtrim, is named as a great benefactor of Trim.[136] When Thomas

122 Ibid., p. 317. 123 Ibid., p. 318. 124 Ibid., pp 330, 332. The entry concerning the death of Margaret Wogan, wife of the Justiciar, and Matilda de Lacy is entered under both 1302 and 1304. 125 Ibid., pp 337–8. 126 Ibid., pp 343–4. 127 Ibid., p. 362. 128 Ibid., p. 390. 129 Ibid., p. 337. For a possible connection between an English family of the name of Pembridge and Mortimer see Flower, 'Manuscripts – British Museum', p. 321n. 130 Ambrose Coleman, 'Regestum monasterii fratrum praedicatorum de Athenry', in *Archivium Hibernicum*, i (1912), pp 204–5. 131 *Chartul. St Mary's, Dublin*, vol. ii, p. 336. 132 Ibid., p. 337. 133 Ibid., p. 391. 134 Ibid., p. 395. 135 Ibid., p. 351. To cut a long story short, John Hussey refused and cut off three heads of the Irish and carried them to Richard de Bermingham who, as a reward, gave John lands and made him a knight. 136 O'Heyne,

Butler died in 1329 Pembridge states that this is to the great damage of Ireland and then we are told that on Tuesday after the feast of St Bartholomew his body was brought to Dublin and placed, still unburied, with the Dominicans until the next Sunday when the body was carried by the citizens with great honour and buried with the Friars Preachers, and his wife held a feast that same day.[137]

The anonymous Dominican continuator also continues that practice of noting the burials of benefactors. On 24 February 1351, he reports that Kendrick Sherman, formerly mayor of the city of Dublin, was buried under the campanile of the Dominicans. Kendrick Sherman was clearly an exemplary figure because we are told that apart from actually erecting that same campanile, glazing the windows in the chapter choir and roofing the church, he had also done many other good deeds. At the end of his life he made his will to the value of 3,000 marks and he left much to the church both religious and secular.[138] In 1355 the death in Dublin Castle, of Maurice fitz Thomas, justiciar of Ireland, is reported and this notice is accompanied by the statement that he was a good and just man who even hanged his own relatives for theft, rape and evil deeds and subdued the Irish. This encomium is, not surprisingly, followed by the announcement of his burial first in the choir of the Dominicans of Dublin and finally in the convent of the Dominicans of Tralee.[139] Another post-Pembridge benefactor was Maurice Doncreff, citizen of Dublin, who, we are told, died on 8 January 1361 and was buried in the cemetery of the Friars Preachers of the same city. We are also informed that he had given forty pounds to the Dominicans for the glazing of the church.[140] Incidentally, in the same year, 1361, we are told of a great storm on 15 January which demolished the Dominican campanile.[141]

Robert Savage, seneschal of Ulster in 1333 and 1343, was evidently of great interest to the anonymous Dominican continuator. In 1352 there can be found a very long anecdote about Robert beginning to build castles in many places in Ulster to counter the Irish resurgence. His son disagreed with his policy and stated that he should have trust in his men. His father conceded but prophesied that afterwards his sons and posterity would be sorry and we are told that this duly happened and the Irish destroyed all that country because of the lack of castles.[142] This comment is useful as it discloses that the continuator was writing later than 1352. His interest in Robert Savage is explained eight years later, in 1360, with the obituary notice and the statement that this man slew 3,000 Irish near Antrim. He then adds a long observation about Robert's liberality, a trait much admired in the middle ages. Apparently before battle Savage ordered that his English soldiers should be given wine or ale. He further ordered that sheep, oxen, fat fowls and venison red deer should be made ready

Epilogus chronologicus … fundationes sacri ordinis praedicatorum, trans. Coleman, p. 32.
137 *Chartul. St Mary's, Dublin*, vol. ii, pp 370–1. **138** Ibid., p. 391. **139** Ibid., p. 392.
140 Ibid., p. 395. **141** Ibid., p. 396. **142** Ibid., pp 391–2.

for the returning victors. Then the continuator states that when it pleased God to give victory to the English, Savage invited them all to eat and he himself said 'I give thanks to God'. Then we are told that Robert Savage was buried in the convent of Dominicans of Coleraine.[143] This burial of one of the Savage family among the Friars Preachers is of interest and gives weight to the statement by O'Heyne, which is not fully accepted by Gwynn and Hadcock, that the Savages founded the Dominican priory of Newtownards.[144] In the light of Robert Savage's inclusion in the Dominican annals this scepticism might be worthy of reassessment.

These entries relating to Dominican benefactors and the references to Irish burial notices alone would be sufficient reason for the claim that both Pembridge and the continuator were Dominican. However to these can be added other Dominican burials. In 1315 there is the information that the Scottish lords, Fergus de Androssan and Walter de Morrey, were buried at Athy in the convent of the Friars Preachers,[145] and the notice in 1312 that Peter Gaveston was buried in the church of the Dominicans at Langly.[146] Pembridge has only positive things to say about Gaveston including the fact that he made an offering to the church in 1309.[147]

Apart from the numerous burial notices, specific references to the Dublin Dominican priory abound in Pembridge again reinforcing the Dominican provenance. For example, on 12 June 1304, a fire burned the Dominican church,[148] and on 2 February following we are told that Eustace le Poer laid the first stone of the choir of the Dominicans.[149] The Friars Preachers evidently proved loyal to the le Poers since in 1328 when Arnold le Poer was in disgrace we are told that the said Arnold le Poer died in Dublin Castle and later lay with the Dominicans without burial.[150] They were evidently willing to take his body and hold it even though he was in disgrace. In 1308 we are told that John le Decer, then mayor of the city of Dublin, apart from building the marble cistern which was to supply water to the city, did many good things for the convent of the Friars Preachers in Dublin, namely providing one stone buttress in the church and one altar stone for the high altar together with its ornaments.[151] In 1316 when the Scots were approaching, we are told that 'the mayor, Robert de Nottingham, together with the citizens of Dublin destroyed the church of St Saviour which is the place of the Friars Preachers and the stones of the same place were transported to build the walls of the city … ' Pembridge adds that later the king of England ordered that the same mayor and community should re-build the convent for the friars just as it had been before. This of course indicates that the information was written after 1316.[152]

---

143 Ibid., pp 393–4.   144 O'Heyne, *Epilogus chronologicus … fundationes sacri ordinis praedicatorum*; trans. Coleman, p. 19.   145 *Chartul. St Mary's, Dublin*, vol. ii, p. 347. 146 Ibid., p. 341.   147 Ibid., p. 338.   148 Ibid., p. 332.   149 Ibid., p. 332.   150 Ibid., p. 369. 151 Ibid., p. 337.   152 Ibid., p. 353.

Apart from the notices of Dominican burials and information concerning the Dominican priory in the annal, its very character is mendicant in tone. The mendicant orders broke away from the most basic principle of traditional monasticism by abandoning the seclusion and enclosure of the cloister in order to engage in an active pastoral mission to society with the result that the friars were a gregarious and mobile order. The ethos of St Francis and his friars was to minister to the people. The raison d'être of the Dominican order was preaching and combating heresy. They were preachers to the people, they heard their confessions and consequently they were involved in city life. This relationship with the daily life of the people of Dublin is fully revealed in these annals. In fact all the mendicant characteristics are to be found in Pembridge, one of the most obvious being their interest in education. It is from Pembridge that we learn the names of the four founding teachers at the newly instituted Dublin university in 1320. We are told that the first *magister* in that university was friar William de Hardits, order of Friars Preachers and the fourth *magister*, in sacred theology, was the Dominican friar Edmund de Kermerdyn.[153] As might be expected there is some, but not much, interest in other mendicant orders. The foundation of the Franciscan order by St Francis at Assisi is noted,[154] as is the information that Robert Bruce slew John Comyn in the cloister of the Franciscan friary of Dumfries in 1305.[155] However, the intense public interest in Bruce would account for that information being included. A few Franciscan burials are noted and the Carmelites are mentioned only once in 1333 when, attending a parliament, the earl of Ormond and his retinue assembled in the house of the Carmelites.[156] Mendicant bias is most clearly evident in the entry, by the anonymous Dominican continuator, concerning the anti-mendicant Archbishop of Armagh, Richard fitzRalph.[157] When he is reporting the great controversy between fitzRalph and the four orders of Mendicants in 1358 he concludes by stating, 'but in the end the friars got the mastery and the pope caused the archbishop of Armagh to hold his peace'.[158] Two years later, in 1360, he reports the death of fitzRalph in Avignon and informs us that his bones were conveyed to Ireland by Stephen, bishop of Meath, for burial in the parish church of St Nicholas, Dundalk, where he was born, after which statement, our mendicant annalist then adds the dismissive rider: 'But it is doubted whether they were his bones or those of some other man.'[159]

The Friars Preachers had originally been founded in order to combat the Albigensian heresy and Pembridge is very interested in any case of heresy

153 Ibid., p. 361. For the identification of Friar Edmund as a Dominican, see E.B. Fitzmaurice and A.G. Little (eds), *Materials for the history of the Franciscan province of Ireland 1230–1450* (Manchester, 1920), p. 108, n. 1.   154 *Chartul. St Mary's, Dublin*, vol. ii, p. 310. 155 Ibid., p. 333.   156 Ibid., p. 379.   157 For an account of FitzRalph, see Katherine Walsh, *A fourteenth century scholar and primate: Richard FitzRalph in Oxford, Avignon and Armagh* (Oxford, 1981).   158 *Chartul. St Mary's, Dublin*, vol. ii, p. 393.   159 Ibid., p. 393.

coming to his ears. In 1287 there is a long entry about the king of Hungary who, forsaking the Christian faith, became an apostate.[160] Nearer to home Pembridge includes in his annals the Alice Kyteler case of 1324 where he has extra information about Kyteler not to be found in either Clyn's annals or in Bishop Ledrede's contemporary 'Narrative'.[161] For example it is in Pembridge that the statement, 'ipsam mundare vicos Kylkennie scopis inter completorium et ignitegium , et scopando sordes usque ad domum Willelmi Utlawe, filii sue, conjurando dixit, tota felicitas Kylkennie veniat ad domum hanc',[162] first appears which later became the doggerel 'Unto the house of William my son – Hie all the wealth of Kilkenny town'. Similarly, only he reports the information that Alice put ointment on a stick called a coultree which she could then ride on throughout the world.[163] These additional details may be true but it is far more likely to be just an example of how quickly rumour can add to and distort truth. Had this been true it would have been included in the contemporary 'Narrative'.[164] Pembridge's interest in heresy is again evident in 1327 when Adam Duff O'Toole, son of Walter Duff, was accused of denying the Incarnation and the Resurrection and said that the Virgin Mary was a harlot and that the sacred scriptures were fables.[165] He was pronounced a heretic and blasphemer and by church decree was burned at the Hogges in the eastern suburb of Dublin on the Monday after Easter in 1328.[166] Perhaps greater weight than heretofore should be placed on such an episode as reported by a Dominican. The following year, 1328, Pembridge reports that another O'Toole, David O'Toole, a thief, a burner of churches and destroyer of people, was taken from Dublin Castle to the Tholsel and the justices. The heretic, as he puts it, was drawn by horse's tails through the midst of the city before being hanged.[167]

Certain comments made throughout the annals confirm the scribe as a cleric and further suggest a preacher.[168] In 1317 he decries the men of Ulster who, he says, when the Scots were in Ireland, had done much harm and moreover had eaten flesh in Lent, and not out of necessity. The result was that much tribulation came upon them and they ate each other. And here, Pembridge says, appeared the vengeance of God.[169] In 1318, after his notice that Roger Mortimer[170] had sailed back to England without paying for the food he had taken from Dublin to the tune of £1000, he reports that by the great grace and mercy of God the value of wheat which had been fifteen shillings was now only

160 *Chartul. St Mary's, Dublin*, vol. ii, pp 319–20.   **161** Ibid., pp 262–4.   **162** Ibid., p. 362.   **163** Ibid., p. 263.   **164** Ibid., p. 179. For the contemporary account written either by the inquisitor, Richard Ledrede, bishop of Ossory, or one of his followers, see *A contemporary narrative of the proceedings against Dame Alice Kyteler, prosecuted for sorcery in 1324, by Richard de Ledrede, bishop of Ossory*, ed., Thomas Wright (London, 1843).   **165** *Chartul. St Mary's, Dublin* p. 189.   **166** Ibid., p. 366.   **167** Ibid., pp 366–7.   **168** Ibid., p. 315, where the term 'a son of Beliel' is used.   **169** Ibid., pp 357–8.   **170** He was a benefactor of the Dominicans of Cork in 1317: O'Heyne, *Epilogus chronologicus … fundationes sacri ordinis praedicatorum*; trans. Coleman, p. 46.

worth seven shillings and there was great plenty of wine, salt and fish. Around the feast of St James (25 July), new bread was made with new corn, a thing that had never or seldom been seen before in Ireland. This, Pembridge tells us, was a sign of God's tender mercy as a result of the prayers of the poor and other faithful people.[171] In 1327, when the Irish of Leinster made Domnall MacMorrough king, Pembridge tells us that God saw his pride and malice and caused him to fall into the hands of one Henry Trahern.[172]

Pembridge, most definitely, sees the hand of God in the death of Ralph Ufford on 9 April 1346.[173] Reportage about Ralph Ufford, justiciar of Ireland 1343–6,[174] and his wife Matilda, daughter of the earl of Lancaster who was formerly the wife of the murdered 'Brown Earl' of Ulster, is a fascinating example of extreme bias. Vitriolic is the adjective that best describes Pembridge's entries concerning Ufford and Matilda and it is worth summarising Pembridge's comments. He begins with pathetic fallacy. When Ufford arrived In Ireland on 13 July 1343 we are told fair weather changed immediately to foul and rain and tempestuous storms were the order of the day until he died. Pembridge tells us that none of his predecessors were like him. He was an oppressor of the people of Ireland and a robber of the goods of both the church and the laity, rich and poor alike. He was a defrauder under the guise of doing good; he neither observed the rights of the church nor the laws of the kingdom. He did wrong to the natural inhabitants, ministering justice to few or none and altogether distrusting – except for a few – the natural-born dwellers of the land. He deprived people of their lands by having charters cancelled, defaced and annulled (echoes of Henry Scorch-villein here!). Other complaints include the accusation that he raised the king's standards against the earl of Desmond without the assent of the magnates of the land and obtained the arrest of the earl of Kildare by treachery. Ufford's death, according to Pembridge, was greeted with joy, the floods ceased and the common people truly and heartily praised the only son of God.[175] It is difficult to imagine anything worse left to say.

There is apparently no single reason for the hatred shown by Pembridge. The explanation probably lies in the many actions taken by Ufford in his short term in Ireland. Ufford's two years in Ireland indeed resulted in the imprison- ment of the earl of Kildare; the earl of Desmond had likewise been forced to become a fugitive among the Irish of the south-west, and there followed the le Poer rebellion of 1345. All these men were important Anglo-Irish figures and many of them were Dominican benefactors. Eustace le Poer had laid the foundation stone of the Dominican priory in Dublin and the earl of Desmond was also a Dominican patron. Less notable figures familiar to Dubliners, and

171 *Chartul. St Mary's, Dublin*, vol. ii, pp 358–9.   172 Ibid., pp 365–6.   173 Ibid., p. 388.
174 For a complete report on Ralph Ufford in Ireland, see Robin Frame, 'The justiciarship of Ralph Ufford: warfare and politics in fourteenth-century Ireland', in *Studia Hibernica*, 13 (1963), 7-47.   175 *Chartul. St Mary's, Dublin* vol. ii, p. 388.

adversely affected by the advent of Ufford, were Elias of Ashbourn, a crown official, who had his goods and chattels seized and been imprisoned by Ufford. It was this Elias Ashbourn who had successfully persecuted and hanged the heretic David O'Toole, as reported by Pembridge in 1328. After Ufford's death Elias was released and compensated. Another such figure adversely affected by Ufford's period in office was John Balscott, former chamberlain of the exchequer and deputy treasurer, who was captured and had his lands seized over a minute administrative error. It might be conjectured that these two figures, familiar in Dublin circles, with properties in Dublin, were friends of the Dominicans.

Less personal reasons for the antagonism towards Ufford might have been the very large retinue that Ufford brought with him to Ireland which would inevitably cause problems of purveyance. Also, many of his retinue were new-comers to Ireland. One of Pembridge's complaints is that Ufford ignored local opinion, 'with a few exceptions, utterly mistrusting the local inhabitant'. Some support for Pembridge's view of Ufford might be detected in a comment emanating from the priory of Holy Trinity which sought to buy cloth for the justiciar's purveyors, 'that they may be more favourable to us'. Robin Frame is inclined to dismiss Pembridge's opinion of Ufford and justifies this by noting that John Clyn of Kilkenny did not have anything bad to say about him,[176] but this can be accounted for by the fact that one of Ufford's chief supporters was Fulco de la Frene, the man whom Clyn praised above all others. Clyn would therefore not be inclined to condemn Ufford. Also, according to Ufford's itinerary, Ufford was never in Kilkenny; a couple of days in Cashel was the nearest he ever came to the city. Therefore a greater weight should be placed on Pembridge's view of Ufford which would probably reflect the opinion held in Dublin by the citizens and the Dublin administration. Pembridge was not 'anti-administration'. An earlier justiciar, Anthony Lucy, is praised by Pembridge for his kindness and care of the Dublin people.[177] Pembridge does concede that Ufford's dependants and his wife sorrowed at his death – while all the loyal subjects of Ireland rejoiced. Matilda, Ufford's wife, had also come under attack from Pembridge who stated that Ufford was misled by the counsel and persuasion of his wife. This may have been so, but may also reflect the quite common mysogynism of clerical commentary in this period. He then paints a pitiful picture of Matilda who, he said, had lived like a queen in the land of Ireland now leaving by the postern gate to avoid the clamour of the people who were calling upon her to pay her debts and so, 'she left Ireland in disgrace, sad and mournful'.[178]

The final point to be explored might popularly be called Dublin news. If the Friars Preachers of Dublin did not live within the city walls they lived

---

176 Frame, 'The justiciarship of Ralph Ufford', p. 37.   177 *Chartul. St Mary's, Dublin*, vol. ii, p. 375.   178 Ibid., p. 386; she had become pregnant while in Ireland because at one time, great with child, she remained at Kilmainham: ibid., p. 387.

nonetheless just across the river and to all intents and purposes were fully part of the town. From Pembridge we get a fascinating insight into many aspects of Dublin medieval life. From him we learn such incidental news that, in 1308, as already noted, John le Decer made a marble cistern for Dublin at his own expense,[179] and in 1313 he built a bridge with arches at Clontarf which, unfortunately, a heavy rainfall destroyed.[180] It is Pembridge who tells us that from 2 December 1338 to 10 February 1339 there was severe frost and snow lying to a great depth in Ireland and the river Liffey froze over. The people of Dublin were dancing, playing ball and running on the ice and used wood and turf to make fires on the frozen river and roasted herrings.[181] From Pembridge we also learn that in 1331, when famine had caused great distress to the people of Dublin, God's mercy caused a mighty multitude, around 500, whales to beach in Dublin at the mouth of the Dodder on the evening of 27 June. The justiciar and certain citizens of Dublin, among whom was the former mayor Philip Craddock, killed about 200 of them and the justiciar ordered that no man was to be forbidden to take them away (stranded whales were the property of the crown).[182]

As stated before, there are many references to prices and naturally a friar would be a frequent visitor to the Dublin market.[183] This scribe shows a deal of interest in marriages and births and the news and gossip constantly related in his text makes it unlike any other Anglo-Irish annal. It is also characterised, as we have seen, by the frequent repetition of the phrase 'news came to Dublin'[184] and, less frequently, 'rumour states'. There is an interest in the city affairs. Reports of the burning of the city one would expect,[185] but not the many fascinating insights into Dublin life afforded by the annals. It is here that we learn that in 1330 there was such a great wind in Dublin that part of the wall of a house belonging to Sir Miles Verdun fell down and killed his wife and daughter.[186] Pembridge reports when feasts were given in the city and one assumes that the Dominican prior at least would be invited to such gatherings. In 1305 the chancellor Thomas Cantock gave a great feast which is described as very sumptuous and rich where the wealthy ate first then the poor – such has had never before been heard of in Ireland. In 1317, at a time of great famine, Pembridge tells us that it was reported as truth that some evildoers were so hungry that they took bodies from the graves and cooked the flesh in the skulls for food and women ate their own children through starvation.[187]

---

179 Ibid., p. 337.   180 Ibid., p. 342.   181 Ibid., p. 381.   182 Ibid., p. 375. For the importance of stranded whales in medieval times, see Arthur E.J. Went, 'Whaling from Ireland', in *R.S.A.I. Jn.*, 98 (1968), p. 31. C.A. Ralegh Radford, 'Stranding of "Whales" at Seaton', in *Devon Historian*, 32 (1986) p. 29. For contemporary account of stranded whales 30 feet long taken from the Thames in 1309, see *Annals of the reigns of Edward I and II*, ed. William Stubbs (RS, London, 1882–3), pp lxxvii, 157, 267. The presence of whales on the Liffey is collaborated by Clyn's annals s.a. 1331.   183 *Chartul. St Mary's, Dublin*, vol. ii, pp 167, 175–6.   184 Ibid., 177.   185 Ibid., p. 174.   186 Ibid., p. 372.   187 This is the last

The location of St Saviour's is reflected in the detail given in the annals about Holy Trinity at Christ Church and Dublin Castle both of which would have been in the constant view of the Friars Preachers across the river. There are many entries referring to Holy Trinity in the annals. One very captivating entry is the account in 1337 when Pembridge says that seven partridges – he does not know what spirit moved them – leaving the open field made their way directly to the city of Dublin and flying most quickly over the market place settled on the top of the brew house belonging to the Canons of Holy Trinity. At this sight the citizens came running and wondered at so strange a sight. However the boys of the city caught two of them alive and killed a third and the rest took flight out of fear and escaped over the fields. Pembridge declares that he cannot tell what this sight portends.[188] One can almost visualise the friars coming out of their priory to watch what was going on just across the river. There are also references to the steeple of Holy Trinity; in 1283 the belfry was burned,[189] and in 1316 the steeple fell again during a storm which overthrew many houses;[190] also Pembridge reports that St Werbugh's church was burned in 1301.[191]

Pembridge is very interested in the city of Dublin but he does not often mention individual people. He is not interested in the Dublin oligarchy; he only mentions John le Decer as mayor because of his donation to the Dominicans and Philip Craddock, another mayor, because of the incident of the whales in the Liffey. On balance it might be said that Pembridge has a greater interest in the administration. He exhibits an interest in the parliaments held in Ireland and even England but especially those held in Dublin. Nearly all known parliaments held in Ireland during the period are mentioned in the annals; twenty one are referred to by Pembridge and the Dominican continuator between 1308 and 1368. Since some of the Dublin ones were held in Holy Trinity, it is more than probable that the prior of the Dominicans would have been present as a guest of Holy Trinity and indeed some of the participants would have been guests of the Dominicans themselves especially those who were benefactors.[192] The Castle also holds Pembridge's interest. It was after all just across the river. Pembridge can tell us that Domnall MacMorrough escaped from the castle of Dublin on 6 January 1330 by a rope which a certain Adam Nangle procured and the said Adam was later drawn and hanged,[193] but he does not mention the similar attempt by William de Bermingham on the 2 July 1332. The explanation must lie in his admiration for William, whose execution in 1332 he laments.[194]

entry for 1317, ibid., p. 358.   **188** Ibid., p. 380.   **189** Ibid., p. 319.   **190** Ibid., p. 298; this item is part of the section that Gilbert has omitted from his edition, merely referring the reader back to a previous annal. It should be on p. 351.   **191** Ibid., p. 329.   **192** The parliament of 11 July 1333, which was attended by the earl of Ormond, was held in the house of the Carmelite friars: ibid., p. 379.   **193** Ibid., p. 372.   **194** Ibid., p. 377.

The identity of the scribe Pembridge as John de Pembridge, head of the Dominican order between 1331 and 1343, seems beyond doubt. Pembridge lived in St Saviour's priory across the river Liffey from Holy Trinity. He was a man who mixed with the people of Dublin and listened to the gossip and news coming into the city. He was always aware of the price of crops, and was interested in the parliaments that took place in Dublin. He saw the hand of God in the events that happened around him and had a lively interest in omens and strange tales such as the barking mania that attacked the populace in 1341.[195] This vital and energetic Dominican annal makes a great contribution to our knowledge of Dublin and Ireland in the early fourteenth century. Pembridge's annals deserve to be re-edited and also to be translated in order that they may be made wholly available to the citizens of Dublin today and for all time.

195 Ibid., p. 383.

Excavations at Dublin Castle, 1985–7

ANN LYNCH AND CONLETH MANNING

INTRODUCTION

Extensive archaeological excavations were carried out at Dublin Castle between 1985 and 1987 in connection with a major rebuilding programme, which was undertaken to provide facilities at the castle for international conferences and in particular the then imminent Irish presidency of the European Union. Some of the older buildings involved, especially those partly founded on the north moat of the medieval castle, had developed serious structural problems and were unoccupied for some time. Those buildings along the north side of the upper yard were to be demolished apart from their front façades and rebuilt with piled foundations (figs 1, 2). Block 10 which extended into the lower yard, was fully demolished. The main block of the old Genealogical Office, crowned by a mid-eighteenth-century clock tower, called the Bedford Tower, was to be retained and conserved intact, but the Guard House, to the north of it, was demolished apart from its east and north façades. The west block of the upper yard was likewise retained and conserved. The programme also involved the construction of some new buildings such as the large conference hall in the north-west corner of the castle precinct and a new kitchen block at the south-west corner.

As the building works were clearly going to involve extensive removal or disturbance of archaeological deposits, a series of archaeological excavations was scheduled into the work plan between the demolition and construction phases. Ann Lynch initiated the work with excavations in the areas of the Cork Tower, the Bermingham Tower and the Children's Court. Conleth Manning continued the work with excavations at the Genealogical Office and finally in the area of the Powder Tower (Blocks 8, 9 and 10). Excavation was confined to the areas threatened with disturbance, which mostly comprised parts of the west and north moat of the castle (fig. 3). Given the restricted areas available for excavation and the proximity of unstable façades, the size, location and stepped profile of cuttings were largely determined by safety considerations, as decided by structural engineers specifically retained for this purpose. Only tiny portions of the interior of the castle were excavated and these were mostly truncated by

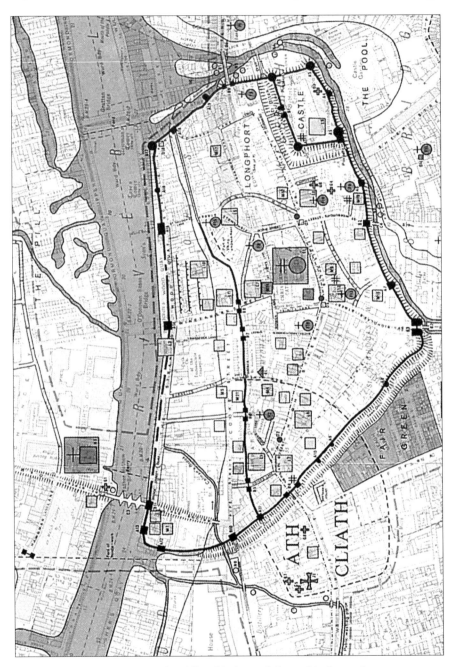

1   The medieval walled town of Dublin with the castle located in the south-east corner, as
    published by the Friends of Medieval Dublin, *Dublin c. 840–1540. The medieval town in
    the modern city* (extract from Ordnance Survey Ireland, copyright Government of Ireland,
    Permit No. MP006800).

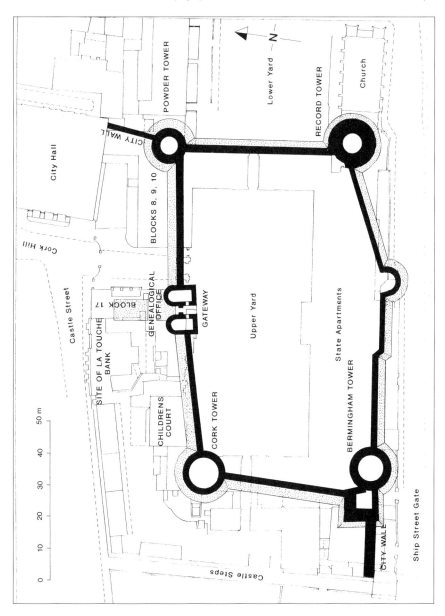

2   Composite map of the buildings existing in 1985 in relation to the walls of the medieval
    castle. The batter and entrance causeway are shown stippled.

later building work and, apart from the centre of the Powder Tower itself, did not contain deposits contemporary with the use of the medieval castle. The moat itself was a massive feature up to 22m wide and in places over 10m deep below contemporary ground level. The curtain walls of the castle were founded on boulder clay with their lower battered faces acting as retaining walls for the inner edge of the moat. From the inner face of the curtain walls to the outer edge of the moat all earlier deposits had therefore been totally removed when the medieval castle was being built. Pre-castle deposits from the Hiberno-Norse town were excavated outside the north-west corner of the moat and within the Powder Tower itself and just inside the adjacent north curtain wall. The moat itself contained deposits and finds varying in date from the thirteenth century up to the eighteenth century.

GEOGRAPHICAL SETTING

The Hiberno-Norse town of Dublin was founded on a low east/west ridge at the confluence of the river Liffey and its tributary the Poddle. This ridge was bounded on the north side by a tidal stretch of the Liffey, while the Poddle bounded it at its short east end and for some distance along its south side. The Hiberno-Norse town filled the east end of the ridge and the thirteenth-century castle was built within the pre-existing south-east corner of the town. The castle was constructed on low-lying ground which sloped gradually upwards towards the west and north and was bounded on its south and east sides by the river Poddle. The massive moat provided defence on the west and north (or townward) sides and the thirteenth-century town walls extended from the south-west and north-east corners of the castle, thereby incorporating the castle in the circuit of the medieval town defences (fig. 1).

HISTORICAL BACKGROUND

The following is a translation of the mandate issued by King John in 1204 for the building of a castle at Dublin:

> The king to his trusty and well-beloved Meiler, son of Henry, Justiciar of Ireland, greetings. You have given us to understand that you have no safe place for the custody of our treasure and, because for this reason and for many others we are in need of a strong fortress in Dublin, we command you to erect a castle there in such a place as you may consider to be suitable for the administration of justice and if need be for the defence of the city, making it as strong as you can with good ditches and strong walls.

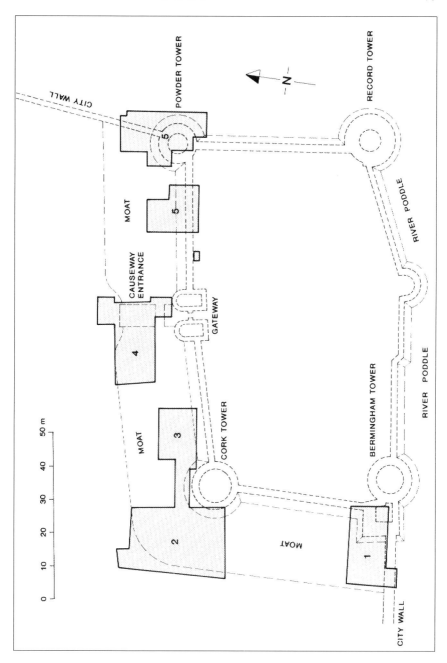

3   Map of the areas excavated showing the castle walls and moat. 1. Bermingham Tower area; 2. Cork Tower area; 3. Children's Court area; 4. Genealogical Office area; 5. Powder Tower area.

But you are first to build a tower, to which a castle and bailey and other requirements may be conveniently added: for all these you have our authority. At present you may take and make use of 300 marks from Geoffrey fitz Robert, in which he stands indebted to us. (Gilbert 1870, 61; Sweetman 1875–84, i, 35)

There are references to a castle at Dublin prior to 1204, about which a number of deductions can be made (Manning 1998). First, it was sited in the same area as the later castle (Orpen 1892, 198–9; Gilbert 1889, 370; Sweetman 1875–84, i, 17–8). Second, it was smaller and took up less ground, because properties had to be acquired to build the later castle (Sweetman 1875–84, i, 120, 126, 267, 269). And third, according to the mandate it was considered insufficient by Meiler and King John for the custody of the king's treasure, the administration of justice and the defence of the city. In short it was not perceived as being large, strong or commodious enough to serve as the administrative centre and main fortress of the king's deputy in Ireland. Again the wording of the mandate might indicate that it did not have sufficiently 'good ditches and strong walls' for this purpose.

The mandate itself was not the most favourable of beginnings for the building of a major new castle. The recommended approach to planning the structure could be seen as haphazard, in that a tower was first to be built, 'to which a castle and bailey and other requirements may be conveniently added' presumably as resources became available. The only money committed to the project was 300 marks owed by Geoffrey fitz Robert, which Meiler was going to have to collect. Even the concept of a great tower or donjon, as was advocated, was already outdated by this time. It is not therefore surprising that little progress appears to have been made with the new castle in the first ten years after the mandate was issued. Opposition from Church interests may also have been a major impediment, as church property, including two churches, had to be acquired and demolished to make way for the new castle (Murphy 1995, 55). The appointment of Henry of London as both justiciar of Ireland and archbishop of Dublin in 1213 would have facilitated the alienation of Church property, and progress with the building of the castle is indicated for the first time in surviving records by compensation claims for property lost for this purpose in the period from *c.*1213 to 1218 (Sweetman 1875–84, i, 120, 126, 267, 269). The only specific reference to the works on the castle dates from 1227–9 and concerns payments to carpenters and masons for the construction of towers and for the making of leaden gutters (*RDKPROI* 35 (1903), 29). It is likely that the castle was nearing completion at that time. A mandate was issued by Henry III in 1243 for the building of a large hall at the castle in preparation for a planned visit by the king, which in fact never took place. The pre-existing hall was presumably not seen as grand enough and the mandate specified that the new hall was to measure 120 by 80 feet with glazed windows 'in the manner of the hall of Canterbury'. It was to have a great portal and a round window, 30 feet in diameter in the gable beyond the dais, above a painting of the king and queen sitting with their barronage (Sweetman 1875–84, i, 389). The hall was rebuilt in the 1320s (*RDKPROI* 43 (1912), 27–8) and survived to be depicted on seventeenth-century plans of the castle (fig. 4).

Dublin Castle was the main centre of administration in Ireland from the early thirteenth century until 1922. Up to the eighteenth century it often served as the official residence of the chief governor of Ireland. The hall was often a venue for law courts and parliaments and the exchequer and armoury were generally housed within the castle. Parts of the complex were used as a prison for persons of quality and accounts of escapes from prison there in the sixteenth century in particular throw light on aspects of its defences. It was never captured by force of arms and was only besieged on one occasion and that was in 1534 during the revolt of Silken Thomas. His limited ordnance made the siege ineffective and it was lifted after a short time (Maguire n.d.). New buildings were erected within the castle by Sir Henry Sidney during his terms of office in the later sixteenth century and these were altered and extended during the seventeenth century (Maguire 1974, 8, 12–3). The oldest surviving depiction of the castle is a print in Derricke's Image of Ireland, published in 1581. It shows the gateway and bridge with Sir Henry Sidney riding out with a troop of horse and the moat and north-west tower in the background (Quinn 1985, pl. VI). This depiction is probably not to be relied on for detail and it is unclear whether the gate shown is the front of a barbicon, like that on the Dublin Gate at Trim Castle (Sweetman 1999, figs 30–33), or the entrance to the gatehouse itself. A descriptive survey survives of the perimeter walls and towers of the castle, dating from 1585 and commissioned by the Lord Deputy, Sir John Perrot (Gilbert 1891–1944, ii, 558–561). It details the number of floors in each of the towers and the number and aspect of the external windows on each floor. The earliest surviving plan of the castle is a sketch done by a man called Wattson in 1606 to illustrate a proposed new access and bridge across the moat from the west directly into the hall (Maguire 1974, 5–8). Despite its sketchy nature, it does illustrate the location of the main structures within the castle. The gatehouse of the castle was largely rebuilt in 1617 (CSPI 1615–1625, 196, 202) and the north-west corner tower, not having its foundation on rock and having long been undermined by the waters of the moat, finally collapsed in 1624 (CSPI 1615–1625, 489). It was rebuilt over the following five years. The earl of Cork completed the tower in 1629 at his own expense and thus it became known as the Cork Tower (Ware 1678, pp 23ff).

The most detailed plan of the castle is that dated 1673 in the collection of the earl of Dartmouth (Maguire 1974, 8–9). This is the first and only surviving measured survey of the internal structures within the castle and for that reason is extremely important (fig. 4). The internal buildings are shown in outline and the towers as if they had flat roofs and parapets. The curtain walls are shown as if they had both internal and external parapets. The overall plan is slightly more elongated than it should be in reality and the north ends of the east and west curtain walls are skewed more to the east than is truly the case. The square tower attached to the west side of the Bermingham Tower (here called Kitchen Tower) is captioned 'platform' because it was adapted to take cannon. We know from the 1585 survey that it was then three storeys high.

In 1684 there was a serious outbreak of fire within the castle and the earl of Arran, who was deputising for his father, the duke of Ormond, caused many of the internal structures to be blown up to prevent the fire spreading to the Powder Tower, where the gun powder was stored, or to the Bermingham Tower, where the records were kept (Maguire 1985, 13–6). Plans were soon after drawn up by William Robinson, the Surveyor General, for grand ranges of buildings to replace much of the castle (Loeber 1980, 63–4, pl. 2). However, when Richard Talbot, earl of Tyrconnell, was made Lord Deputy in 1687, Robinson fled to England and the first section of the grand design, the east end of the south range, was erected under the supervision of William Molyneux (Loeber 1980, 66). In 1685 Thomas Phillips had produced a survey of the castle which showed none of the internal buildings but only the curtain walls and towers (Maguire 1974, fig. 1). This appears to show the outline of the castle more accurately than the 1673 plan.

Building work came to a halt as a result of the Williamite wars and was not resumed until soon after 1700. The view of the castle on Brooking's map of Dublin (1728) shows less than half of the Upper Yard completed, namely the east and west blocks as well as the section built by Molyneux. This drawing is particularly valuable in that it shows the gatehouse as rebuilt in 1617, the ruined Bermingham Tower and adjacent buildings to its east, part of the north curtain wall and the Record Tower, which still survives. The building ranges around the upper yard were not completed until around the middle of the eighteenth century (see Rocque's map of 1756) with the building of the central structure on the north side, crowned by the Bedford Tower and later used as the Genealogical Office. This was built on the site of the old gatehouse.

In 1775 the Bermingham Tower was taken down to the top of its battered base and rebuilt with thinner walls. In 1796 the northern part of the east block (known as the Cross Block) was taken down and rebuilt. At the same time Block 8, immediately east of the main or Justice Gate, was to be doubled in width to the north. The builder, George Darley, having bored down 36 feet into the medieval moat, failed to reach solid ground and decided to use a shallow foundation of granite blocks bolted to timber beams, which he also used for the rebuilt section of the Cross Block (NAI OP/94/8).

The next major development at the castle was the result of political and security considerations following on the 1798 rebellion. Much of the outer part

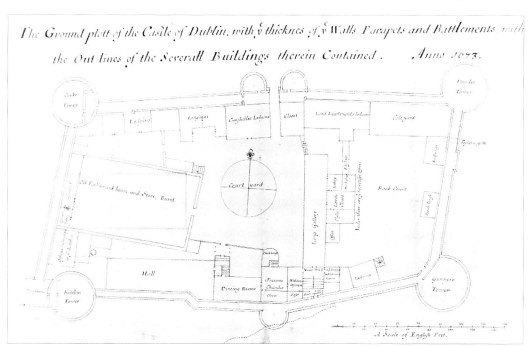

4   The 1673 map of Dublin Castle. Reproduced by kind permission of the Staffordshire
     and Stoke-on-Trent Archives Service (Staffordshire Record Office).

of the original moat on the west and north sides of the castle had been sold off
for the building of houses in the seventeenth century and as a result the
buildings on Cole Alley and Silver Court backed onto the buildings of the
upper yard (fig. 5). Discussions were held about buying up these two streets but
nothing was done until the Emmet rebellion of 1803 spurred the administration
into action. An act was quickly passed for this purpose and some of the
buildings were soon after purchased and demolished (NAI PW I/1/2/1/1).
The only building allowed to remain was the La Touche bank, which was
eventually acquired by the State in 1870 and demolished in 1945 apart from the
vaults and ground-floor façade. The massive boundary wall along the west side
of the castle precinct and along part of Castle Street was not completed until
1806 and a new thoroughfare, called Castle Steps, provided outside it to connect
Castle Street and Ship Street (NAI PW I/1/2/1/1).
    In 1814 the new Chapel Royal in the Lower Yard was completed to the
design of Francis Johnston (Lawlor 1923, 57) and at the same time the adjacent
Record Tower was fitted out as a repository for State papers and had the present
upper floor and battlements added to it (*RCPR*, I, 471, Pls. xix, xx). In the
1820s the dormer attic floor on most of the buildings around the upper yard was

replaced by a full storey and, before 1843, Block 10, connecting the Cross Block and the Treasury in the lower yard, was built.

By the middle of the twentieth century the Cross Block was again in a dangerous condition due to foundation failure and a decision was taken to rebuild it with pastiche façades. Demolition in 1961 revealed archaeologically-rich deposits beneath its basement floor. Salvage excavations were carried out by Marcus Ó hEochaidhe at three locations; (i) at the junction of the Cross Block with the Record Tower, (ii) mid-way along the Cross Block and (iii) at the northern end of the Cross Block where the east and north curtain walls meet the Powder Tower. In addition to exposing portions of the curtain walls and part of the Powder Tower, a sequence of layers with post-and-wattle houses, predating the castle, was also revealed. This was the first scientific excavation to be carried out in medieval Dublin. It was, unfortunately, never completed (access to the early habitation deposits is still possible) and subsequent building work at the castle in the 1960s at the east end of the State Apartments and at the east end of the lower yard was carried out without any archaeological input or investigation.

SUMMARY OF EXCAVATION RESULTS

The Hiberno-Norse or pre-castle layers
Layers pre-dating the castle only survived outside the moat and inside the castle walls. The only area excavated which lay outside the edge of the moat was in the north-west corner of the castle precinct, just inside the high boundary wall erected in 1806, where Castle Street meets Castle Steps (fig. 3). A small cutting, in keeping with engineering safety requirements, was excavated through these deposits in 1985. However, during the construction phase, a larger area of these deposits was exposed and had to be excavated as an urgent salvage operation (pl. 1).

In this limited area, where pre-Norman deposits were up to 1 metre in depth, nine separate phases of activity were identified. These ranged from a large cess pit and cobbled walkway in phase 1 to possible property boundaries (phases 2, 4 and 6), metalworking (phase 3), post-and-wattle houses (phases 5, 8, 9; pl. 1) and a period of abandonment (phase 7). These deposits were aceramic but produced numerous artefacts including pins, needles, beads, gaming pieces, combs, knives, nails, textile fragments and items made from wood and leather. One of the wooden pieces has been tentatively identified as the cross-beam from a small light loom. Another unusual artefact recovered was a small saw frame made from a piece of antler (fig. 6). There is a good parallel for this among the finds from York (Hall 1996). Amongst the antler combs is an example with a runic inscription. The comb in question, which was recovered

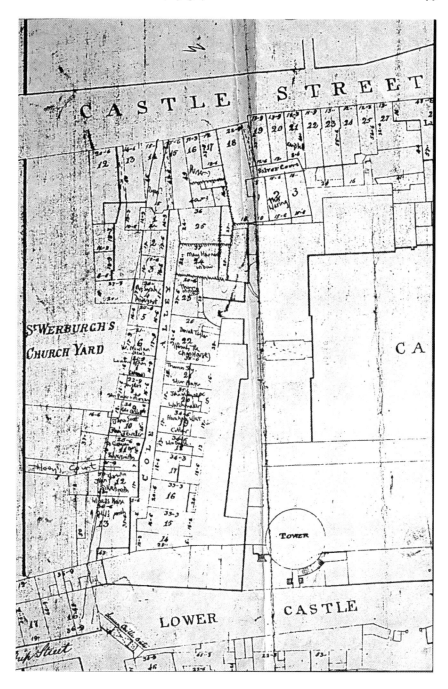

5 Plan of Cole Alley and Silver Court prepared by Robinson and Green, 1803.

Plate 1   Pre-Norman habitation levels in the north-west corner of the castle precinct. Note
the remains of house, timber-lined pit to right and the edge of the castle moat to
the rear left. (Photo: Con Manning.)

from deposits belonging to the latest phase of occupation (phase 9), comprises
part of a toothplate with fragments of the slightly-arched sideplates riveted in
place. The central portion of one of the sideplates has incised linear decoration
with lightly-scratched doodles on one side and the runic inscription on the
other (fig. 7). The inscription consists of six graphs, lightly scratched and has
been interpreted as a possible monogram of the personal name *Uni* (Barnes,
Hagland and Page 1997, 44,45). No definitive dating evidence was recovered for
these early habitation levels but a date of around the tenth/eleventh century is
suggested.

Under Blocks 8 and 9 in the Powder Tower area, a narrow strip of ground
was excavated just inside the north curtain wall of the castle, and between it and
the retained south façade of the eighteenth-century building (fig. 3, pl. 7). This
narrow strip, having been cut on its north side by the construction of the
curtain wall in the thirteenth-century and on its south side by the foundations
of the south wall of Blocks 8 and 9, had dried out and consequently did not

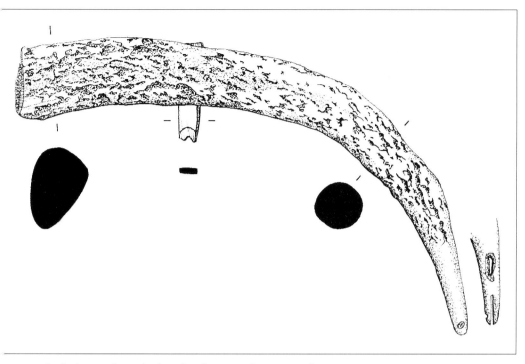

6 Antler saw-frame (scale 1:2) and suggested reconstruction.

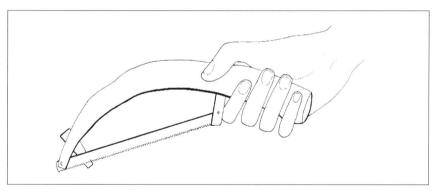

have good organic preservation. For most of its length it was also truncated by the excavation for the basement floor. However, at its extreme west end beyond the west end wall of the block and adjoining the Justice Gate, a narrow column of deposits survived to a much higher level (2.4m). Some lines of stake holes were uncovered in the long strip and also deposits of clay that appear to represent the floors of houses.

Within the circular interior of the Powder Tower, and below its lowest floor level, a circular area of pre-castle deposits survived, bounded all around by the

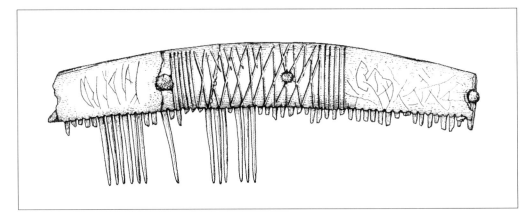

7 Antler comb with runic inscription to the left of incised linear decoration on the sideplate (scale 1:1).

deep foundation wall of the tower. The earliest feature uncovered here was part of the outer face of a north/south stone-faced bank, which was built on the shelving rocky shore of the Poddle estuary. The bank material was clay and stone and the facing, which was without mortar, had an average slope of about 45 degrees (figs 8, 9; pl. 2). A short stretch of post-and-wattle fencing was found in front of the southern section of bank and this may have served as a breakwater. On the north side the bank and its facing had slumped forward, presumably due to water action. The surviving portion of the bank was 2.7m high and 2.6 wide and on present evidence it is not possible to say what its original height might have been. Layers of refuse were dumped over the bank and part of the timber-revetted face of a later bank was found at a higher level. These banks appear to be the eastern defences of the pre-Norman town and the limited available evidence from excavation in this area indicates that this corner was similar in its layout to other parts of the town.

Vestiges of a possible ditch or fosse were also recorded in the boulder clay core encapsulated within the foundations of the square tower, adjacent to the Bermingham Tower. This feature may represent the remains of a defensive fosse belonging to the Hiberno-Norse town.

The medieval castle
Since the rebuilding programme, and consequently the excavations, were largely focused on the west and north ranges of the upper yard, in general only the outer facings of the west and north curtain walls and of the corner towers, were exposed. None of the buildings or structures inside the castle walls were revealed. The moat which encircled the west and north sides of the castle was investigated at a number of points as were those portions of the town walls which abutted the Bermingham Tower and Powder Tower (fig. 3).

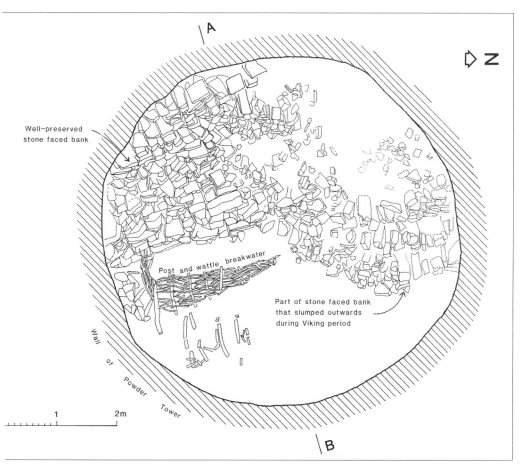

8   Plan of interior of Powder Tower showing remains of Viking period stone-faced bank.

The Bermingham Tower As noted above, the south-west corner tower, known as the Bermingham Tower, was demolished to the top of its battered base in 1775 and rebuilt with thinner walls. The excavations exposed a segment of the thirteenth-century battered base and the associated curtain wall which extended northwards from it. At a distance of *c*.2m north of the tower, a 7m long curved stretch of earlier masonry had been incorporated in the thirteenth-century structures (pl. 3). This early wall, constructed of massive limestone blocks and founded on the boulder clay, had been breached to insert the tower and was then incorporated in the curtain wall. Since it is probable that the pre-1204 castle was also located on this site (see above p. 174) it is tempting to interpret this early masonry as being part of an enclosing or enceinte wall belonging to an earlier fortification.

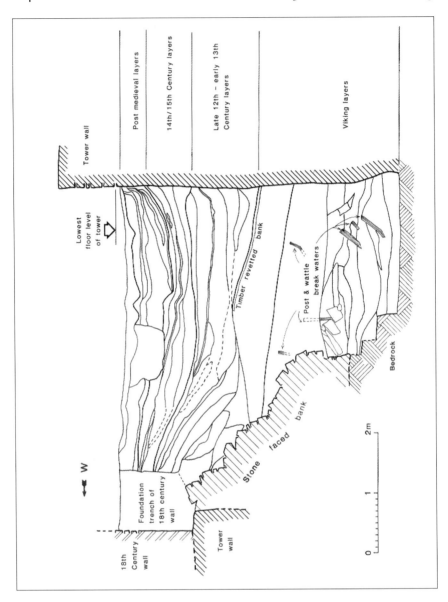

9 Section (see fig. 8, a–b) through deposits below the floor of the Powder Tower.

Plate 2 View of the stone-faced Viking-period bank within the Powder Tower, as now displayed in the Undercroft.

Early masonry

Plate 3 The Bermingham Tower area during excavation showing in the background the possible enceinte wall incorporated in the thirteenth-century curtain wall with the remains of the square tower in front and the town wall with blocked-up arch on the right.

The excavations uncovered the foundations of a square tower abutting the base of the Bermingham Tower and coeval with it. The digging of the moat and addition of a battered base to the early masonry wall also date to this time. The foundations of the square tower were constructed by scarping the boulder clay and facing it with mortared limestone masonry. The 1585 survey of the castle describes this 'little square tower' as being three stories high with 'spickes' flanking the gardens southward, into the town to the west and along the wall northwards towards the north-west tower later called the Cork Tower. As mentioned above, by the time the plan of 1673 was drawn up the square tower is captioned as a 'platform' which suggests that it had been reduced in height and adapted to take cannon. The excavations also revealed that this seventeenth-century adaptation included the addition of an extra skin of masonry to the base of the tower to provide additional support and revetment for the ordnance platform.

The Cork Tower The north-west corner tower was described early in 1624 as being 63 feet high, 124 feet in circumference with walls 10 feet thick, at a time when plans were being drawn up by Lord Faulkner, the Lord Deputy, to demolish and rebuild it. Events overtook him, however, and in May 1624 the tower collapsed, also weakening the adjoining curtain walls. It is likely that the tower had become structurally unstable over the centuries but an explosion of over 6 tons of gunpowder at nearby Wood Quay in 1596 must have contributed to the weakening of the castle walls. The rebuilding of the tower commenced in September 1624 and the project was completed in 1629 when the earl of Cork (who resided nearby) came to its financial assistance. The tower thus became known as the Cork Tower.

When the west range of the upper yard was built in the early eighteenth century, the front façades were founded on the remains of the medieval curtain wall and the base of the Cork Tower. The excavations revealed a portion of the battered base of the rebuilt Cork Tower (fig. 10; pl. 4) which survived to a height of *c*.5m below the eighteenth-century façade (retained in the current building programme). The limestone masonry of this seventeenth-century tower was very finely coursed in comparison with the more open masonry style of the thirteenth-century structures. Due to the waterlogged conditions in the moat-deposits around the tower, a series of intra-mural timbers had survived in its base. These consisted of three concentric rings of oak timbers within the masonry, the outer one of which was visible in the face of the tower. Immediately below these timbers, a series of radial oak beams extended back towards the centre of the tower. The use of intra-mural timbers in building construction has been recorded since Roman times. The technique was employed to help stabilise and consolidate masonry while the mortar was setting and drying out and is most commonly found where ground conditions were unstable, where corners needed reinforcement and where a collar was required to hold a tower together (Wilcox 1972, 193–220).

Entrance area No part of the gatehouse itself was excavated or even located because the excavation was confined to an area north of the old Genealogical Office, which stands on the site of the gatehouse. The area excavated was under the old Guardhouse (Block 17) and the La Touche Bank. The truncated base of the causeway leading across the moat to the gatehouse was uncovered (fig.11; pl. 5). This was up to 6.9m wide, consisting of a 2.5m-wide core of undisturbed boulder clay revetted at each side by vertically faced mortared masonry some 2.2m thick. The causeway had been partly refaced on the west side in later medieval times with masonry which was slightly set back from the original work and resembled the blocking of the arches, in the city wall which spanned the moat. There was an original gap in the causeway, 2.5m wide, about half way across the moat, which appears to have been a drawbridge pit and is marked as such on one of the seventeeth-century maps (pls 5, 6). This was at the southern extent of the area available for excavation and only its eastern end could be investigated. Two later buttresses were found here supporting the corners of the causeway on the east side. Also a late narrow wall was inserted between the two corners and this had a narrow arch in it.

To the north of the causeway the base of an early ditch was found running east/west. This was either an early defensive ditch for the causeway itself or may have predated the early thirteenth-century castle. Like the causeway itself it was heavily truncated by eighteenth-century basements and these had destroyed its stratigraphic relationship to adjacent medieval features. The finds from it dated to the late twelfth or early thirteenth century.

Plate 4   The moat at the Cork Tower during excavation. Note in the foreground the masonry from the original tower which collapsed in 1624.

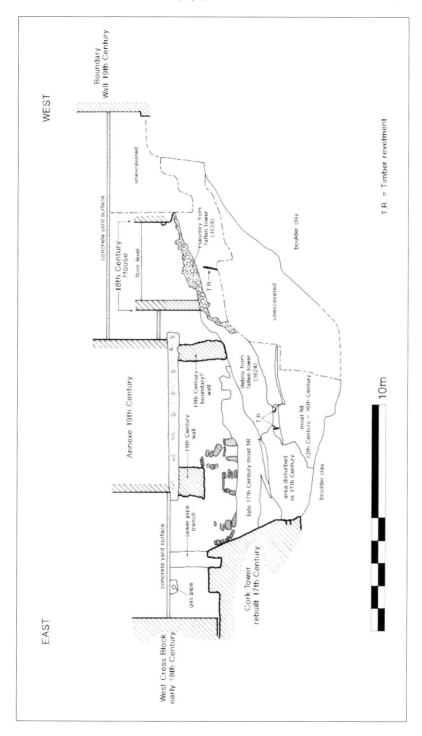

10 Composite and simplified section across the moat at the Cork Tower.

The curtain wall Excavations on the site of the old Children's Court exposed a short stretch of the thirteenth-century curtain wall which linked the Cork Tower with the castle gateway to the east (fig. 3). The battered face of the curtain wall which was founded on the limestone bedrock, survived to a height of 3.15m underneath the eighteenth-century façade of the Children's Court.

Plate 5 A view from above of the remains of the entrance causeway.

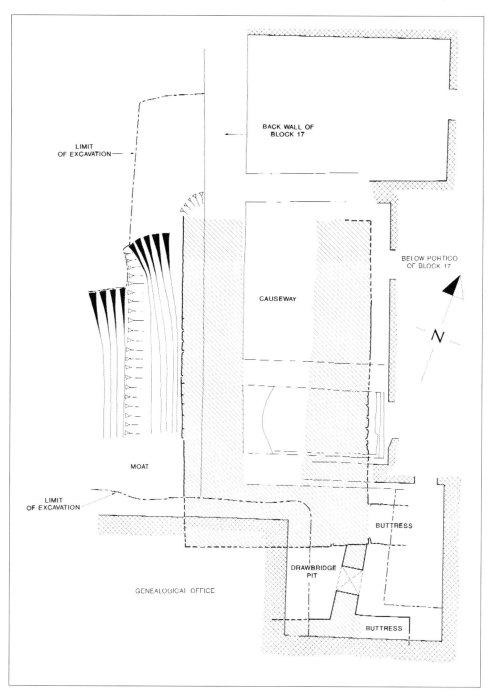

11 Plan showing remains of truncated entrance causeway in relation to later buildings.

Plate 6 A view of the drawbridge pit from the east showing later flanking wall with arch and later buttresses.

The façade of the north range of the upper yard is on a slightly different alignment from the north wall of the castle so that, while the façade of the Children's Court was founded on the batter of the curtain wall, the remains of the curtain wall (where exposed) at the east end of the upper yard were entirely to the north of the eighteenth-century façade. The remains of an *c.*15m length of curtain wall were excavated here beneath the basement of Blocks 8 and 9. The curtain wall itself was founded on boulder clay and the trench for it was cut vertically through pre-castle deposits exactly where the inner or south face was to be built so that the wall face abutted the earlier deposits. The same practice was recorded within the Powder Tower itself. The remains of the curtain wall had been severely robbed during the building of Blocks 8 and 9 including much of the batter well below basement floor level (pl. 7). This showed that the batter

Plate 7 A view from above of the remains of the curtain wall under Blocks 8 and 9.

was mostly a thin façade revetting the upper part of the south side of the moat where it was cut through boulder clay. The lowest courses of the batter sat on bedrock.

The east end of the north curtain wall was excavated as part of the Cross Block excavations in the 1960s and contained the lower part of an original postern with steps descending into the moat immediately to the west of the Powder Tower.

The moat The strategic position of Dublin Castle at the eastern end of a ridge, was greatly enhanced by the river Poddle which flowed along its southern and eastern sides before joining the Liffey and by a wide moat which skirted its western and northern curtain walls (figs 1–3). Since the castle was built in the south-east corner of the medieval town, the moat was designed to provide effective defence from the townward side.

The full width of the moat was exposed at only one location, the north-west corner, where it measured almost 22m (fig. 10; pl. 4). It was roughly U-shaped in section and had a maximum depth of *c.*10m below contemporary ground level. The lower part of the moat was rock-cut along most of its length with the exception of the area around the Cork Tower where it was cut entirely through boulder clay, because the bedrock was at a lower level there. The moat, where rockcut, would in fact have been a convenient quarry for much of the calp limestone which was used for the construction of the castle walls.

The large arches in the town walls would have allowed the tide to ebb and flow around the moat throughout the thirteenth century. Once the arches were blocked up however, in about the fourteenth century, the only water source would have been derived from natural springs, ground water and seepage from the Poddle. If the moat was dug today, the water level would settle at about 8m OD which would provide a depth of at least 3m of water. The moat narrowed towards the openings in the city wall and evidence of narrowing was also found to the west of the causeway leading to the main entrance.

When the Cork Tower was being rebuilt, the moat deposits were removed/ disturbed for a distance of about 3m from its base. Further to the east, at the Children's Court, there was evidence for re-cutting or cleaning out of the moat with the result that seventeenth-century material lay directly on thirteenth/ fourteenth-century deposits. The deposits in the moat beneath Blocks 8 and 9 were greatly disturbed by eighteenth-century building activity. Closer to the city wall and Powder Tower the deposits were less disturbed and a wattle fence, a tree stump in situ, and a drain were uncovered within the fill. The blocking of the arch in the city wall was sitting on up to 1.3m of fill (pl. 9a) and this same fill further to the west contained local medieval pottery dating from around the fourteenth century.

Elsewhere within the moat, however, there was an accumulation of refuse deposits ranging in date from the thirteenth to the seventeenth centuries. In some areas, stratification of deposits was difficult to discern due to the homo-genous nature of the waterlogged material but where tip-lines were recorded, they indicate that the refuse in the moat was derived from the townward side and not from the castle (fig. 10). A large percentage of the 100,000 or so artefacts recovered from the excavations were retrieved from the moat deposits. Ceramics form a large proportion of this material and over 40,000 sherds of medieval pottery have been identified. Locally-made ceramics predominate but imported wares have also been recorded, mainly from France and England. Many decorated floor tiles were retrieved, some of which may have originated from Christ Church Cathedral. A wide variety of metal objects was recovered, including coins, tokens, pins, needles, knifes, fish hooks, arrowheads, spearheads and spurs. The damp and waterlogged conditions in the moat also ensured the preservation of organic material such as leather shoes and scabbards and fragments of clothing, both leather and textile. Wooden artefacts including small knobs, handles, plates and bowls also survived.

Powder Tower This was the only one of the large circular corner towers whose interior was available for excavation (pl. 8). It formed the north-east corner of the castle and according to the 1585 descriptive survey had five storeys and a spiral stairs on the north-west side. At that time the Lord Deputy Perrot had his chamber on the top floor. In the seventeenth century the tower was used for storing gunpowder from which it derived its name. It was demolished to its lowest floor-level in the early eighteenth century but was not fully built over until the early nineteenth century, when Block 10, which connected the ranges around the upper yard to the Treasury building in the lower yard, was built.

Up to 6m of the tower survives above its bedrock foundation, which is some 2m below high-water mark. At the base the walls are 5.5m thick and enclose a roughly circular area 5.5–6.0m in diameter. The lowest 2m or so of the outer face is vertical on the north side. Above this point, which corresponds roughly with the mean tidal high-water level, the wall has a batter of 72 degrees and at the upper surviving level it is still battered and over 4m thick. At most only a few courses (up to 1m high) of a finished inner face survived and the bottom of these courses marked the lowest original floor-level within the tower (fig. 9). This floor was originally of mortared masonry but was removed during medieval times leaving a ragged masonry scar around the inner face. Beneath this the pre-castle levels were left in place within the tower and the wall was built against the roughly vertical cut.

Most of the deposits encapsulated within the base of the tower predate it but 0.3 to 0.8m of deposits dating from the fourteenth/fifteenth centuries were excavated immediately above the pre-castle deposits and below the missing masonry floor. These deposits contained evidence for metal-working in the form

Plate 8 A view of the Powder Tower under excavation with the Record Tower in the background.

of many pieces of iron, offcuts of sheet bronze and bronze objects such as mounts, rivets, strap tags and pieces of chain. Coin and pottery evidence indicate a fourteenth/fifteenth century date and a thin plain gold ring, set with a small green stone, was also found in these layers.

The city wall In the Powder Tower area the moat was excavated up to the west face of the city wall where it joined the tower. The city wall here survives to almost the same height as the Powder Tower and is 1.55m thick. An arched opening, about 7m wide, allowed the tide to ebb and flow through the moat and may even have allowed small boats access at high tide to the postern in the north wall. Above the arch was a subsidiary relieving arch to help spread the weight of the wall. The opening in the wall was blocked in the late fourteenth or fifteenth century to judge from the local pottery found in moat deposits below the blocking (pl. 9).

The thirteenth-century town wall also abuts the base of the square tower adjacent to the Bermingham Tower and extends westward from it across the castle moat. The city wall was just over 2m in width at this point and an arch was incorporated in the wall where it spanned the deepest part of the moat. At some stage, probably in the fourteenth century, this arch was blocked up and refuse deposits began to accumulate against it (pl. 3).

Post-medieval activity

By the seventeenth century, the accumulation of refuse in the moat was such that its dimensions had been almost halved both in width and in depth. Trees were now growing in the moat, property boundaries had extended onto it from the townward side and a series of simple timber revetments had been built along its sides. Stone-built drains were also being constructed in the moat at this time, many of which had foundations consisting of reused timbers. Included in these timbers were structural elements from a timber-framed house, fragments of a staircase and pieces of a wheeled vehicle. A substantial stone-built house had also been built in the edge of the moat, close to its north-west corner.

The moat had long since ceased to serve any defensive function by the time the castle was being remodelled in the late seventeenth century and at this time over 2m of domestic refuse and builders' rubble was deposited in the moat to finally level it off and allow building works to proceed. To the west of the castle, a laneway called Cole Alley was laid out linking Ship Street with Castle Street and in the early eighteenth century houses were built fronting onto this and nearby Silver Court which lay just to the north of the north-west corner of the upper yard (fig. 5). These houses were occupied by silk-dyers, wig-makers, gold and silver smiths, surgeons and attorneys. The political instability brought about by the 1798 rebellion which was followed quickly by the Emmet rebellion of 1803, caused renewed fears about the security of the castle. Consequently, in

Plate 9 Blocked arch in city wall beside Powder Tower: a) during excavation and b) *(opposite page)* as now displayed to visitors in the Undercroft.

1803 the houses of Cole Alley and Silver Court were bought up by a Jeremiah d'Olier on behalf of the State and demolished shortly thereafter (NAI OP 185/7). The castle precinct was then enclosed by the high boundary wall still in existence today.

The remains of these eighteenth-century houses together with their drainage and sewage systems, were fully recorded during the excavations (fig. 10). Most of the houses had been demolished to within about 1m of ground level before they were covered with rubble and sealed by a concrete yard surface. The walls of the houses were constructed of brick or a mixture of brick and stone and had internal and external plaster render. Flagstones set in mortar covered most of the floor surfaces but some cobbled floors were also recorded. The remains of two brick-built ovens had survived. Water was supplied to the houses via a complex system of lead pipes. Only a small portion of the cobbled surface of Cole Alley had survived but a large drain or culvert which ran under Cole Alley was largely intact.

The late-seventeenth-century infill of the moat and the Cole Alley/Silver Court remains (particularly the culvert) produced large quantities of seventeenth- and eighteenth-century artefacts, probably the largest such assemblage ever to be systematically recorded in Dublin. Almost 55,000 ceramic pieces were recovered including stonewares, earthenwares and porcelains originating from China, Germany, the Netherlands, Spain, Portugal, France and England. Ceramic roof, floor and wall tiles were also found. Metal finds include keys, buckles, needles, pins and lace-points and the glass assemblage includes drinking glasses, wine bottles and medicine bottles. Clay pipes were plentiful as were wig curlers. Leather and wood artefacts survived in the upper levels of the moat and include a leather-bound wooden book cover.

The construction of new government buildings over the moat in the eighteenth-century was handled in various ways. When building the rear wall of Blocks 8 and 9 in about 1730 most of the moat at this point must have been dug out to get a solid continuous foundation for the wall. The archaeological excavation, which was prevented from reaching the base of this wall by safety considerations, revealed that the moat fill here was totally disturbed. Further west along the north moat, pier foundations were used to support the rear of the Children's Court and parts of the Genealogical Office. This involved the digging of large square pits and shuttering the sides of them with timber to keep the water out and prevent collapse. Once rock or solid ground was reached a mortared masonry pier was built to fill the pit, and arches between the piers supported the continuous main walls of the building. When in 1796 George Darley was carrying out site investigations for a building to double the size of Blocks 8 and 9 it is recorded that he bored down 36 feet without reaching solid ground. The remains of his timber-shuttered trial pit were found during the excavation below water-table level against the original rear wall of Blocks 8 and 9. Darley built the building on a poor foundation of large blocks of granite bolted to timbers, which rotted in due course. Block 10, built before 1843, was partly founded on concrete foundations laid over moat fill.

CONCLUSION

The Dublin Castle excavations have contributed significantly to our knowledge of the building history of the enclosing elements of this major thirteenth-century fortification and its relationship with the contemporary town defences. The great width and depth of the moat were surprising, though one seventeenth-century source had claimed that the tide formerly flowed around the walls (Maguire 1974, 9). The excavation confirmed that this was indeed true. The changing role of the castle moat from defensive feature to refuse dump to building site reflects changing social and military conditions within the town. The artefactual evidence from the excavation also throws light on the social and economic conditions pertaining in the town adjacent to the castle from the thirteenth to the eighteenth centuries. The excavations included the first systematic recording of eighteenth-century house remains and associated features in Dublin – features which are often regarded as non-archaeological and therefore ignored.

Dublin Castle represents an important link in the development of castles in western Europe. Already in the late twelfth century the concept of a great tower, serving possibly as a last resort, was going out of fashion and the defensive elements of castles were being concentrated on the perimeter walls. In the early thirteenth century large twin-towered gatehouses were coming into fashion along with rounded towers at the corners and interspersed along the walls, which provided flanking fire to protect the curtain walls. Few if any major castles were being built from scratch in Britain at this time, resulting in little scope for putting these new castle-building theories into practice except in adding to or partly rebuilding older castles. Dublin however could be seen as almost a greenfield site where the new theories could be tried out in a single integrated plan. Its roughly rectangular plan with round corner towers has parallels of slightly earlier date in France but none of such an early date in Britain. Other contemporary parallels in Ireland are Kilkenny and Limerick. This type of plan became very popular in the later thirteenth century and was brought to a fine art with some of the great Edwardian castles in Wales. In Ireland, Roscommon, Ballymote and Ballintubber are later variations on the same plan. Dublin, with its innovative plan, may have continued to influence the design of castles in Ireland and Britain for many decades after it was built.

The excavations benefited from the lessons learnt during the Wood Quay controversies of the previous decade. The archaeological implications of the proposed development at Dublin Castle were considered from the very earliest stages of the project and there was close liaison at all times between the archaeologists and the project architects and engineers. In most areas, separate contracts were awarded for the demolition and construction, with the archaeo-logical excavations slotted in between. This offered some protection against the scenario of costly delays if the excavations overran their time limit (in the event, all phases of excavation were completed on schedule). Archaeologists were also retained to monitor ground disturbance during some of the construction phases and this proved to be a very worthwhile exercise as it became clear that site drawings often bore little relation to what actually happened on the ground. The archaeological project to date has amounted to about 3% of the total project budget.

As masonry elements of the medieval castle were exposed during the excavation, discussions were entered into with the project's design team to ensure the preservation of these structures and, in some instances, their presentation in the completed development. The preservation *in situ* of the square tower adjacent to the Bermingham Tower was achieved by sacrificing a basement floor in the new kitchen block and the remains, while not on public display, are easily accessible. The foundations of the new conference centre are partly set into the remains of the Cork Tower which involved some removal of seventeenth-century masonry. A segment of the tower is however exposed to view, underlying both the conference centre and the eighteenth-century west range and illustrating clearly the different phases of building in this part of the castle site (pl. 10).

The portions of the medieval castle which were found in the Powder Tower area lent themselves ideally to public presentation, in that there was sufficient headroom under the original basement floor-level of Block 10 to provide for public access. The architects and engineers involved drew up plans for this project with enthusiasm and official approval for the extra expenditure was granted in due course. The substructure had to be completely redesigned with most of the internal weight being placed on a few very large columns. It was also found possible to include the section of the north curtain wall, with the postern

Plate 10 A segment of the seventeenth-century Cork Tower exposed to view underlying the eighteenth-century west range and twentieth-century conference centre.

and steps, which had been uncovered in the 1960s under the north end of the Cross Block.

The main features displayed in this area, which has become known as the Undercroft, are: the base of the Powder Tower with the remains of the stone-faced Viking-period bank within it (pl. 2); the postern and steps in the north curtain wall; and the moat of the castle and adjacent section of the city wall with its blocked-up arch, which spanned the moat (pl. 9b). The water level in the moat is kept artificially low with the aid of a self-activating pump, allowing the visitor to view the Powder Tower and city wall from a suspended gangway low in the moat.

The defensive bank within the Powder Tower is the only *in situ* Viking-age monument in the city of Dublin which is on display to the public. The Undercroft allows visitors to experience at close quarters the strength and massiveness of the medieval defences. It is accessed from the lower yard through a room in the basement of Block 10, where panels illustrate aspects of the history and archaeology of the castle. This area is now part of the official tour of Dublin Castle and the vast majority of the visitors (170,000 in 1999) are brought through the Undercroft.

Post-excavation research and analysis followed on the excavation and specialist reports were produced on different types of finds such as medieval pottery, post-medieval pottery, wooden artefacts, ridge tiles, floor tiles, metal artefacts, etc. Animal bones, human bones and environmental samples were also studied and reported on. The site supervisors produced provisional accounts and interpretation of the stratigraphy and a report was produced on the history of the castle with emphasis on sources relating to the building history of the areas excavated. This work was completed before 1990 but the increasing workloads of the authors since then have militated against the preparation of the final report for publication. It is hoped that this summary will go some way to filling the gap in dissemination of information until such time as a more complete report on the excavation and its findings can be published.

ACKNOWLEDGEMENTS

The authors wish to acknowledge the contribution of the site supervisors, assistants and workmen who toiled during the years of the excavation. The post-excavation team and specialists also deserve special mention. Our thanks to Gerard Woods and Muiris de Buitléir for the plans and sections and to Patricia Johnson and Sadbh Model for the artefact illustrations. Unless otherwise stated, the photographs are the work of Con Brogan of Dúchas the Heritage Service. The historical summary is largely based on research carried out for the project by Thaddeus Breen.

BIBLIOGRAPHY

Barnes, M.P., Hagland, J.R. and Page, R.I. 1997 *The runic inscriptions of Viking Age Dublin.* Royal Irish Academy. Dublin.
CSPI Calendar of state papers relating to Ireland (1509–1670) 24 vols, London 1860–1912.
Gilbert, J.T. (ed.) 1870 *Historic and municipal documents of Ireland A.D. 1172–1320.* London.
—— (ed.) 1889 *Register of the Abbey of St Thomas, Dublin.* London.
—— (ed.) 1889–1944 *Calendar of ancient records of Dublin* 19 vols. Dublin.
Hall, R. 1996 "A dashing old blade" (Old Saws). *Archaeology in York* Vol.21, no. 1, 20–27.
Lawlor, H.J. 1923 The chapel of Dublin Castle *RSAI Jn.* 53, 34–73.
Loeber, R. 1980 The rebuilding of Dublin Castle: thirty critical years, 1661–1690. *Studies.* 69, 45–69.
Lynch, A. and Manning, C. 1990 Dublin Castle: The archaeological project. *Archaeology Ireland* 4, 65–8.
Maguire, J.B. n.d. *Dublin Castle: historical background and guide.* Dublin.
—— 1974 Seventeenth-century plans of Dublin Castle *RSAI Jn* 104, 5–14.

—— 1985 Dublin Castle: Three centuries of development. *RSAI Jn* 115, 13–39.

Manning, C. 1998 Dublin Castle: The building of a royal castle in Ireland. *Chateau Gaillard* 18, 119–22.

Murphy, M. 1995 Balancing the concerns of church and state: The archbishops of Dublin, 1181–1228, in T.B. Barry, R. Frame and K. Simms (eds.) *Colony and frontier in medieval Ireland*. London.

Orpen, G.H. (ed.) 1892 *The song of Dermot and the Earl*. Oxford.

Quinn, D.B. (ed.) 1985 *The image of Irelande with a discovery of woodkarne by John Derricke 1581*. Belfast.

RCPR Report from the commissioners appointed by his majesty to execute the measures recommended in an address to the House of Commons respecting the public records of Ireland. 3 vols (1815–1825), London.

RDKPROI Reports of the deputy keeper of the public record office of Ireland. Various dates.

Sweetman, H.S. 1875–84 *Calendar of documents relating to Ireland vol.1, 1171–1307*. 5 vols. London.

Sweetman, P.D. 1999 *Medieval castles of Ireland*. Cork.

Ware, R. 1678 The History and antiquities of Dublin. Dublin Public Libraries, Gilbert Collection, Ms. 74.

Wilcox, R.P. 1972 Timber reinforcement in medieval castles *Chateau Gaillard* 5, 193–202.

Women in medieval Dublin: an introduction

JESSICA McMORROW

According to a civic ordinance, the women of Anglo-Norman Dublin were to be fined six pence if they wore kerchiefs dyed in saffron, in the style of Gaelic Irishwomen.[1] Such legislation demonstrates how Dublin's position as a colonial outpost on the periphery of the Anglo Norman empire shaped the lives of the women who lived there. The ban on saffron-coloured kerchiefs may have been intended to protect the women of Dublin in times of war; if hostilities arose between the Anglo-Norman settlers and their Irish neighbours, it was important that the women of Dublin were not mistaken for Gaelic Irishwomen.[2] It also reflects concern on the part of the Anglo-Norman settlers to protect their cultural identity from the influence of a native community which they regarded as inferior to their own.[3] Indeed, women were intimately associated with the Irish customs of which Anglo-Norman observers most disapproved. Gaelic marriage customs, which permitted polygamy and divorce, had earned the Irish a reputation for sexual promiscuity, and were frequently condemned by clerics and chroniclers alike.[4] In this context, it is not surprising that the governors of Dublin wished to ensure that the women of the city did not adopt the customs of Gaelic Irishwomen in any form, however superficial.

Medieval Dublin was the administrative centre of the Anglo-Norman colony in Ireland. As such, it was governed by English laws and customs. Dublin was also a thriving centre of commerce, having extensive trading contacts with Britain and the continent. Its political, cultural, and commercial links with the rest of Europe meant that the position of women in medieval Dublin was more similar to that of their British and continental counterparts than it was to that of their Irish neighbours.[5] Women's names appear frequently in the wills and deeds which have survived from medieval Dublin. These documents provide valuable information about women's lives, and help to illuminate their legal and

1 T.K. Moylan, 'Dubliners, 1200–1500', *Dublin Historical Record*, 13 (1952), 79–93, at p. 87. 2 This was the justification given for legislation prohibiting men from adopting Irish costume at a meeting of the Anglo-Norman magnates of Ireland in 1297: see Philomena Connolly, 'The enactments of the 1297 parliament', in *Law and disorder in thirteenth-century Ireland*, ed. James Lydon (Dublin, 1997), p. 159. 3 That the Anglo-Norman settlers regarded Gaelic culture to be inferior is indicated by the fact that they described the English who adopted Irish customs as 'degenerate'. See Seán Duffy, 'The problem of degeneracy', in ibid., 87–106. 4 Seán Duffy, *Ireland in the middle ages* (Dublin, 1997), pp 25–27.

social position. Women did not participate in municipal government like men; however, they enjoyed certain similar legal and economic privileges. They owned property, were eligible for membership of guilds, and played an important role in the economic life of the community. They also made invaluable contributions to society as wives, mothers, and managers of households, and were highly respected in these roles.

WOMEN'S LEGAL POSITION AND PROPERTY RIGHTS

Women were eligible to become citizens of medieval Dublin.[6] Indeed, if a woman married a man who had not yet been admitted to the civic franchise, he obtained the right of citizenship through her. For example, in 1482, Meiler Trevers, a goldsmith, was admitted a freeman of Dublin in right of his wife.[7] As citizens, women in European towns did not enjoy the same political privileges as their male counterparts; however, they enjoyed similar legal and economic privileges.[8] Women could instigate legal proceedings and act as witnesses in court. When they committed a crime, they were responsible for their own actions, and had to stand trial. In 1478, a Dublin woman named Matilda, wife of Henry Russell, was excommunicated and sentenced to death for an unspecified crime, the suit against her having been instigated by a woman named Isabelle, wife of Richard Nangle.[9] Women in medieval Dublin could also own and alienate property in their own right. According to common law, a woman's property passed into the hands of her husband upon their marriage.[10] It is evident, however, that in practice, property was often considered to belong jointly to husband and wife in medieval Dublin. In the *Register of wills and inventories of the diocese of Dublin in the time of Archbishops Tregury and Walton, 1457–1483*, wills are preceded by an inventory of the goods of the household of the deceased, which are often described as being jointly held by the testator and his or her spouse.[11] Out of the fifty-four wills in the register which were made

5 Dublin's links with Bristol were especially important, as Henry II had granted the Irish town to the men of Bristol in his 1171–2 charter, 'to be inhabited and held by them from him and his heirs, with all liberties and free customs which they [had] at Bristol and throughout his entire land'. See J.T. Gilbert (ed.), *Historic and municipal documents of Ireland, A.D. 1172–1320* (London, 1870), p. 1. 6 Moylan, 'Dubliners', p. 92. They presumably obtained citizenship by virtue of owning urban property, which they could acquire by inheritance, marriage, or purchase, as was the case in other European towns. See Shalamith Shahar, 'Townswomen', in *The fourth estate: a history of women in the middle ages* (London and New York, 1983), p. 175. 7 H.F. Berry, 'The Goldsmiths' company of Dublin (Gild of All Saints)', *R.S.A.I. Jn.*, 31 (1901), p. 120. 8 Shahar, 'Townswomen', pp 175–6. 9 H.F. Berry, *The register of wills and inventories of the diocese of Dublin in the time of Archbishops Tregury and Walton, 1457–1483* (Dublin, 1898), p. 181. 10 Richard H. Helmholz, 'Married Women's wills in later medieval England', in *Wife and widow in medieval England*, ed. Sheridan Walker (Michigan, 1993), p. 165. 11 For example, on p. 55, there is an 'inventory of all the goods

by individuals who were clearly married, fourteen are preceded by inventories which specify that the goods listed belonged jointly to husband and wife. The idea of joint ownership is made even more explicit in Peter Higley's will: he bequeaths to his wife 'the residue of the term which I hold in and of 40 acres of land near Killeight from the Baron of Skreen, and the third part of *all common goods acquired between us* to Millane, my wife, during her life'.[12] It is in fact surprising that Peter felt the need to state that he was bequeathing a third of their property to his wife; it was customary under the English common law system for a widow to receive a third of her husband's property upon his death. During Henry II's visit to Ireland in 1171–2, a synod of Irish bishops convened at Cashel for the purpose of conforming to the practices of the English church. At the synod, the making of testaments was discussed, and it was laid down that a testator should divide his moveable goods into three parts, leaving one part to his wife, one to his children, and the third part for funeral expenses. If the couple had no lawful children the goods were to be divided between the testator and his wife; if the wife was deceased, then the goods were to be divided between the testator and his children.[13] The surviving wills show that these rules were adhered to in the diocese of Dublin throughout the middle ages.

It was customary in Dublin in the later middle ages for a husband to appoint his wife as one of the executors of his will. Out of 35 wills in the register of Archbishops Tregury and Walton which were made by men who were clearly married, 29 appointed their wife as one of their executors.[14] This demonstrates that women were considered to be competent partners in the management of family affairs, and suggests that they were valued and respected as wives, mothers, and managers of households. It also shows that women were educated enough to keep proper accounts, as it was illegal to appoint as executors of wills persons who could not render correct accounts.[15] Wives were not usually the sole executors of their husbands' wills; in most cases, the couple's eldest son or a male friend of the family was appointed co-executor. This should not necessarily be interpreted as a slur on women's abilities to administer their husbands' property; rather, it is likely that in most cases a husband merely wished to ensure that his wife could obtain reliable help and sound advice if she needed it. The administration of a will could sometimes involve litigation or other forms of legal inquiry, on which many men would probably have sought advice.[16] John Chever appointed his wife as the administrator of his will and his

moveable and immoveable of Geoffrey Fox and Jonet Cristore his wife'. The portion of Jonet, the deceased, is given to be one-half the total worth of these goods.   **12** Berry (ed.), *Register of wills and inventories*, p. 130.   **13** Berry (ed.), Introduction to *Register of wills and inventories*, p. x.   **14** Berry (ed.), *Register of wills and inventories*, passim.   **15** Berry (ed.), Introduction to *Register of wills and inventories*, p. xi.   **16** See M.J. McEnery (ed.), 'Calendar to Christ Church Deeds', in *Report of the deputy keeper of the public records in Ireland*, vols 20, 23, 24, 27 (1888–96), vol. 20, pp 90–1, for an instance of the former; see H.J. Lawlor (ed.), 'Calendar of the Liber Niger and Liber Albus of Christ Church, Dublin', *R.I.A. Proc.*, 27

children's portion of his property during their minority, 'with the counsel and advice' of Philip Bermyngham, James Ailmer, and John Stokis. The former appears to have been a relative of Chever's wife, Anne Bermyngham, and the latter was a chaplain. These three individuals had no power to dispose of Chever's goods, but were available to advise Anne should she require it.[17] Married women also usually appointed their husbands as the executors of their wills, though there are some exceptions.[18]

Under common law, a wife was not permitted to make a will without her husband's permission, although most medieval legal commentators advocated that the husband ought to grant such permission.[19] Canon law differed from common law with regard to women's testamentary capacity, upholding the right of married women to make wills disposing of their own portion of the property which they held jointly with their husbands.[20] In 1266, the Lord Edward issued letters patent to Dublin, which specified that pleas concerning chattels or debts against the citizens of Dublin could be held in ecclesiastical courts only if they arose out of testamentary or matrimonial causes.[21] Thus, it is clear that testamentary matters were governed by canon law in Dublin. A high percentage of wills in medieval Dublin were in fact made by married women. Approximately one-third of the wills listed in the register of Archbishops Tregury and Walton were made by women; of these, seventeen appear to have been married. Thus, married women's wills account for 23.6 per cent of the total registered in this source. By comparison, in medieval England at this time, married women's wills occur much less frequently in the surviving records. For example, in 1477 at Canterbury, only six out of fifty estates administered (12 per cent) belonged to women, none of whom was definitely married at the time of her death.[22] In 1457 at Rochester, only two out of 123 wills (1.6 per cent) registered belonged to women who were clearly married.[23] A study of wills in 1340s Rochester, by contrast, reveals that eighteen per cent of wills registered belonged to married women.[24] Helmholz has argued that the frequency with which married women made wills in medieval England decreased towards the end of the period. He attributed this to a growing acceptance of the idea that women did not have separate property rights, the increasing testamentary freedom of husbands, and the growth of trusts for married women, which eliminated the need for them to make a will.[25] In Dublin, the situation appears to have been different. Perhaps this was due to its distance from the centre of royal government, and the

(1907–9), C, p. 28, for an instance of the latter.   **17** Berry (ed.), *Register of wills and inventories*, pp 146–7.   **18** For example, Agnes Duff did not appoint her husband, Thomas Hydon, as executor of her will, though he was clearly living when she made her will. See Berry (ed.), *Register of wills and inventories*, p. 6.   **19** Helmholz, 'Married women's wills', p. 166.   **20** Ibid.   **21** Lawlor (ed.), 'Calendar of the Liber Niger and Liber Albus', p. 65. **22** Helmholz, 'Married women's wills', p. 169.   **23** Ibid.   **24** Ibid., p. 167.   **25** Ibid., pp 172–3.

continuing importance of the church in administering the affairs of the city: the archbishop was the wealthiest landowner in County Dublin, usually doubled as a secular official, and acted as royal judge, diplomat, and bureaucrat.[26]

WOMEN'S ECONOMIC ROLE

Though they did not play any direct role in the political affairs of urban communities, women played an important role in the commercial life of towns across medieval Europe.[27] The surviving evidence indicates that the experience of women in Dublin fits this pattern. In Dublin, women were permitted to belong to craft guilds, including the merchant-tailors' guild and the barber-surgeons' guild, and probably others as well.[28] There were guilds for weavers and embroiderers in medieval Dublin,[29] and as weaving and embroidery were traditionally female tasks, it seems likely that women belonged to these guilds. Women belonged to embroiderers' guilds in other parts of Europe; in Paris, the officers of the guild of embroiderers included one married woman, and in England embroiderers trained girl apprentices.[30] While women in Dublin were allowed to belong to guilds, it seems that they were not eligible to become masters or wardens of the guild, nor to elect these officers. The fifteenth-century charter for the barbers' guild gave the founders freedom to found 'of themselves and other persons, as well men as women, a fraternity or guild of the art of Barbers of our city of Dublin, and [to] receive as brethren and sisters any honest and fitting persons willing freely to join them'.[31] Yet while it was specified that both brothers and sisters might join, the charter only mentioned brothers when granting the power to elect masters and wardens, stating 'that the brothers of the said fraternity or gild so founded may elect each year a master and two wardens belonging to the art of Barbers, for the rule and governance of the fraternity'.[32] Thus it seems that although women could belong to craft guilds in Dublin, there were some restrictions upon their participation. This too corresponds to the pattern in other European towns.[33]

In England and other parts of Europe, the wives and daughters of craftsmen usually helped in the family workshop. It was also common for widows to continue to practise their husband's occupation after his death.[34] It is likely that

26 Duffy, *Ireland in the middle ages*, pp 104–5.   **27** Shahar, 'Townswomen', p. 175.   **28** H.F. Berry, 'The merchant tailors' guild: that of St John the Baptist, Dublin, 1418–1841', *R.S.A.I. Jn.*, 48 (1918), p. 19; H.F. Berry, 'The ancient corporation of barber-surgeons, or Gild of St Mary Magdalene, Dublin', *R.S.A.I. Jn.*, 30 (1900), p. 219.   **29** See H.S. Guinness, 'Dublin Trade Guilds', in *R.S.A.I. Jn.*, 52 (1922), 143–63.   **30** Shahar, 'Townswomen', pp 192–3. **31** Quoted in Berry, 'Barber-surgeons' gild', p. 219 and in M.V. Ronan, 'Religious customs of Dublin medieval gilds', *Irish Eccles. Rec.*, 26 (1935), p. 229.   **32** Ibid.   **33** Shahar, 'Townswomen', pp 196–9.   **34** Ibid., p. 190.

this was also the case in Dublin. In the 'Calendar of Christ Church deeds', there are deeds which show husbands and wives jointly leasing or selling plots of land which had shops situated on them.[35] Among the Christ Church deeds are instances of a merchant and his wife making a grant to Christ Church cathedral, and of a skinner and his wife making a joint grant of land; there is also a deed in which Alice Brode, wife of John Ferreys, tailor, consents to an alienation of land made by her husband.[36] In these cases, it appears that the husband and wife jointly conducted affairs relating to business and property. Women also owned and managed shops independently. There is a reference in the Christ Church deeds to a widow named Margaret Dowoke leasing a messuage with two shops and a garden in Oxmantown.[37] It was common in other parts of Europe for a widow to continue practising her husband's trade upon his death, so it is possible that such was the case for Margaret Dowoke. Women did not always practise the same trade as their husband, however, so this need not necessarily have been the case. It was common for women to sell food and other goods at shops and stalls, and in markets and fairs, in all parts of medieval Europe.[38] A statute banning pigs from Dublin refers to the danger which these animals were to the children under the stalls in the marketplace; this indicates that women were selling goods at stalls along the streets of Dublin, and that, if they had babies or small children, the children customarily napped or played beneath the stalls while their mothers worked.[39] Civic legislation which required that women selling fish on Fishamble Street pay a farthing a week for the cleaning of their stalls also attests to the existence of women trading at the city's markets.[40]

The success of women in their capacity as traders in medieval Dublin is demonstrated by statutes which restricted their activities: they were not allowed to sell meat or wine, and they were penalised for brewing inferior beer.[41] In general, such restrictions were placed on the activity of women when the competition which they provided affected men's businesses and jobs.[42] In medieval Bristol, weavers were forbidden from hiring female servants to help in their workshops; the weavers' wives and their wives' servants were the only women permitted to work in these workshops. It was stated in Bristol that the employment of hired female labour was responsible for the fact that many male weavers were unable to find work.[43] Women's wages were typically lower than men's, and this gave them a competitive advantage in the job market.[44] Thus, the restriction on women's right to sell certain types of goods in medieval

---

35 McEnery (ed.), 'Calendar to Christ Church deeds', p. 122, no. 34; p. 127, no. 781.
36 McEnery (ed.), 'Calendar to Christ Church deeds', p. 114, no. 428; p. 109, no. 1026; p. 129, no. 789.   37 Ibid., p. 110, no. 1032.   38 Shahar, 'Townswomen', p. 194.   39 T.K. Moylan, 'Vagabonds and sturdy beggars: poverty, pigs and pestilence in medieval Dublin', in *Dublin Historical Record*, 1 (1939), pp 11–12; reprinted in H.B. Clarke (ed.), *Medieval Dublin: the living city* (Dublin, 1990), pp 192–3.   40 Moylan, 'Dubliners', p. 82.   41 Ibid., p. 92. 42 Shahar, 'Townswomen', p. 200.   43 Ibid., p. 198.   44 Ibid.

Dublin suggests that their activities were providing unwelcome competition for male wine merchants and meat sellers. In addition, the aforementioned guild legislation from Bristol demonstrates that women were sometimes hired to help in the workshops of craftsmen; it is likely that craftsmen in Dublin also hired women on occasion, as Dublin and Bristol had close political, commercial, and cultural links.[45]

Women participated in the economic life of medieval Dublin in a variety of ways. The legislation prohibiting women from brewing inferior beer and selling it in taverns shows that women were both brewers and vendors of beer, and suggests that they commonly managed or worked in taverns. In fact, women were the principal brewers and vendors of beer in most medieval towns.[46] It was also common for women to manage inns in other parts of medieval Europe.[47] This may apply to Dublin as well. In his will, Thomas Sneterby left a piece of property called 'Burgey's Innys' to his wife; it seems likely that this was an inn, from which she managed and derived income.[48] We know of at least one laundress in medieval Dublin, who is mentioned in the 'account roll' of the priory of Holy Trinity, and probably many women engaged in this occupation.[49] Many women also worked as maidservants, and are commonly referred to in the wills of their employers. The Christ Church deeds contain records of women renting out property, thus demonstrating that they commonly acted as landladies.[50] Women's wills also reveal that they acted as moneylenders on occasion; Ellen Stiward had a brass pot belonging to Stephen Kery in pledge for 5*s*., and a set of beads, five rings, and a brooch which belonged to Agnes Broun in pledge for 5*s*.[51] Thus, the surviving evidence indicates that women played an important and varied role in the economic life of medieval Dublin.

WOMEN AND THE HOME

In addition to their role in the urban economy, the women of Dublin fulfilled classic domestic roles, managing households and caring for their children. The custom of appointing one's wife as executrix of one's will, and the numerous legacies to wives and mothers in the wills of medieval Dubliners show that women were valued in their domestic roles. John Kempe (d. 1471), a tenant farmer from County Dublin, demonstrated his regard for his mother and his concern for her welfare by leaving her in his will a cow, a heifer, and one bullock.[52] When Michael Haillan died intestate, the administration of his goods was granted to Ellen Foill, 'his natural mother'.[53] John Gogh appointed his wife

---

45 See note 5, above.   46 Shahar, 'Townswomen', p. 194.   47 Ibid.   48 Lawlor (ed.), 'Calendar of the Liber Niger and Liber Albus', p. 38.   49 Moylan, 'Dubliners', p. 87.   50 See, for example, vol. 24, p. 102, no. 978 and p. 104, no. 993.   51 Berry (ed.), *Register of wills and inventories*, pp 1–2.   52 Ibid., p. 15.   53 Ibid., p. 72. He was presumably unmarried.

as an executor of his will, and gave her custody of all his goods during the minority of their children.[54] These examples suggest that women were perceived as able administrators of the affairs of their children and their households.

Women's domestic tasks probably included cooking, gardening, tending children and domestic animals, washing and mending clothing, and doing other household chores, such as changing the bedding (which as most people did not have bedsteads, probably consisted of straw or bracken)[55] and the layer of rushes on the floor. Those Dubliners who were more prosperous had servants to assist with household tasks. Such help was undoubtedly needed, as women would have had a difficult task in attempting to keep their homes clean and orderly in the medieval urban environment. Historians of daily life in medieval Dublin have tended to emphasise the low standard of living in the medieval city.[56] Houses were generally quite small, made of wood or wattle, with thatched roofs. A limited number of residences were constructed of stone. The floors of houses were usually made of clay, and covered with rushes. In some cases, floors were extremely unhygenic, as the scraps and refuse were not always cleared away before a new layer of rushes was laid down.[57] Nonetheless, cleanliness and orderliness must have varied from home to home. Craftsmen and wealthy citizens lived in greater comfort than the other inhabitants of the town, and since they could afford to keep servants, used wax candles which enabled them to see the dirt, and probably had more leisure to care about it, they may have been able to keep their homes cleaner. Regardless of her social position, the cleanliness of a household probably depended greatly on the personality and resources of the woman who managed it. Lydon has argued that most inhabitants of medieval Dublin slept on beds of bracken which were infested with fleas and bedbugs.[58] Presumably, however, a housewife who did not fancy sharing her bed with bloodthirsty insects would have made an effort to have the bedding changed frequently.[59] A fastidious housewife might also have demanded that her servants swept the floors before laying down a new layer of rushes. It was, however, difficult to dispose of waste in medieval Dublin; people tended to pile their refuse in the streets, a practice which made the condition of the streets deplorable, and inspired a continual stream of civic legislation.[60] While this legislation reveals that Dublin's streets were quite dirty, it also shows that the citizens of the medieval town were not inured to squalor, but rather that they wished to find ways of dealing with it. Thus, it is not unlikely that there were many housekeepers who attempted to keep their homes clean and orderly, challenging though this may have been.

---

54 Ibid., pp 41–2.   **55** On the bedding, see James Lydon, 'The medieval city', in *Dublin through the ages*, ed. Art Cosgrove (Dublin, 1988), p. 36.   **56** Lydon, 'The medieval city', pp. 25–6; Moylan, 'Dubliners', pp 82–3.   **57** Moylan, 'Dubliners', p. 83.   **58** Lydon, 'The medieval city', p. 36.   **59** A fourteenth-century housekeeping manual written in Paris for merchants' wives recommends a number of methods for ridding homes of such pests. See

The inventories which precede medieval wills help to illuminate the standard of living in the households which the women of medieval Dublin managed. At his death in 1463, Thomas Sneterby, 'gentleman,' with Katherine Nangle, his wife, owned a great deal of land in Ardee, Co. Louth, including mills and an inn, and also possessed gold, silver, jewels, lands, grain, and livestock. His household goods included 3 basins with 2 ewers, 6 pairs of blankets and 8 of sheets, 2 little pans, 3 candlesticks, and other household utensils worth 10s., which possibly included items such as spoons and knives.[61] Thus, there was bedding sufficient for 6 people; 3 basins and 2 ewers for them to use when washing themselves; 2 pans and other utensils for cooking; and 3 candlesticks to hold candles and provide light.[62] That a man dignified by the title of 'gentleman' and possessed of what seems to have been such a great deal of land, had such a relatively limited number of household possessions (by modern standards) suggests that, despite his status, he inhabited a fairly modest place of residence, perhaps with two or three rooms only.

By comparison, Dame Margaret Nugent, the widow of a knight and former mayor of Dublin, Sir Thomas Newbury, possessed a greater quantity of household possessions, including many luxury items. She had silver items, including primarily cups and spoons, worth 99s. 12d., three silver girdles, 3 gold rings, several vessels of brass, 3 coverlets, a featherbed, and 2 mattresses, 2 'tables for cups called cupboards', 3 coffers, one buckram bed with 3 curtains, household utensils worth 20s., 'one cover of a silver salt cellar', one small brass pot for holy water, one piece of wooden furniture called a 'scrine', 2 pairs of coral beads, 5 bankers with 5 cushions, and pewter vessels worth 4s.[63] As she was a widow, it is likely that this was only a portion of the goods which she and her husband possessed during his lifetime. Her greater material wealth indicates that her residence was probably larger and better appointed than that of Thomas Sneterby but, based upon the inventory of her goods, it seems unlikely that it could have had more than four or five rooms. It is not clear where Dame Margaret Nugent was dwelling at the time of her death; she did not have any house or land to bequeath, and thus it is probable that she had only a life interest in her place of residence.[64] She must have had an unusually luxurious

Shahar, 'Townswomen', p. 204. See also Bonnie S. Anderson and Judith P. Zinsser, 'The townswoman's daily life: the twelfth to the seventeenth centuries', in *A history of their own: women in Europe from prehistory to the present* (London, 1988), vol. 1, pp 375–6, for more information on medieval housekeeping.   **60** Moylan, 'Dubliners', p. 82.   **61** Lawlor (ed.), 'Calendar of the Liber Niger and Liber Albus', p. 38.   **62** Only the more prosperous could afford to use wax candles during the medieval period; even with the benefit of wax candles, homes were probably quite dark: see Moylan, 'Dubliners', p. 85.   **63** Berry (ed.), *Register of wills and inventories*, pp 78–9. A 'buckram bed' was used for storing clothes, to protect them when they were not being worn. See ibid., p. 216, note. A banker was a cover of cloth or tapestry for a bench (Moylan, 'Dubliners', p. 84).   **64** It is also interesting to note that despite the relative luxury of her way of life, Margaret Nugent was greatly in debt when she bedroom, with a featherbed and a 'coverlet of arras and 2 other small ones', and a buckram bed for storing her garments. Perhaps the wooden 'scrine' was a screen for privacy? It is likely that she also had some sort of sitting room; the 5 bankers accompanied by 5 cushions and the 'cupboards' sound like suitable furnishings for a sitting area. Presumably there was also in her residence a kitchen or area for cooking.

Most Dubliners had a more modest catalogue of possessions than Dame Margaret Nugent or Thomas Sneterby and his wife. Richard Porter, who seems to have been a farmer (as no occupation is listed and he had 17 cows, one hundred sheep, and a quantity of corn), his wife, Rose Tirrell, and their children, had four brass pots, two brass skillets, three spits, six silver spoons, and other household items worth 40s.[65] The total value of these household goods was 94s. 12d. Alice Cassell and her husband shared a similarly modest way of life, having one cart horse, two cows, a sow and four young pigs, 12 sheep, a boat, 14 sea nets, other ship's gear worth 2s. 8d, brass vessels worth 40s., leaden vessels worth 20s., 3 mease of herrings, and other household utensils worth 6s. 8d.[66] The total value of the household items listed here is 66s. 8d.; which is slightly less than that of those belonging to Rose Tirrell and her husband. Alice Cassell and Rose Tirrell would have shared a modest way of life with their families, the latter being slightly better off. Both women enjoyed a higher standard of living than Joan White, a single woman or childless widow who leased a small farm in the parish of Leixlip, and had only one pan, two small old pots, two old chests, and household items worth 4s., in addition to a few cows, farm horses, sheep, pigs, wheat and barley.[67] It seems likely that as a tenant with so few possessions, she lived in a one-room cottage.

Those households which were fortunate enough to possess a garden probably depended upon it a great deal to supply they household with fruit, herbs, and vegetables. For many women, managing a household probably involved tending the garden, or supervising servants in this task. There are numerous references to gardens in medieval deeds. In the Christ Church deeds, there is a lease by Johanna Seys, the widow of a man named Philip Payne, to William Chamerleyne of Dublin, of 'an orchard or garden lately called "paradise" in St. Brigid's-st., suburbs of Dublin, for 9 years; rent a grain of corn; lessor covenants to repair the applehouse thereon'.[68] This evokes a very pleasant picture in contrast to the vision of urban squalor created by sanitary legislation; the name of the garden also suggests that Johanna Seys or another of the garden's previous owners perceived the garden as a refuge from the less pleasant aspects of urban life. Medieval Dublin may have had dirty streets and tiny houses, but it also contained some lovely gardens.

---

died.   **65** Berry (ed.), *Register of wills and inventories*, pp 41–2.   **66** Ibid., pp 52–3.   **67** Ibid., p. 47.   **68** McEnery (ed.), 'Calendar to Christ Church deeds,' vol. 24, p. 101, no. 974.

It is evident that managing a household was a challenging task in medieval Dublin. The urban environment was very dirty, and there were no adequate facilities to dispose of household waste. However, the continuous stream of legislation directed at dealing with sanitation shows that the inhabitants were not inured to dirt and grime, but rather were attempting valiantly to combat it. Cleanliness and orderliness probably varied from home to home, depending on the resources and priorities of the inhabitants. Women who kept lovely gardens may have been more concerned to keep their homes clean and tidy than women who left fish entrails strewn on the streets beneath their stalls at the market.

The status of women in medieval Dublin was not equal to that of men. Women did not participate in municipal government, and husbands, not wives, were considered to be the heads of their families. Nonetheless, the numerous references to women in the wills, deeds, and statutes which have survived from the medieval city demonstrate that women played an active role in social, economic, and religious life. Women were remembered fondly in the wills of the men of medieval Dublin as wives, mothers, sisters, neighbours, and servants. It is thus apparent that although they did not enjoy the same political rights as men, Dublin women enjoyed many of the same legal and economic privileges of citizenship, and were valued members of medieval society.[69]

69 There are other aspects of women's role in the society of medieval Dublin which I have not been able to cover; for example, some women entered into the religious life at St Mary de Hogges, Dublin's only nunnery. Women were active philanthropists, a notable example being the sisters who nursed the poor and ailing at the hospital of St John the Baptist. Laywomen also belonged to religious fraternities, which functioned as both social and religious institutions (see Ronan, 'Religious customs of the Dublin medieval gilds').

A cut above: cranial surgery in medieval Dublin

BARRA Ó DONNABHÁIN

INTRODUCTION

The principal focus of archaeology is on the people of the past and the infinitely
diverse cultural responses they devised to cope with their physical and social
environments. The sub-discipline of bioarchaeology involves a recognition of
the biological template shared by all humanity and of the interplay between
biology and culture that is the subtext to much of human existence. When
viewed from this perspective, human burials can be seen to form a special type
of archaeological feature that afford us a unique opportunity to study the
interaction of ancient culture and biology. Burials are the only type of physical
remains that tie a variety of classes of information directly to individual
participants in the past. They consist of the physical remains of the people
themselves deposited in a manner that is governed by strong ideological
considerations that are specific to particular historical contexts. As a result, the
funerary practices of earlier societies have traditionally received a lot of
attention in archaeology. Ironically, human skeletal remains have not always
been included in this concern with past mortuary behaviour. The skeleton
contains a record of individual biology and life history while also preserving a
record of the genetic heritage of the person and of the biological population
from which they are drawn. In Ireland, while there has been a strong tradition
of concern with past funerary behaviour, detailed osteological analysis of
human remains retrieved from all archaeological sites only became standard
practice during the late 1980s and 1990s. Prior to that time, remains from
prehistoric sites were usually curated while the standard of the associated
osteological reporting varied from detailed to cursory. In contrast, remains from
sites dating to the historic period tended not to be curated and were usually
reburied at the site or disposed of elsewhere. While there were some notable
exceptions (for example, Howells 1941; McLoughlin 1950), osteological data
were not recorded in remains from the historic period. This situation has
changed in recent years and the curation and analysis of remains from all
periods is now mandatory (Buckley et al. 1999).

The importance of the retention of all remains is clearly demonstrated by
the wealth of cultural and biological information that can be gleaned from the
single human bone that was curated as a result of excavations that were carried

out at the site of the church of St Michael le Pole in Dublin in 1981 (Gowen, Chap. 1 above). A number of burials were uncovered during this work. While most of the remains post-dated the construction of the twelfth-century church, this latter activity had cut through an earlier series of burials that included a lintel grave. A radiocarbon date ranging from the late tenth to eleventh centuries was obtained from the burial in this grave (Gowen, ibid.; Simpson 2000). As the excavation was considered to be a site assessment rather than a research exercise and as was common practice at the time on archaeological sites dating from the medieval period, the bulk of the human remains were not submitted for osteological analysis and were reburied at the site. Unusual markings and a hole that appeared to have been drilled were noted on one bone that came from a disturbed context. This was submitted to the author for analysis. While the results were published soon thereafter in summary form (Ó Donnabháin et al. 1985), the detailed report belongs with that on the excavation and is presented here with a consideration of the broader context of the surgical procedure involved. Unfortunately, it was not possible to determine the date of the bone in question. While the majority of the human remains at the site post-dated the Anglo-Norman invasion, others were contemporary with the Hiberno-Norse settlement of Dublin and the presence of pre-Norse burial activity cannot be ruled out. The curated bone could date from any of these periods.

The remains from the church of St Michael le Pole

The bone that was recovered during the excavation consists of the greater part of a human left parietal that had been trepanned (pl. 1).[1] The size of the bone suggests it belonged to an adult. None of the observable sutures (the bregmatic portion of the coronal suture, the sagittal suture, the lambdoidal and median portions of the lambdoidal suture and the squamosal suture) had begun to fuse. This may indicate that the individual was a younger adult. In suggesting this age estimate it must be stressed that the correlation between age at death and suture closure is relatively weak (Key et al. 1994; Masset 1989) but it is the only indicator of age available in this case. It is not possible to determine the sex of this individual based on the morphological examination of this single bone.

The trepanation procedure had been carried out in the area immediately anterior to the parietal eminence. An oval roundel of bone was detached; the excised bone was not recovered. At the ectocranial or outer surface, the resulting perforation measures 20.9mm anteroposteriorly and 19mm medio-laterally. On the cerebral or inner surface, the trepanation measures 14.99mm anteroposteriorly and 17.1mm mediolaterally. The margin of the trepanned

---

1 Trepanation is the removal of a portion of bone from the skull vault by various methods. The word is derived from the Greek *trupe*, a hole, and *trupanon*, a boring device. A trepan is a cylindrical saw used in the operation. A trephine (hence trephination) is an improved form of trepan with a guiding centre-pin.

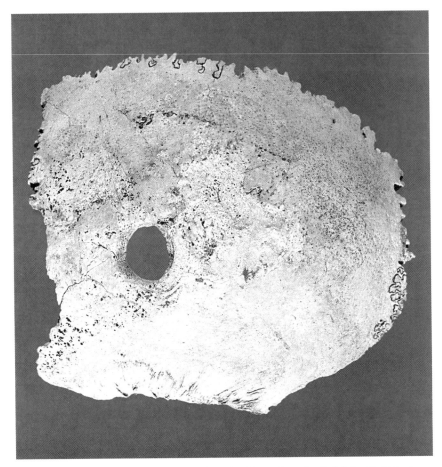

Plate 1 General view of the trepanned left parietal bone from the St Michael le Pole site.

cavity is slightly bevelled in both its anterior and posterior aspects, while it is almost vertical medially and laterally. The margins of the perforation are located 27mm from the coronal suture (the latter is broken post mortem), 85.5mm from the lambdoidal suture, 60mm from the sagittal suture and 48.7mm from the inferior border of the squamosal suture. There is some post mortem cracking of the bone between the coronal suture and the area subjected to the surgical procedure.

On the outer surface, the trepanation is ovoid in shape (pl. 2). The perforation has cut through the anterior end of a linear depressed fracture of the outer table alone that extends posteromedially from the trepanation (pl. 2, a). The original extent of this injury cannot be assessed as the posterior end of the

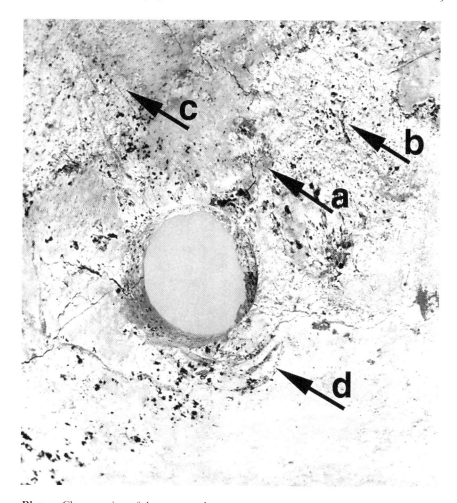

Plate 2 Close-up view of the trepanned area.

wound has been obscured by a large area of post mortem deterioration of the surface of the bone (pl. 2, b). The depressed area was at least 5mm wide and survives to a length of 15mm. The fracture produced localised crushing of outer table bone only in a linear lesion, suggesting it was due to a blow from an object with a blunt edge. If, as seems likely, this wound was incurred prior to the trepanation procedure, symptoms that were perceived to be associated with the injury may have suggested the need for the operation. The outer surface of the parietal also has two other sets of features. The first of these consists of at least four straight, shallow incisions that radiate antero-medially and posteriorly from the trepanation (pl. 2, c). These were made with a sharp instrument and the longest extends 48.5mm from the trepanned opening towards bregma (the

Plate 3 Endocranial view of the trepanation.

junction of the frontal and parietal bones). Unfortunately, the incisions are also partially obscured by post mortem flaking of the bone's outer surface (pl. 2, b). The second set of features on the outer surface of the bone consists of three shallow, semi-circular grooves that are immediately infero-lateral to and running into the perforation (pl. 2, d). The uniform shape and size of these arcs and that of the perforation itself suggest that the grooves were made by a cutting instrument with a cylindrical blade that had a diameter of about 19mm.

While the perforation is ovoid on the outside of the cranium, it is D-shaped on the inner surface (pl. 3). The rounded anterior, medial and lateral sides are smooth while the straight-sided posterior margin is quite jagged. The form of the margins of the roundel that was removed indicates that the instrument cut cleanly through the inner table bone at the anterior, medial and lateral sides. The cutting instrument must have been applied at an angle from the front to produce both the oblique anterior margin and the vertical medial and lateral margins. Once the inner table of bone had been penetrated anteriorly, the operator straightened the trepan, thereby prising out the disc of bone. While the roundel had been cut free anteriorly, it snapped at the posterior inner margin producing the jagged edge described above. This suggests that the person carrying out the procedure was trying to minimise the risk of the cutting instrument penetrating the *dura mater*, the tough outer lining of the brain. Unfortunately perhaps, a groove for a branch of the left middle meningeal artery lay directly under the cut lateral margin (pl. 3). This artery runs in the most superficial layer of the *dura mater*.

Reconstructing the surgical procedure
The constellation of features noted on the bone offers clues to the motivation for the operation, the procedure that was followed and its outcome. It seems likely that this individual incurred a skull fracture some time prior to undergoing the operation. This lesion was probably due to a blow to the left side of the head from an object with a blunt edge. The resulting wound was confined to the outer table bone and is unlikely to have been lethal. While it is possible that this injury was incurred accidentally, it could also be the result of some form of interpersonal violence. As most people are right-handed, head wounds that are the result of face-to-face combat tend to be more common on the left side of a victim. The fact that the area of the fracture was cut by the trepanation procedure suggests that two features are directly related. Pain, some degree of loss of consciousness, or other symptoms perceived to be associated with the fracture may have suggested the need for the operation. It is likely that the scalp was lacerated at the time the fracture was incurred. The straight incisions (pl. 2, c) probably mark the initial stages of the surgical intervention where the scalp was cut again. If the patient was conscious during the surgery, alcohol or herbal preparations (Voights and Hudson 1992) are likely to have been the only pain relief that was available. The initial incising of the scalp would have been the most painful part of the procedure and the cut soft tissues would have bled profusely. Turning back the scalp flaps would have staunched the bleeding as well as exposing the outer surface of the cranium. The semi-circular arcs and the shape of the perforation itself suggest that the skull was then cut with a cylindrical saw or trepan such as the nineteenth-century example illustrated in Plate 4. The three semi-circular grooves probably represent some initial failure by the operator to get a good grip on the bone. This may have been due to the presence of blood and the periosteum or may reflect the struggles of a squirming patient. The bones of the skull do not have the rich supply of

Plate 4 Nineteenth-century trepanation saw similar to the one used in the operation described here.

sensory nerves that is found in the scalp, so this part of the procedure would not have been painful *per se* but, if the patient were conscious, it is likely that they were in considerable discomfort. The cutting instrument must have been applied at an angle from the front to produce both the oblique anterior margin and the vertical medial and lateral margins of the perforation. Once the inner table of bone had been penetrated anteriorly, the operator straightened the trepan and snapped out the roundel of bone. It is possible that the penetration of the inner table bone with the saw involved nicking the branch of the left middle meningeal artery that lay directly underneath (pl. 3). The laceration of this vessel would have resulted in haemorrhaging that would have been difficult to stop. Any attempt to do so would have been dangerous, as it would have run the risk of causing direct damage to the brain.

Whether or not the blood vessel was cut, it is clear that this person did not survive for long after the procedure. Neither the scalp incisions nor the perforation itself show any signs of healing having occurred. Lisowski (1967) described the healing and repair process in a trepanation. The diploë produces a small amount of endosteal callus, while the periosteal callus of the epicranium grows only a little. While the perforation would never close, the healing process leaves characteristic new bone at the site of the procedure. This slight osseous regeneration results in the smoothening of the trepanned margin. Macroscopic examination of the margins of the St Michael le Pole trepanation shows that these are quite smooth anteriorly, medially and laterally. However, the use of a trepan would account for the form of these margins. Similar smooth diploic surfaces have been observed in skulls with sword cuts from which the victim could not possibly have survived (Ó Donnabháin 1985). In the St Michael le Pole trepanation, the diploë is still visible in the cut margin and the jagged posterior margin shows no sign of regrowth. Moreover, the straight incisions, which probably resulted from the operator incising the scalp and reflecting it back over the area to be trepanned, show no sign of healing. These would have been obliterated quickly if healing had taken place. The absence of any osteitis further supports the view that the patient did not survive for long after the trepanation.

While it is not possible to determine with certainty the cause of death, a fatal haemorrhage due to the laceration of the branch of the middle meningeal artery seems most likely. Direct injury to the brain could also have occurred. A catastrophic infection is also a possibility as it is unlikely that the procedure was carried out under aseptic conditions.

Trepanation in Ireland
Trepanations have been reported from a number of different archaeological contexts in Ireland (Buckley and Ó Donnabháin 1992). A comprehensive study of these has yet to be produced but a preliminary inventory is listed here in chronological order (so far as that can be determined) to facilitate comparisons with the remains from the church of St Michael le Pole. Some of the remains listed here are from contexts that are poorly documented. In some of the older examples, only the skull or the portion thereof with the possible trepanation was curated while the current location of a few examples mentioned in the literature is uncertain. Unlike the case detailed in this paper, it is not always possible to determine with certainty if a defect observed in a skull is the result of surgical intervention. There are a number of taphonomic processes and pathological conditions that can produce defects that can be difficult to distinguish from healed trepanations. Brothwell (1967; Brothwell et al. 1978), for example, reported on an example of what he termed a pseudotrephination of supposed Iron Age date from Gortnacargy, Co. Cavan. He concluded that the skull defect was a post-depositional feature that was probably caused by rodents gnawing on bone. Weapon wounds can occasionally be confused with the effects of trepanation, especially if healed. Dysraphism, a congenital herniation of the

skull, can also produce a defect that, in dry bone, can mimic a trepanation (Ortner and Putschar 1985). This herniation often occurs at the site of the fontanelle, the soft spot on the head of an infant, and can lead to the incomplete fusion of the frontal and parietal bones of the skull. As a result, this defect often occurs close to bregma, the point where these bones meet. It is possible that some of the cases that have been found in archaeological contexts in Ireland represent the operation of these taphonomic processes or the presence of such pathological conditions.

Only one possible example has been noted to date in remains from the prehistoric period. This is from the Early Bronze Age flat cemetery at Edmondstown, Co. Dublin (Buckley in Mount and Hartnett 1993). The skull of a young adult male has a teardrop shaped lesion on the left temporal bone. Buckley (ibid.) concluded that the defect could be a perimortem trepanation or, perhaps more likely, that the fragment of bone could have been removed after death. The cut surfaces in this case have some marks that are reminiscent of rodent gnawing so the operation of taphonomic processes cannot be ruled out.

Rynne has argued for a date in the Iron Age for a supposed case of trepanation that was noted in one of five skeletons found at Ballinlough, Co. Laois (Lisowski 1967; Rynne 1974). His suggestion of an Iron Age date was made on the grounds that the corpses had not been buried at a Christian cemetery a few hundred metres from the site and on the presence of an isolated human skull. The latter skull, which did not have a trepanation, had been reburied at some time in the past with a small collection of other human bones. This is commonplace is more recent cemeteries where earlier remains are disturbed during grave digging and it is not necessary to resort to Iron Age head cults to explain this occurrence. The fact that the burials were aligned east-west and in the absence of diagnostic artifacts, a date in the historic period does not seem unreasonable. The skull that was described as having a trepanation had been uncovered prior to the arrival of the archaeologist at the site so the form of its deposition and relation to other remains is unknown. It is currently not available for inspection but photographs taken in the 1980s indicate that this was the skull of an adult male. The defect is located on the right frontal, about 10mm posterior to bregma and close to the sagittal suture. The perforation is roughly circular with a diameter of about 20mm and is irregularly bevelled. Erskine, the anatomist who wrote a five-line report on the skull as an appendix to Rynne's report (ibid.), considered this to be a trephination (*sic*) and suggested that the margins of the wound had some signs of healing but that this was obscured by post-mortem cracking. Examination of photographs of the defect suggests that the entire margin of the perforation could have been produced by cracking and the defect has the appearance of an exit wound. Two large cracks radiate from the defect. Erskine considered these to be post mortem but they could also be perimortem. There was no obvious entry wound to account for this perforation

Plate 5   An image taken from John Derrick's *Image of Ireland* where heads of defeated
Irish are carried impaled on swords by victorious English soldiers.

but it is possible that it was produced by an object that was introduced into the
cranium through the foramen magnum and then forced through the top of the
head. Unfortunately, it is not currently possible to check the base of the skull
for associated damage. It seems possible then that this was not a case of
trepanation but rather one where a head had been mounted in some way prior
to its disposal. The practice of displaying trophy heads has been documented
from a number of medieval contexts in Ireland (Ó Donnabháin, 1995) and it is
possible that the people buried at Ballinlough had been treated in a manner
similar to that depicted in a woodcut from John Derrick's *Image of Ireland*
where heads of the defeated Irish are carried impaled on swords by victorious
English troops (pl. 5). Rynne (ibid.) did mention that some of the post-cranial
remains at Ballinlough had weapon wounds though these bones were not
curated. If these remains do represent individuals killed in a violent conflict
during the historic period, this may explain the location of the burials: close to
but outside the boundaries of the nearby cemetery. People dying violently, being
spiritually suspect, were perhaps buried outside.

Walmsley (1923) described a trepanation thought to be of early medieval date
that was recovered from the monastic site at Nendrum, Co. Down. The skull
was that of an adult and the trepanation was reported to be on the left parietal.

Martin (1935) mentioned that the skull was in Queen's University, Belfast though it cannot now be located.

In his description of the post medieval trepanation from Armagh friary (see below), Lynn (1975) mentioned that he had found a skull with a trepanation (on the left parietal) during trial trenching at the early medieval church at Banagher, Co. Derry. The context or dating of the example from Banagher was not discussed and the trepanation was not mentioned in Waterman and Hamlin's (1976) subsequent report on the excavations. This skull has been examined by the writer and is an example of a trepanation that had healed. The perforation is on the left parietal in a location almost identical to that in the case of the St Michael le Pole example described above. The trepanned defect in the Banagher example is roughly circular and slightly larger than that in the Dublin example and lacks the straight margins of the latter. This suggests that it was probably produced by scraping the bone rather than using a cylindrical saw.

Three trepanned skulls of early medieval date were recovered during recent excavations of an early medieval cemetery at Cabinteely, Co. Dublin (Conway 1999; 2000). Six stratigraphic phases of burial were identified at the site. Radiocarbon dates are not yet available but the earliest phases have been dated by artifactual associations to the fifth or sixth centuries AD. The trepanations were found in burials from each of the three later phases identified at the site. While the *modus operandi* used in the trepanations is very similar in all three cases, the stratigraphic data suggest that the particular method used in the procedure had a history in the community that used the site for burial. This cemetery is located about 10km southeast of the site of the church of St Michael le Pole and it is possible that the trepanation from the latter is contemporary with one of the three from Cabinteely. Of the three, one has signs of some partial healing having taken place prior to the death of the individual, while the degree of remodelling in the other two suggests that the people involved had survived for a long time after the operation. In each of the three cases, the techniques used involved scraping the bone rather than sawing it. This produced similar bevelled lesions in each case. Each of the lesions is oval and two are on the right parietal while one is on the left. Two of these lesions are quite extensive with maximum lengths of 52mm and 65mm.

McLoughlin (1950) examined the skeletal remains of over 140 individuals from an early medieval cemetery at Castleknock, Co. Dublin. The excavation was carried out in 1938 and the resulting report is an interesting though redundant example of the typological approach that dominated physical anthropological discourse in the first half of the twentieth century. The report concentrated on metrical analysis and on the determination of 'racial type'. Little mention was made of pathological changes but he did note that

There were two cases of perforation of the parietal bone over the left lateral

> lacuna, a large one in the skull of a woman of about 45 and a smaller one in the skull of a man of about the same age (McLoughlin 1950, 1).

It is not clear from this statement if McLoughlin considered the perforations to be trepanations carried out during life. The remains from Castleknock are not currently available for inspection though arrangements are being made to place the collection in the care of the National Museum of Ireland. As a result of this move, it may be possible to identify the two crania mentioned by McLoughlin and provide a more detailed analysis.

Martin (1935) mentioned a trepanned skull from Collierstown, Co. Meath that was recovered along with many other skeletons from a medieval cemetery. This was found in 1934 during excavations carried out by personnel attached to the National Museum of Ireland. The skull is that of an adolescent or young adult and that the trepanation is located on the right frontal. The perforation is oval, measuring 29mm by 22mm and had been made by scraping the bone. It is surrounded by a large rectangular area of healed osteitis that may have resulted from inflammation of the area of reflected scalp. Remodelling of the margins of the trepanation and of the area of osteitis indicate that the patient had survived for some time after the procedure.

Five possible examples of trepanation are known that are thought to be of later medieval date. In two of these, one from Maganey Lower, Co. Kildare (Prendergast 1962) and the other from the cemetery at the site of the medieval hospital of St Stephen, Dublin (Buckley 1993; Buckley and Ó Donnabháin 1992), the defect occurs at bregma and a diagnosis of dysraphism (described above) cannot be discounted. A further potentially confounding factor is the poor preservation of the example from Maganey Lower. If the example from the site of St Stephen's hospital is a trepanation, the individual survived the procedure. The irregularity of the lesion suggests that if it is a trepanation, a cylindrical saw was not used.

Another possibly late medieval example was recovered during excavations at the site of the church of the Holy Trinity, Carlingford, Co. Louth (pers. comm., Laureen Buckley).

The remaining putative case of late medieval date is from Moyle Abbey, Co. Kildare (unpublished file in the National Museum of Ireland). This may be a healed weapon wound though trepanation cannot be ruled out. The defect occurs on the left side of the frontal bone of an adult and the angle of the cut surface is on a single plane. This is consistent with a glancing blow to the side of the forehead from a weapon such as a sword.

Two cases of trepanation are known from post-medieval contexts. Lynn (1975) found one at the Franciscan friary in Armagh among a group of skeletons thought to date from the late seventeenth century. The perforation is on the occipital bone at the back of the head and had healed. Another post-medieval trepanation has recently been noted during excavations of an eighteenth-century cemetery at North King Street in Dublin (pers. comm., Jenny Coughlan).

DISCUSSION

Cases of trepanation have been found in archaeologically retrieved skeletal remains from all world areas. In Europe, the earliest known example was found during excavations carried out in the 1950s at the Vasilyevka II cemetery in the Ukraine. This skeleton has recently produced a radiocarbon date that places it in the Mesolithic period (Walker 1998). Trepanation has also received some attention in the ethnographic literature (Magretts 1967; Oakley et al. 1959), which includes eyewitness accounts (for example, Crump 1901). In his discussion of a dramatic example of Early Bronze Age date from southern Britain, Piggott (1940) suggested that the idea of trepanation had originated in prehistoric Europe. While this type of eurocentric and diffusionist reasoning that was typical of the traditional school of archaeology of the first half of the twentieth century is no longer considered valid in archaeological interpretation, Piggott's idea is still being repeated in the bioarchaeological literature (Roberts and Manchester 1995). It seems more plausible to suggest that this is a procedure that has been developed independently by many peoples in different contexts over many millennia. This diversity is presumably matched by an equally diverse set of motivating factors. Among the many potential motives that have been suggested in both the bioarchaeological and ethnographic literature, the majority fall under two general headings: magico-religious and curative. In the former, the focus is on both the perforation and the bone that was removed which many suggest may have been retained as a powerful amulet (Ortner and Putschar 1985). There is strong circumstantial evidence for the curative motivating factors where the emphasis would have been on the effects of producing the perforation rather than on the excised piece of bone. Trepanations associated with trauma and other pathological conditions have been reported in archaeological material from a diverse range of cultural contexts (Brothwell et al. 1978; Lisowski 1967; Mann 1991; McKinley 1992; Wells 1982). As with the case from the site of the church of St Michael le Pole, the association between the trepanation and other lesions suggests that the perforation was perceived in many different socio-cultural settings as a means of relieving at least some somatic conditions. While it is likely that medical knowledge systems in many early societies were conceptualised in a way that was radically different from modern western biomedicine, they probably had a strong empirical basis. Trepanation can indeed be an effective treatment in cases of trauma to the head that produces sub-dural bleeding. The procedure reduces the pressure placed on the brain by the resulting haematoma. The effects of such intra-cranial pressure will vary according to the location of the haematoma but can include symptoms such as loss of consciousness, headache, cognitive impairment and peripheral neurological signs. In the case of many head wounds, it would be clear to any observer of the victim that there was a direct relationship between the injury and the onset of such symptoms. As seems to have been the case in the St Michael le Pole example, the location of the initial injury would point to the site where the pressure-relieving operation would be most likely to be effective. If the efficacy of the treatment could be demonstrated, it may have encouraged early practitioners to use the procedure for other disorders while also assuring the co-operation of other potential patients. Perhaps it is misleading though to present the surgery as an experimental operation. It seems likely that the surgeon who operated on the individual from the church of St Michael le Pole was using an instrument specifically designed for an intervention that had a long history in the medical knowledge of the particular cultural milieu. McDougall (1992) has noted the similarity between descriptions of surgical procedures in thirteenth- and fourteenth-century Icelandic manuscripts and those in contemporary and earlier texts from southern Europe. He has argued that this demonstrates the transmission of medical knowledge systems throughout medieval Europe. No doubt the population of medieval Dublin were also both generating and at the receiving end of the exchange of medical knowledge and expertise.

In the 1950s, Stewart (1958) examined 214 trepanned skulls from pre-Columbian contexts in Peru. From the evidence of healing at the site of the surgery, he concluded that in more than half of these cases, the patient had survived for a considerable time after the procedure. This indicates that even when carried out by practitioners who had little understanding of sepsis and in conditions that would seem primitive today, this operation had a success rate that may have been considered reasonable. Of the seventeen trepanations and putative trepanations from Ireland reviewed above, the majority, including the example from the site of the church of St Michael le Pole, date from the historic period. Information about the extent of healing was available in eleven cases. Remodelling of the bone suggested that seven of the individuals involved had survived the operations, though in at least one case this was only for a short period of time.

As the occurrence of trepanation varies widely both temporally and spatially, the technology associated with the procedure also shows considerable variation. While subsequent healing can obscure the evidence of the techniques that were used, unsuccessful attempts, such as that from the church of St Michael le Pole, can offer clues as to the form of the cutting instrument that was used and the manner in which it was applied. The various techniques of trepanation that have been documented in archaeological contexts have been reviewed by a number of writers (Lisowski 1967; Oakley et al. 1959; Ortner and Putschar

1985) and involve a diverse range of cutting and scraping techniques and instruments. Brothwell (1974) described a set of trephining equipment that was found in a Roman period context at Bingen-am-Rhein in Germany. This type of equipment, including the cylindrical saw, was well known in the Classical World, as was the associated head surgery. The medical treatises attributed to Hippocrates (late fifth century BC) indicate that trepanation was used to relieve the effects of skull fracture and contain descriptions of cylindrical toothed saws. Similar objects were described by the Roman medical writer Celsus (*c*.AD 3–64) who also left instructions on how the instrument should be used. These instructions imply that the instrument had a central pin that could be removed once the saw had begun to penetrate the bone. The cylindrical saw from Bingen described by Brothwell (ibid.) had a central anti-slip pin such as that mentioned by Celsus. The presence of the three semi-circular grooves on the bone from the church of St Michael le Pole suggests that a centre pin was not present in the cylindrical saw that was used during that procedure. However, the use of the cylindrical saw in the case from the St Michael le Pole site seems to be unique in the Irish context.

The possibility that there were two trepanations at Castleknock, others of possibly similar date from Banagher, Nendrum and St Michael le Pole as well as the three confirmed examples at Cabinteely may suggest that this was a practice that was not uncommon in early medieval Ireland. It is likely that the literati of that society would have been familiar with late Roman medical technology and the associated literature mentioned above. The trepanation from the church of St Michael le Pole is a clear indicator of the presence or perhaps the survival of this technology and associated expertise. The chief importance of this example of trepanation is a function of the premature death of the patient: the absence of healing allows a forensic-like reconstruction of the details of the operation. We know very little about the medical knowledge systems and expertise that obtained in medieval Dublin. This single parietal bone offers us a tantalising glimpse of the level of medical intervention that was practised and is a graphic reminder of the interaction between biological and cultural systems that is fundamental to understanding the human career.

ACKNOWLEDGEMENTS

I would like to thank Robin O'Sullivan for being so generous with his time and expertise during the initial study of the Ship Street trepanation. I would also like to thank Jenny Coughlan and Laureen Buckley for information about unpublished trepanations. Finally, I am grateful to Chris Lynn, Andy Halpin and Mary Cahill for facilitating access to some of the material.

REFERENCES

Brothwell, D.R. 1967 Human remains from Gortnacargy, Co. Cavan. *R.S.A.I. Jn.* 97, 75–84.
—— 1974 Osteological evidence of the use of a surgical modiolus in a Romano-British population: an aspect of primitive technology. *Journal of Archaeological Science* 1, 209–11.
—— Powers, R., and Denston, B. 1978 The human skeletal remains from Amesbury Barrow 51 with special reference to the case of trephination and its position in the history of trephining in Britain *Wiltshire Archaeology Magazine*, 43–60.
Buckley, L. 1993 A bone to pick. *Technology Ireland* 25, 29–31.
—— Murphy, E., and Ó Donnabháin, B. 1999 *The treatment of human remains: technical paper for archaeologists.* Dublin: Irish Association of Professional Archaeologists.
—— and Ó Donnabháin, B. 1992 Early cranial surgery in Ireland *Archaeology Ireland*, 10–12.
Conway, M. 1999 *Director's first findings from excavations in Cabinteely.* Dublin: Margaret Gowen and Company Transactions 1.
—— 2000 Mount Offaly, Cabinteely: early medieval enclosed cemetery. In I. Bennett (ed.): *Excavations 1998: summary accounts of archaeological excavations in Ireland.* Bray, pp. 36–7.
Crump, J.A. 1901 Trephining in the south seas. *Journal of the Royal Anthropological Institute* 31, 167–172.
Howells, W.W. 1941 The Early Christian Irish: the skeletons at Gallen priory. *R.I.A. Proc.* 46C, 103–219.
Key, C.A., Aiello, L.C., and Molleson, T. 1994 Cranial suture closure and its implications for age estimation. *International Journal of Osteoarchaeology* 4, 193–207.
Lisowski, F.P. 1967 Prehistoric and early historic trepanation. In D.R. Brothwell and A.T. Sandison (eds.) *Diseases in antiquity: a survey of the diseases, injuries and surgery of early populations.* Springfield, Illinois, 651–672.
Lynn, C.J. 1975 Excavation in the Franciscan Friary church, Armagh. *Ulster Journal of Archaeology* 38, 61–80.
Magretts, E.L. 1967 Trepanation of the skull by the medicine-men of primitive cultures, with particular reference to present-day native east African practice. In D.R. Brothwell and A.T. Sandison (eds.) *Diseases in antiquity: a survey of the diseases, injuries and surgery of early populations.* Springfield, 673–701.
Mann, G. 1991 Chronic ear disease as a possible reason for trephination. *International Journal of Osteoarchaeology* 1, 165–168.
Martin, C.P. 1935 *Prehistoric man in Ireland.* London.
Masset, C. 1989 Age estimation on the basis of cranial sutures. In M.Y. Iscan (ed.) *Age markers in the human skeleton.* Springfield, Illinois, 71–103.
McDougall, I. 1992 The third instrument of medicine: some accounts of surgery in medieval Iceland. In S. Campbell, B. Hall and D. Klausner (eds.) *Health, disease and healing in medieval culture.* London, 57–83.
McKinley, J.I. 1992 A skull wound and possible trepanation from a Roman cemetery at Baldock, Hertfordshire. *International Journal of Osteoarchaeology* 2, 337–40.
McLoughlin, E.P. 1950 *Report on the anatomical investigation of the skeletal remains unearthed at Castleknock in the excavation of an early Christian cemetery in the summer of 1938.* Dublin.

Mount, C. and Hartnett, P.J. 1993 Early Bronze Age cemetery at Edmondstown, Co. Dublin. *R.I.A. Proc.* 93C, 21–79.

Ó Donnabháin, B., O'Sullivan, V.R., and Fraher, J.P. 1985 A trepanned parietal bone. *Journal of Dental Research* 64, 727.

Ó Donnabháin, B. 1985 The human remains from Tintern abbey, Co. Wexford. Unpublished thesis presented to Department of Archaeology, University College, Cork for an MA degree.

—— 1995 Monuments of shame: some probable trophy heads from medieval Dublin *Archaeology Ireland* 9, pp 12–15.

Oakley, K.P., Brooke, M.A., Akester, A.R., and Brothwell, D.R. 1959 Contributions on trepanning or trepanation in ancient and modern times. *Man* 59, 92–6.

Ortner, D.J., and Putschar, W.G.J. 1985 *Identification of pathological conditions in human skeletal remains.* Washington.

Piggott, S. 1940 A trepanned skull of the Beaker period from Dorset and the practice of trepanning in prehistoric Europe. *Proceedings of the Prehistoric Society* 6, 112–133.

Prendergast, E. 1962 Archaeological acquisitions for the year 1960. *R.S.A.I. Jn.* 92, 152.

Roberts, C. and Manchester, K. 1995 *The archaeology of disease.* Ithaca, New York.

Rynne, E. 1974 Ancient burials at Ballinlough, Co. Laois. *Journal of the Kildare Archaeological Society* 15, 430–433.

Simpson, L. 2000 Forty years a-digging: a preliminary synthesis of archaeological investigations in medieval Dublin. In S. Duffy (ed.) *Medieval Dublin I. Proceedings of the Friends of Medieval Dublin symposium 1999* Dublin 11–68.

Stewart, T.D. 1958 Stone Age skull surgery: a general review with emphasis on the New World. *Annual Report of the Smithsonian Institution 1957*, 469–91.

Voights, L.E. and Hudson, R.P. 1992 A drynke pat men callen dwale to make a man slepe whyle men kerven him: a surgical anesthetic from late medieval England. In S. Campbell, B. Hall and D. Klausner (eds.) *Health, disease and healing in medieval culture.* London, 34–56.

Walker, A.A. 1998 Mesolithic surgery Archaeology:http://www.archeology.org/online/news/trepanation.html.

Walmsley, T. 1923 A trephined Irish skull. *Man* 23, 108.

Waterman, D.M. and Hamlin, A. 1976 Banagher church, Co. Derry. *Ulster Journal of Archaeology* 39, 25–42.

Wells, C. 1982 The human burials. In A. McWhirr, L. Viner and C. Wells (eds.) *Romano-British cemeteries at Cirencester.* Cirencester: Cirencester Excavation Committee, Corinium Museum.

The rise and fall of Geoffrey Morton, mayor of Dublin, 1303–4

PHILOMENA CONNOLLY

Among those who held the office of mayor of Dublin in the early 14th century, three men stand out – John le Decer, who was responsible for a number of public works, Robert de Nottingham, who held office during the Bruce invasion and took the unprecedented step of arresting and imprisoning the earl of Ulster, and Geoffrey Morton, the subject of this paper. Geoffrey was notorious for extending his own house onto the city wall, thereby compromising the defence of the city, obtaining a grant of murage for his own benefit, not that of the city, and being constantly at loggerheads with the royal administration in Dublin. Such a colourful character obviously merited closer investigation.

The first step was to examine his background and associates, and here arises the usual problem of the survival of records. While official records for the late 13th and early 14th centuries are quite good by Irish standards of survival, they are far from complete and very often do not give us the whole story. There is no contemporary Dublin chronicle for this period to throw light on his actions and what his fellow citizens might have thought of him. But perhaps the most important gap in the sources is the absence of records of the municipality of Dublin itself, especially records of the hundred court and the guild merchant, which would certainly have contained a wealth of information on Geoffrey's dealings with his fellow merchants. However, the existing records could be used to build up a picture of Geoffrey's circle of associates, both social and business. It was possible to identify people in the following categories: people whom Geoffrey appointed as his attorneys, or who appointed him as their attorney; people appearing with him as co-plaintiffs or co-defendants in legal cases; people against whom he took legal action, usually for debt, implying a previous business transaction; people whose charters he witnessed; people who acted as surety for him in legal cases, or for whom he acted as surety; people on whose behalf he received money; people who named Geoffrey as their executor.

Geoffrey first appears in the Irish records in 1295, as a merchant based in Dublin, and from then until his death in the winter of 1314–15 his life is fairly well documented.[1] It would seem from his relations with other members of the

1 There is no reason to believe that the drawing on an Irish plea roll for 1281–2 of a head labelled 'Mortone' is intended to represent Geoffrey Morton. (*Hist. & mun. doc. Ire.*, xxxvii

Morton family based in London that he may originally have been a Londoner, though he had widespread connections elsewhere in England.[2] In 1295, Geoffrey is mentioned as trading in hides and other unnamed commodities with two merchants of Bruges, Giles de Courtray and William Sonte. Four other Dublin merchants are also named as trading with Giles at this time – Robert le Woder, John de Hereford, Peter de Bristol and Henry le Mareschal – and it is possible that they formed some sort of joint trading enterprise.[3] It may even have been this association that brought Geoffrey to Dublin in the first place. Three of these merchants were close associates of Geoffrey in the years that followed – John de Hereford acted with him as royal purveyor for the war in Gascony in 1296–7; Geoffrey was a surety for Robert le Woder in legal actions on two occasions, in 1299 and 1300; and Geoffrey witnessed a grant made by Henry le Mareschal in 1299. Henry, Geoffrey and Robert de Wileby appear to have been involved in a business enterprise together in 1305, and Geoffrey maintained close connections with the Mareschal family throughout his life.[4]

In the following year, 1296, Geoffrey is described as a citizen of Dublin, implying that he had been admitted to the freedom of the city, but since the records do not survive, we do not know when this occurred.[5] In October 1296 he and one of his associates, John de Hereford, were appointed as royal purveyors, to purchase corn in Ireland and ship it to Gascony for the king's war there. They served in that capacity for over a year.[6] The choice of Geoffrey as a purveyor is an indication of his standing as a merchant, as is the fact that he refers to nine of this own men and servants being involved in the enterprise. This involved collecting corn, not only in Leinster, but also in Cos. Cork, Limerick and Waterford, hiring ships, repairing them and fitting them out for the voyage, loading the wheat and oats and transporting them to Gascony. Whatever benefits might be expected to accrue from being a royal purveyor, Geoffrey considered that it left him out of pocket and eight years later he was petitioning the king for recompense for his labours and expenses – unsuccessfully, as he was still trying to get payment in 1314, shortly before his death.[7]

It was at about the same time that Geoffrey began to establish or develop contacts with important people in the Dublin administration, and especially

---

n.2). **2** William Morton, citizen of London, acted as Geoffrey's attorney in England in 1309 and 1313 (*Cal. pat. rolls, 1308–1313*, p. 99; *1313–18*, pp 10, 79). Richard Morton was an executor of Geoffrey's will (NAI, RC 8/10, pp 140–3). In 1307 Geoffrey's mainpernors in England came from Derbyshire, Sussex, Rutland and Yorkshire (*Hist. & mun. doc. Ire.*, p. 226). **3** *Cal. doc. Ire., 1293–1301*, p. 109. **4** P.R.I. *rep. D.K.* 38, p. 44; *Cal. justic. rolls Ire., 1295–1303*, pp 293, 380, *1305–07*, p. 197; J.L. Robinson, 'On the ancient deeds of the parish of St John, Dublin, preserved in the library of Trinity College', *R.I.A. Proc. 33* (1916–17) sect. C, p. 180; M.J. McEnery and Raymond Refaussé, *Christ Church Deeds* (Dublin, 2000), no. 180; *Hist. & mun. doc. Ire.*, p. 505 **5** P. Connolly, *Irish exchequer payments, 1270–1446*, (Dublin, 1998), p. 135. **6** *P.R.I. rep. D.K.* 38, p. 44. **7** PRO, SC 8/124/6193; F.W. Maitland (ed.) *Memoranda de Parliamento, 1305*, (Rolls Series, 1893) p. 251; *Hist. & mun. doc. Ire.*,

with the legal side of that administration, members of the judiciary and king's pleaders. The fact that many of these were of English origin and had previously worked in the royal courts in England suggests that Geoffrey may have known them there.[8] His association with John de Fresingfield, the keeper of the records of the common bench and later a justice, lasted from 1299 to 1314.[9] He was involved in some business transaction with Walter de Kenley, the chancellor of the exchequer, and acted as pledge for Simon de Ludgate, the chief justice of the Dublin bench.[10] He was also closely associated with William de Bardfield, one of the king's pleaders, and in view of these legal connections, it is quite likely that William de Morton, the clerk of the common bench, was related to Geoffrey.[11] It was legal connections of this kind that led to Geoffrey's first known brush with the law, in 1296. Acknowledgements of debts of merchants in the city of Dublin were made, in accordance with the statute of merchants, before the mayor and a king's clerk specially appointed for the purpose, each of whom had a seal to seal the recognisances. In 1297 Henry de Cumpton, the king's clerk, was accused of having given his seal to certain Dublin merchants to seal these recognisances during his absence. The merchants named are Robert de Wileby, a former mayor (and associate of Geoffrey), Hugh de Carlton, a former bailiff of the city, and Geoffrey himself. The inclusion of Geoffrey, who did not yet hold any municipal office, indicates his importance as a merchant and probably also reflects his legal connections. Geoffrey admitted that he had used the seal during Henry's absence, but said it was done in the presence of someone appointed by Henry, and the matter went no further as far as he was concerned.[12]

So by 1297 Geoffrey was established in Dublin, well-regarded by the royal administration, obviously doing well for himself and building up a useful network of connections, mercantile and others. The next step in his career was to find a suitable wife, and in this he was spectacularly successful. Matilda de Bree was the widow of Robert de Bree, a former mayor of Dublin who had died in 1295, leaving a widow and six daughters, some of whom were already married to members of the Dublin merchant community. He had left his family well off – his legacies to his daughters amounted to £200 in money, with land

pp 293–4; NAI, RC 8/9 pp 473–7.   8 For the background of members of the judiciary and royal legal officers in Ireland see two articles by Paul Brand, 'The early history of the legal profession of the lordship of Ireland, 1250–1350', in D. Hogan and W.N. Osborough (eds.), *Brehons, serjeants and attorneys*, (Dublin, 1990), pp 15–50, and 'The birth and early development of a colonial judiciary: the judges of the lordship of Ireland, 1210–1377', in W.N. Osborough (ed.), *Explorations in law and history*, (Dublin, 1995), pp 1–47.   9 *Cal. pat. rolls, 1313–18*, p. 10; *Cal. justic. rolls Ire., 1295–1303*, p. 220, 1305–7, p. 197; *Ormond deeds, 1172–1350*, no. 479.   10 *Cal. justic. rolls Ire., 1295–1303*, pp 99, 220, 364.   11 Bardfield was mainpernor for Geoffrey in 1306 (*Hist. & mun. doc. Ire*, pp 526–7) and Geoffrey witnessed several grants of property to him and his wife (Robinson, 'Parish of St John', pp 181, 183). 12 *Cal. justic. rolls Ire., 1295–1303*, p. 123.

in the city and Co. Dublin, and his widow also inherited property in the city.[13] One of the executors of Robert de Bree's will was Nigel le Brun, the son of a former chancellor of Ireland. Nigel was later a close associate of Geoffrey's and named Geoffrey as his own executor in 1310, but we do not know whether their association predated Geoffrey's marriage to Matilda, or arose out of their joint activities in connection with the administration of Robert's estate. Similarly, we do not know whether Robert and Geoffrey had ever been involved in business dealings together. As far as wealth and social standing were concerned, Matilda was a good match. Not only was she well-connected – her eldest daughter, Loretta, was married to Robert de Nottingham, the future mayor – but she was also an astute businesswoman, acquiring more land in Co. Dublin by lease during the time of her widowhood,[14] and was to prove a zealous defender of her family's interests, especially Geoffrey's.

Geoffrey's activities as a purveyor in 1296–7 seem to have left him out of pocket and given him little inclination to repeat the experience. However, in his private capacity he did provide supplies for the war in Scotland and seems to have spent some time there himself in 1301. In February 1302 a Geoffrey Morton was pardoned for the death of Giles le Bouchier 'on account of his good service in Scotland', but unfortunately we know nothing of this episode.[15] He brought two ships laden with food for the army to Scotland in the summer of 1303, but one of them was destroyed in a storm and the contents of the other rotted away while waiting for the arrival of the king's army, because Geoffrey did not dare to put them up for sale in the meantime. Again he claimed compensation for his losses, but as in the case of his claim relating to purveyance for Gascony, he was still unpaid at the time of his death.[16] It was probably through his involvement with the Scottish campaigns that Geoffrey became acquainted with Richard de Burgh, earl of Ulster, a connection which was to prove extremely useful to him in the future. De Burgh was a leader of the Irish expedition to Scotland in the summer of 1303, and in Geoffrey's petition for payment, presented at the beginning of 1305, he calls himself 'merchant of the earl of Ulster'.

At Michaelmas 1303, Geoffrey was elected mayor of Dublin for the year beginning on 30 September of that year, and took his oath in the exchequer that he would serve the king faithfully in that office. The charter issued to the citizens of Dublin in 1229 authorising the annual election of a mayor specifically permitted the re-election of the outgoing mayor.[17] Geoffrey's predecessor, John le Decer, was not re-elected in 1303. This was not due to any incompetence on his part, and he was to hold the office on a further five occasions, and be recorded in the Dominican annals as someone who had

13 *Hist. & mun. doc. Ire.*, pp 542–3.   14 *Cal. justic. rolls Ire., 1295–1303*, p. 257.   15 *Cal. pat. rolls, 1301–07*, p. 15.   16 PRO, SC 8/9/430; Maitland, *Memoranda de parliamento*, pp 249–50; *Hist. & mun. doc. Ire.*, pp 291–5; NAI, RC 8/9 pp 473–7.   17 *Hist. & mun. doc. Ire.*, p. 91.

carried out various public works for the benefit of the city.[18] There was no animosity between them, as in the following year John was acting as Geoffrey's attorney.[19] The choice of Geoffrey as mayor is rather surprising, since he had not held municipal office before, and neither had he held any major royal office connected with the city, such as collector of customs. The evidence of the witness lists of charters for the period of Geoffrey's career up to his election shows him acting as witness in only five known transactions, and in each of these one or both of the parties were known associates of his.[20] This is a contrast to the many other Dublin merchants whose names recur with great frequency and regularity as witnesses in the 1290s and early 1300s. One can only conclude from this that Geoffrey's energies were being diverted elsewhere – to his trading and other business activities, and to the numerous legal actions in which he was involved, both in relation to Robert de Bree's estate and to his own interests. He does not appear to have been involved to any great extent in the official life of the city prior to his election as mayor. This was distinctly unusual. If we look at the twenty years immediately preceding Geoffrey's election, we find that a total of eight men held office as mayor, and of these seven had previously been bailiffs of the city.[21] In the case of John le Decer, his father, recently deceased, had been a bailiff.

It is true that Geoffrey could hardly be called an outsider. He was associated with some merchants in business ventures and was related to others through the marriages of his step-daughters, the children of Robert de Bree. He and his wife owned property in the city, which had belonged to Robert de Bree, and he was without doubt a wealthy individual. However, it was probably his close connections with members of the judiciary and legal officers of the crown that made him especially attractive as a prospective mayor. The city of Dublin had been taken into the king's hand in 1301 and direct rule imposed, as a result of the city authorities refusing to acknowledge the jurisdiction of the king's marshal. In this the fault clearly lay with the marshal, and the citizens recovered control of the city the following year.[22] To prevent any recurrence of such incidents, it would obviously be useful to have a mayor with good connections with the administration, and especially with members of the legal profession. In this context, it is perhaps significant that one of Geoffrey's early actions as mayor was to appoint an attorney in the court of common bench 'to claim the liberty of the city of Dublin if that should be necessary'.[23]

18 *Chartul. St Mary's, Dublin*, ii, pp 337, 342, 377. **19** NAI, RC 8/2 p. 351. **20** The persons involved were Henry le Mareschal, Roger de Nottingham and William de Bardfield (Robinson, 'Parish of St John', pp 180–2). **21** H.F. Berry, 'Catalogue of the mayors, provosts and bailiffs of Dublin city, AD 1229 to 1447', in H. Clarke (ed.), *Medieval Dublin: the living city* (Dublin, 1990), pp 157–8. **22** *Hist. & mun. doc. Ire.*, pp 221–2. **23** NAI, RC 8/2, p. 290.

From Geoffrey's point of view the office of mayor was obviously worth having. He was the highest civic officer within the city and the voice of the citizens in their dealings with the royal administration. The prestige was great, and the fact that the mayor presided over the hundred court made the office especially attractive. The salary was only £10 a year, but the opportunities for exploiting the office were immense. If all went well, Geoffrey could count on being re-elected for a second and possibly further terms. Again, if we look at his eight predecessors as mayor during the period 1284–1303, only two had been single term mayors – one had died shortly afterwards and the other, John le Decer, was to be re-elected on a further five occasions in the future. Of the rest, most held office for two or three years, including Robert de Bree, while William de Bristol was elected for a total of four terms.[24] Geoffrey, however, was to hold the office for one year only, and may even have been removed from office shortly before the completion of his term.[25]

The most notable feature of Geoffrey's year as mayor was the beginning of his feud with the Irish treasurer, Richard de Barford. We do not know what lay behind it. Barford had been treasurer since 1300 and had not had any major problems with Geoffrey's predecessors. The initial dispute was over the landing of wine at Dalkey, which Barford thought was being done to avoid the payment of prise, a toll due to the king on wine landed in Ireland. The merchants, including Geoffrey, claimed that they were only unloading part of the wine at Dalkey in order to lighten the ship and enable it to be brought to port in Dublin, and that they were paying prise on the total amount of wine landed. Barford was unconvinced and confiscated the wine. The merchants, led by Geoffrey, immediately petitioned the king in England and obtained an order for the restoration of the wine until further notice.[26] We do not known why Barford suddenly decided to attack the practice of landing wine at Dalkey, but this should have been the end of the matter. The fact that it was not was due to Geoffrey's further dealings with the exchequer as mayor and his propensity for seeing the actions of exchequer officials as a personal attack on himself.

As mayor, he was responsible for ensuring that the farm of the city and any other debts owed to the king, such as arrears of accounts, were paid. He and the bailiffs were jointly responsible for accounting for the city at the exchequer. Fortunately, some exchequer records for 1303–4 have survived, and they show that from the exchequer's point of view, Geoffrey was a most unsatisfactory character. On one occasion, he falsely claimed to have levied money due to the

---

24 Berry, 'Catalogue', pp 157–8.   **25** The evidence for Geoffrey's removal is circumstantial but suggestive, consisting of the use of the word *amocio* in referring to his leaving the office of mayor, and the fact that on 28 July 1304, the unnamed mayor disavowed previous complaints made against the treasurer and barons of the exchequer, which were probably those made by Geoffrey against Richard Barford and his colleagues (*Hist. & mun. doc. Ire.*, pp 523–4).   **26** *Hist. & mun. doc. Ire.*, pp 222–7; *Cal. justic. rolls Ire., 1295–1303*, pp 316–17.

king, when he had done nothing in the matter. He delayed in making payments into the exchequer, putting forward various unacceptable and unsatisfactory excuses. He absented himself from the exchequer without permission, failed to appear in person when required to do so, and on one occasion sent an attorney in his place without providing him with the necessary formal authorisation. He contradicted the evidence of the official record of receipts from taxation, a major offence, and persisted in this, despite imprisonment.[27] In fact, most of these offences led to Geoffrey being imprisoned for several days at a time until he found sureties for his further appearance at the exchequer, a total of 36 days.[28] He complained to the justiciar about the treasurer and barons of the exchequer and obviously felt personally aggrieved.

However bad his relations with the exchequer officials were, Geoffrey was happy to use the exchequer for his own purposes. He accused the two bailiffs of the city in the preceding year, Thomas de Coventry and John le Sergeant, of concealing money which they had collected instead of paying it into the exchequer. Although the exchequer records showed that they were not guilty of this, Geoffrey persisted in his accusations, demanding to see the detailed records of receipts kept by the bailiffs, which, as he probably knew, had recently been lost in the fire in Bridge Street where John lived. Not surprisingly, the exchequer officials decided to believe the bailiffs rather than Geoffrey, and he was imprisoned for making false accusations.[29]

Perhaps the most potentially dangerous action of Geoffrey as mayor, from the city's point of view, was his interference with the activities of a royal purveyor in Dublin in the spring of 1304. The purveyor had been appointed to buy corn for the war in Scotland. Merchants generally disliked purveyors, as they paid lower prices for the corn and other goods than the merchants might have been able to get on the open market. So when they heard the purveyor was coming to town, they intercepted the corn before it came to the market and hid it in various places in the city. The purveyor was understandably furious and sought the mayor's assistance in arresting those responsible and seizing the corn. Geoffrey, whose sympathies were more with his fellow merchants than with the purveyor, refused to help, claiming that a special warrant was needed. The matter eventually came before the Irish council and Geoffrey was found to be in breach of his oath of office and sent to prison. The case was adjourned until July, when Geoffrey was to appear again before the council.[30] We do not know the outcome, but if Geoffrey was indeed removed from office in the summer of 1304, it was probably as a result of this episode, and so done at the instance of the council rather than by his fellow citizens.

Although at the end of his year of office Geoffrey was on the worst terms possible with Barford and the exchequer officials, there is nothing to show that

---

27 *Hist. & mun. doc. Ire.*, pp 519–24, 527–8; NAI, RC 8/2 pp 351, 357, 359.   **28** PRO, SC 8/176/8773.   **29** *Hist. & mun. doc. Ire.*, pp 521–2.   **30** Ibid., pp 503–7.

he had alienated his fellow citizens. They were apparently quite happy for him to retain custody of the two city seals until they should be needed by his successor.[31] His stand on purveyance would have been approved by most of them as merchants, as would his defence of the landing of wine at Dalkey. Although he was the only one to follow up with complaints against Barford's confiscation of the wine, it is likely that he did so with the support of many of the other merchants. And while one is not surprised that a jury in 1306 exonerated Geoffrey of any wrongdoing in the case of the wine, since to convict him would mean incriminating other merchants, two other juries in that year also found in favour of him. One set of jurors said that Matilda's refusal to return the city seal to the mayor was entirely her own idea, done to prevent letters disowning Geoffrey's actions from being sent to England. The jurors went on to imply that Geoffrey had not used the seal to illicitly seal documents for his own advantage.[32] The other jury exonerated him from a charge, probably brought by Barford, that he had appropriated money due to the king while he was mayor, and these jurors stated categorically that he 'never, when mayor of the city, made any concealment of the king's money'.[33] We know the names of the jurors in all of these cases, and they cannot be identified as Geoffrey's associates. Given that the mayor of Dublin at the time was John le Sergeant, the same man whom Geoffrey had accused of concealing revenue in 1304, and someone who could quite easily have handpicked a jury to convict Geoffrey, it is clear that there was not any organised opposition to him in the city.

The real problem was that Geoffrey's personal feud with Barford had become entangled with relations between the city and the crown, since much of what Geoffrey had done was in his capacity as mayor. The city authorities, with the recent memory of the city being taken into the king's hand, were profoundly uneasy about this, and so some sort of damage limitation was called for. The new mayor disavowed complaints made by Morton against the treasurer and barons of the exchequer in the name of the mayor and commonalty of the city.[34] This covered complaints made to the justiciar and council in Ireland, but when the city authorities heard that Geoffrey was going to England to continue his campaign against Barford there, they decided to send letters to inform the courts there that 'no suit that Geoffrey did there was by the wish, order or assent of the citizens'.[35]

Geoffrey's campaign against Barford dragged on through the courts in both countries for at least the next five years, with accusations and counter-accusations proliferating on both sides.[36] As we have seen, Geoffrey was exonerated of any wrongdoing in the episode of the wine, but before this he had

31 Ibid., pp 228–30, 524.   32 Ibid., pp 228–30.   33 *Cal. justic. rolls Ire., 1305–07*, p. 229.
34 *Hist. & mun. doc. Ire.*, p. 523.   35 Ibid., p. 229.   36 *Cal. justic. rolls Ire.1305–07*, pp 316–17, 1308–14, p. 60; *Cal. Chancery Warrants, 1244–1326*, pp 244, 261, 278; *Hist. & mun. doc. Ire.*, pp 222–7; PRO, KB 27 /296 m. 102, KB 27/198 m. 141; P. Connolly, 'List of Irish

been imprisoned in the Tower of London for causing inordinate delays in the progress of the case. A list of accusations brought by Geoffrey against Barford, probably at the end of 1304, has survived.[37] In addition to mentioning the confiscation of the wine, he accuses Barford of preventing Geoffrey from getting payment of debts owed to him, demanding payment of money due when Geoffrey had been granted a respite in this, taking bribes not to levy debts, and attempting to prevent Geoffrey from leaving the country when he was going to England to seek remedy. In most cases it is impossible to tell whether there was any truth in the accusation, but one charge made by Geoffrey had no basis in law. He accused Barford of wrongly imprisoning him for a debt owed by Robert de Bree, stating that he, Geoffrey, was not Robert's pledge or his executor. He ignored the fact that by marrying Matilda, Geoffrey became a co-executor with her and thus jointly answerable for Robert's debts.

Perhaps the most extraordinary feature of this petition is his attempt to claim damages from Barford for imprisoning him for a total of 36 days while mayor, damages which Geoffrey estimated at £100 per day. This was of course totally unrealistic, but can be seen as an indication of Geoffrey's paranoia when it came to his dealings with Barford. Needless to say, he did not receive any compensation. Geoffrey was to use his previous contact with the earl of Ulster to secure the appointment of justices to hear his complaints of wrongs done to him by the king's ministers, and since these justices included Geoffrey's old friend Nigel le Brun, now escheator of Ireland, one can hardly regard them as impartial. It is not surprising, therefore, that Barford found himself imprisoned in Dublin castle as a result, and had to be specially released to be allowed to go to England for the audit of his account. The extent to which Geoffrey saw Barford's actions as treasurer as signs of personal animosity and his tenacity in pursuing these questions through various courts in England and Ireland show that he was apt to get things out of proportion. It is a pity that the existing records do not reveal the end of the matter. Geoffrey was cleared of any offence in landing the wine, and Barford himself was back in the king's favour by 1314 when he was appointed chancellor of Ireland, so it appears that neither side suffered unduly as a result.

While his wrangle with Barford was in progress, Geoffrey had turned his attention to a novel way of enriching himself. Early in 1308 he was in England and may have attended the parliament held at Westminster in the April of that year.[38] His idea was to procure a new grant of murage for the city of Dublin and ensure that he would himself be the one to collect the tolls. Grants of murage had been made to the city on numerous occasions since the early 13th century. They were essentially licences to charge tolls on specified types of merchandise

entries on the memoranda rolls of the English exchequer, 1307–27', *Anal. Hib.*, 36 (1995), pp 168, 170.   **37** PRO, SC 8/176/8773.   **38** *Cal. justic. rolls Ire., 1308–14*, p. 60.

being brought for sale into the city. The grant was made for a specified number of years and the proceeds were to be spent on building or repairing the city walls. Normally the grant was made to the bailiffs and men of the city. The bailiffs would either collect the murage themselves or appoint other trustworthy citizens to act as collectors and the collectors would eventually have to appear in the Dublin exchequer to account for their receipts and expenses. The annual income from murage was estimated to be in the region of £30, so it was worth having.[39]

As has been suggested, Geoffrey was not motivated by public spirit. In one of two surviving petitions addressed to the king, he states that the tower at the head of the bridge of Dublin and the adjoining wall had been burned and knocked down. He goes on to say that he 'seeing the great damage and peril that could befall the king and his city' employed masons to rebuild the wall and tower and had spent £80 already and continues to spend money on these works. He asks for the grant of murage so that he might recoup his expenditure.[40] What he does not say is that he is the tenant of the property in question.

Any petition to the king had a greater chance of success if it were backed or supported by an influential member of the royal circle. Geoffrey may have been known to the king, as a previous inquiry into injuries done to him had been authorised at the request of Edward II when he was prince of Wales. Piers Gaveston, the king's favourite, later stated that the murage had been granted at his request, but there appears to be no definite evidence of any prior association between Gaveston and Geoffrey.[41] It is possible that Gaveston was at this time acting as a patronage secretary or channel for petitions addressed to the king and that the support for Geoffrey's petition came from Richard de Burgh, earl of Ulster.[42] We know that they had both been involved in the wars in Scotland at the beginning of the century. In 1305, Geoffrey referred to himself as 'merchant of the earl of Ulster', and the authorisation of the inquiry into offences committed against Geoffrey, in May 1307, was done at the request, not only of the prince of Wales, but of the king's cousin, Richard de Burgh, earl of Ulster.[43] The clinching evidence is that the date of the warrant authorising the grant of murage is 15 June 1308, the same day that the earl of Ulster was appointed the king's lieutenant in Ireland.[44]

39 *Hist. & mun. doc. Ire.*, pp 96–7, 124–5, 187–195. The figure of £30 is given in an inquisition held in November 1312 (PRO, C 47/10/18/3).   40 PRO, SC 8/240/11985. The other petition submitted by Geoffrey at this time is *Hist. & mun. doc. Ire.*, p. 270.   41 J.S. Hamilton, 'Edward II and the murage of Dublin: English administrative practice versus Irish custom', in J.S. Hamilton and Patricia J. Bradley (ed.), *Documenting the past: essays in medieval history presented to George Peddy Cuttino*, (1989), p. 90. Hamilton's account of the murage episode and the transcripts of portions of PRO, C 47/10/18/3 and 4 contain a number of inaccuracies (ibid., pp 90–91, 95–7).   42 For this suggestion as to Gaveston's role, see Pierre Chaplais, *Piers Gaveston: Edward II's adoptive brother*, (Oxford, 1994), pp 102–3.   43 *Cal. Chancery Warrants, 1244–1326*, p. 261.   44 Ibid., p. 273; *Cal. pat. rolls, 1307–13*, p. 83.

When the grant was made, it was for six years, not the ten which Geoffrey had asked for, but in conformity with previous murage grants to Dublin which had been for five or seven years. The grant made specific mention of the tower at the bridge and the adjoining wall as being in need of repair, and it is stated to have been made at the request of Geoffrey. The letters patent authorising the collection of the murage were issued on 20 July 1308 and given to Geoffrey to bring back to Dublin so that they might be put into effect there.[45]

This grant, however, was to satisfy nobody. Nothing was said in it of Geoffrey being the collector, although Gaveston later stated that this was the king's intention in making the grant. Geoffrey had no authorisation to do anything other than bring the sealed grant to Dublin and hand it over to the city authorities, and it was highly unlikely, in view of his previous actions while mayor, that they would appoint him as collector. This was not at all what he had intended, and we can assume that he made his feelings in the matter clear. On the other hand, there was opposition in Dublin to the terms of the grant, which were essentially the same as those of the 1295 grant, also made under the English great seal. Then, however, there had been complaints and a revised list of commodities and amounts had to be issued in 1297, the main differences being the omission in the second grant of fleeces, woolfells, fish, and numerous kinds of cloth, and the imposition of tolls on ships bringing goods to Dublin for sale there. The 1297 list had formed the basis of a further grant in 1302 and probably also of another in 1304, which does not survive.[46] Now, however, the 1295 grant was being virtually repeated and again, this gave rise to complaints that certain items in it were 'too burdensome' to the king's people in Dublin.[47] In March 1309, the chancellor of Ireland was sent a schedule from England, giving a list of commodities and amounts payable. The original grant was to be cancelled and a new one issued under the Irish great seal incorporating the items listed in the schedule. The schedule also specifically stated that the customs were to be paid to Geoffrey during the term of the grant, and that he was to have powers of forfeiture in case of non-payment.[48] This new grant would be broadly similar to the 1297 and 1302 grants, with more specific tolls on shipping, and should have satisfied any objectors. It should also have satisfied Geoffrey, since he was now mentioned by name as collector.

However, Walter of Thornbury, the Irish chancellor, was not at all happy about cancelling the original grant and issuing a new one to Geoffrey.[49] This was not necessarily due to any personal animosity towards or distrust of Geoffrey. Cancelling a grant under the English great seal on the basis of an order under the English privy seal might have given him a few qualms, but his main problem seems to have been with the form of the grant which he was

45 *Hist. & mun. doc. Ire.*, pp 270–73. **46** *Cal. doc. Ire., 1293–1301*, nos. 250, 435, *1302–07*, no. 239. **47** PRO, C 47/10/18/4. **48** Ibid. **49** The account of the dispute over the issuing of a new grant is given in detail in PRO, C 47/10/18/4.

ordered to make. Grants of murage in the past had been made to the bailiffs and men of Dublin, not to a named person, and now he was being told to issue a commission in Geoffrey's name authorising him to collect the tolls. He and the council, including William de Burgh, the deputy justiciar, expressed disquiet that the king's orders in this matter did not agree with the common form of murage grants made in the past in Ireland. Gaveston was by now the king's lieutenant in Ireland, and presumably Geoffrey complained to him about the delay. Eventually, in May 1309, after repeated orders to Thornbury to do as he was told, Gaveston sent Nigel le Brun, the Irish escheator and close associate of Geoffrey's, to the council in Dublin with a further demand from Gaveston that they would comply with his instructions and make out a new murage grant for Geoffrey.

Nigel turned up at a council meeting in Dublin on 17 May armed with Gaveston's latest letter and the original grant of murage made in 1308, indicating that Geoffrey had handed it to Gaveston and had done nothing about putting it into effect. The chancellor was ordered to issue the new grant 'putting aside all interpretations, delays and excuses', and the council eventually agreed that although they were being asked to approve something that was unusual and not in accordance with Irish practice, it was the duty of the king's ministers in Ireland to obey the king's orders in all things without prevarication, and not to resist or attempt to interpret them. Even with this, it was not until Gaveston himself arrived in Dublin twelve days later, that the original grant was formally cancelled, and on 1 June 1309 a new grant was made to Geoffrey to last for seven years.

Now at last Geoffrey had what he wanted and he lost no time in putting it into operation. There seems to have been no complaint about the commodities and rates in the new murage grant, but whether it was due to Geoffrey's methods of implementing the grant, or the city authorities' realisation that they had been duped, things started to go wrong almost immediately. In October 1309, four months after the grant had been made, the king's sergeant at law complained that Geoffrey had been exempting his friends from paying the murage tolls, and as a result of this, the repairs had not been carried out, to the danger of the city. Geoffrey asked for time to consider his response to this and the matter was deferred until the following January, when Geoffrey was summoned to appear in the exchequer to account for what he had received and spent so far, and to answer the charges brought against him.[50] Unfortunately, we hear no more of this case, but Geoffrey certainly continued to collect the murage. His commission had given him the power to seize goods in cases where the owner refused to pay. At the same time as he was being accused of favouritism, he took an action in the exchequer against Robert de Nottingham saying that he refused to pay the murage.[51] Robert had been the husband of Loretta de Bree, Geoffrey's stepdaughter, but Loretta's death and Robert's

50 *Hist. & mun. doc. Ire.*, pp 273–4.   51 NAI, EX 1/1, mm 13, 19d.

subsequent remarriage had weakened any family feeling there may have been. Nor was Robert alone in his resistance to the murage. A letter from John Wogan, the justiciar, in November 1309, states that various citizens of Dublin had complained that Geoffrey was unjustly exacting murage from them contrary to the liberties previously granted to the citizens by the king's ancestors, and that the matter was under discussion before the justiciar. Further action in this was deferred until January 1310, but again, unfortunately, we know nothing of the outcome.[52]

Resistance continued and Geoffrey was forced to have recourse to his contacts in England. In May 1311 the king wrote to the Irish chancellor telling him that 'we have heard that certain people disturb and dispossess the said Geoffrey and do not permit him to receive the murage'. The chancellor, the escheator and the chief justice of the Dublin bench were appointed as justices to hear and determine any such trespasses, but again, there is no record of any actions heard by them.[53] But Geoffrey was not the only one who was complaining to the king. By July 1311, the king had been told by many people that Geoffrey had procured the grant under false pretences – the tower at the bridge actually belonged to Geoffrey and he was bound to repair it at his own expense; the wall at the time of the grant was whole and crenellated and not knocked down or ruinous in any way; Geoffrey had broken the wall on his own authority to enlarge his house which adjoined the wall, thereby impeding the citizens' access to the wall for defensive purposes. In addition, he was exceeding the terms of the murage grant and exacting tolls and oppressing people coming to the city by what are referred to as 'various distraints and serious extortions'. As a result of this, the city and people visiting it have suffered.[54] This information can only have come from the by now totally infuriated citizens of Dublin. Faced with their accusations and Geoffrey's counter-accusations of interference with the collection of the murage, the only thing to do was to order the justiciar to conduct an inquiry and find out just what was going on.

So on 17 July 1311 John Wogan, the justiciar, was ordered to examine the grant made in 1309 and summon a jury composed of men of the city and the adjacent parts to inquire into the truth of the allegations made against Geoffrey.[55] Geoffrey was to be present at this if he wished. Wogan was also to go personally to the tower at the bridge and examine it and the adjoining wall to see what damage, if any, had been done by Geoffrey's building works. The order for the inquisition arrived in Dublin on 14 November and Wogan obviously lost no time in organising a jury as he was able to hold the inquisition four days later on 18 November 1311. Unfortunately, the text of the inquisition as it survives today is faded, damaged and illegible in parts. However, it appears that a jury of eighteen, rather than the more usual twelve, was empanelled. When we examine

52 NAI, RC 8/4, p. 558.   **53** PRO, C 47/10/18/4.   **54** PRO, C 47/10/18/3.   **55** This account of the inquisition is based on PRO, C 47/10/18/3.

such jurors' names as are legible and identifiable, we can see that this was not necessarily a jury packed with people hostile to Geoffrey. They were reputable men from the city and county. Four of them had served on a jury in a totally unrelated matter in the justiciar's court in the previous July and three of them had served on juries in 1306 which had exonerated Geoffrey of charges brought against him.[56] Geoffrey would have been well known to them, and those jurors who were merchants would have been familiar with the payment of murage tolls. Three of them had acted as royal purveyors,[57] and two had held office in the past as bailiffs of the city, Edward Colet who had been bailiff in 1303–4 when Geoffrey was mayor, and Thomas de Coventry, whom Geoffrey had unsuccessfully accused of concealment of city revenue.

The jury first had to deal with questions relating to the circumstances of the grant in 1308. Did the tower belong to Geoffrey Morton when the grant of murage was made and was he obliged to repair it? The jurors said that Geoffrey and Matilda held the tower and the adjacent gate as permanent tenants from the city, in succession to Robert de Bree, and were bound to pay for the upkeep of the property. Was the wall in good condition and crenellated at the time of the grant, or had it been knocked down, as Geoffrey had claimed? The jurors answered that the wall had not been knocked down at the time, but was ruinous in some places. So the findings in these two matters showed that Geoffrey's grant of murage had been obtained fraudulently. The jurors also pointed out that Geoffrey had procured the grant for himself when the previous murage grant made to the city had two years more to run, and had failed to mention the existence of this grant when petitioning the king.

The jury proceeded to consider two further questions. Did Geoffrey encroach on the wall by his building works? The jurors stated that Geoffrey had caused damage to the wall by building a hall adjoining it which reduced the thickness of the walls. The encroachment on the wall prevented access for defensive purposes, since the only way onto the wall was through the hall. He had removed battlements from the wall and put windows in instead. Did he extort money in collecting the murage? Previous accusations against Geoffrey had referred in general terms to his extortions and oppressions, but the inquisition tells us exactly what these consisted of.

Murage tolls were payable only on goods being brought into the city for sale there, and not on anything else, and that the commodities and the rate of toll were specified each time in the grant. Geoffrey, however, operated differently. In addition to the tolls paid by the sellers of wine, salt and hides, he charged the

---

56 Thomas de Kent, William de Fynglas, Warin Owain and John de Hereford were jurors in July 1311 (*Cal. justic. rolls Ire.*, 1308–14, p. 218). Thomas Coliz, William de Callan and David Wodeward had been jurors in 1306 (*Cal. justic. rolls, Ire., 1305–7*, pp 29, 315–16).   57 John de Hereford, Thomas Coliz and Thomas de Kent.

same amount again to non-Dublin merchants who had bought these items in Dublin and wanted to take them out of the city – his own export tax, in fact, which was totally illegal. Tax on salt was 1/4*d*. per crannock. Geoffrey charged this on smaller amounts as well, which should have been exempt, and applied this same system of a compulsory minimum charge to fish, corn, flour and other commodities. Merchants of London, Bristol and other cities had a general exemption from paying tolls throughout the king's dominions, but this made no difference to Geoffrey. He forced them to pay up, presumably using his powers of forfeiture if they resisted. As a result of this, these merchants avoided coming to Dublin and the city suffered. The tax payable by ships only applied to those bringing goods for sale in Dublin, but Geoffrey charged all ships regardless. Fishing ships from Picardy in France suffered particularly from this. Not only did they have to pay 8*d*. per ship when they were not bringing anything for sale, but Geoffrey also charged them tolls on the salt which they carried in their ships for the purpose of salting the fish they caught.

The jurors estimated the damage to the city at £40 a year and pointed out that as a result of the grant to Geoffrey the city quay and Isolda's tower were both ruinous, whereas if the city had the murage grant, the revenue could have been used to repair them. However, in attempting to maximise his income from murage tolls, Geoffrey had been too greedy. The jurors said that when the city had it, the murage was worth £30 a year at most, and at first Geoffrey, through his extortions, was getting £60 a year out of it. However, by 1311 his receipts had gone down considerably, as merchants had been deterred from coming to Dublin by his extortions. So his efforts were counter-productive in the end.

In all, the inquisition's findings were damning for Geoffrey. Wogan sent the inquisition and a copy of the 1309 grant to England, and after the council there had discussed it, it was decided that the justiciar should be ordered to revoke the grant to Geoffrey, that Geoffrey should be compelled to satisfy the citizens for his receipts during the two years that still had to run of their grant of murage from Edward I, and to satisfy the king for his receipts during the remainder of the term. The justiciar was to proclaim that anyone wishing to complain of Geoffrey's extortions should appear before him to prosecute their cases and he was further ordered to compel Geoffrey to repair the tower at his own cost. An order to this effect was issued on 20 March 1312, the same date as another letter to Wogan, ordering him and the chief justice of the Dublin bench to go to the site of Geoffrey's encroachments on the wall, to remove everything hindering free passage on the wall and cause the wall to be restored to its former state, again at Geoffrey's expense.[58] Shortly afterwards a new murage grant was made to the bailiffs and men of Dublin as a result of their petition asking for such a grant to carry out repairs in the neighbourhood of the new gate on the western

---

58 *Cal. close rolls, 1307–13*, pp 455–6.

side of the city.[59] No mention is made of the quay and Isolda's tower which had been described as ruinous in the 1311 inquisition.

We do not know how long it took for the letters to Wogan to reach him. Since the murage grant and the orders to Wogan were all issued within three weeks of each other while the court was celebrating Easter at York, whoever brought the petition from the citizens of Dublin could have brought the letters back to Dublin with him after the murage grant had been made. However, progress was not fast enough for the citizens of Dublin. In the summer of 1312 they petitioned the king again, complaining that the justiciar had delayed in executing the orders. A further order was issued in October 1312 ordering him to put the previous orders into immediate execution.[60] Wogan himself had left Ireland in August 1312, though he did not relinquish the office of justiciar until June 1314. During the period of his absence Edmund Butler was keeper of Ireland, and he seems to have been disinclined to carry out the king's orders, and a further letter to the same effect had to be sent to him in April 1313.[61] This delay may have been due to Geoffrey's activities in England, and the possibility that the king might change his mind as a result of his representations.

Even after the inquisition had shown up Geoffrey's misdeeds, he was not prepared to give up without a fight. In the autumn of 1312 he appeared personally before the king and council at Windsor and was charged by the citizens of Dublin, among other things, with collecting and receiving the murage tolls other than he ought to have done and otherwise than had been done in the case of similar grants in the past. In response, he said that he had done nothing against the form of the warrant and the particulars contained in the schedule which the king had sent to Dublin in 1309. This schedule had been sent under the king's privy seal, so a copy would not normally have been enrolled in the English chancery. Perhaps Geoffrey was gambling on the possibility that the contents of the schedule would not be available. Certainly no transcript could be found in England, and no-one could remember its contents, so the Irish chancellor had to be asked to provide a copy of the schedule together with copies of the original grant of 1308, cancelled on Gaveston's instructions, and the grant made to Geoffrey in 1309. Fortunately, or unfortunately for Geoffrey, these could be located in the Irish chancery and copies were duly sent to England.[62] A comparison of these documents and the findings of the inquisition in 1311 would have been enough to convince anyone that Geoffrey had indeed exceeded his powers.

Having failed to win the argument based on the his authority to collect the murage. Geoffrey proceeded to challenge the findings of the jury, apparently on the grounds that he had not been present at the inquisition.[63] The writ ordering

59 *Hist. & mun. doc. Ire.*, pp 308–12.   60 *Cal. close rolls, 1307–13*, p. 553.   61 NAI, RC 8/9, pp 493–9.   62 PRO, C 47/10/18/4.

the inquisition had said that he was to be present if he wished, and Wogan's note on the transcript of the inquisition says clearly that Geoffrey was present at the examination of the tower and wall but was not admitted to take exception to any of the jurors because the writ did not intend that the claims of the interested parties to the dispute should be heard. Geoffrey might have objected to the presence of certain jurors as biased, but it was unlikely that this would have had much effect, and Wogan was probably within his rights in not allowing either Geoffrey or the city authorities to put forward their side of the story.

By this stage, the king and his council in England must have been heartily sick of the whole subject of the Dublin murage and of everything to do with Geoffrey Morton. However, his latest claim had to be given a fair hearing and it was referred to the parliament to be held in June 1313. In the meantime, Wogan was ordered to postpone the execution of the orders relating to the murage and the wall. Unfortunately for Geoffrey, his petition had not been discussed or examined by the time parliament was prorogued, but he was given a further postponement until Christmas 1313.[64] The final outcome of all of this is not known in detail. We hear nothing of any further complaints of extortion brought by individuals against Geoffrey, as they were encouraged to do. The encroachment on the wall was removed, but we do not know when, and it might not have been done until after Geoffrey's death, but we do know that in the summer of 1314 he appeared in the exchequer to account for the murage, an indication that the whole matter had been resolved by then.[65]

While Geoffrey was in England in the summer of 1313, waiting for parliament to deal with the murage case, the city authorities decided to take further action against him on their home ground. The question of the murage and tower was *sub judice*, but they could proceed against him on other counts. In July 1313 they brought an case in the justiciar's court, claiming their right to a property called the Fishhouse, near the bridge, originally granted by the city to Robert de Bree. Judgement was given in favour of the city, which was to recover the property and damages, and Geoffrey and Matilda were to be amerced for their action in dispossessing the city.[66] As with most things involving Geoffrey, delays resulted, and it was not until 1317 that Matilda and their daughter Alice agreed to hand the property back to the city authorities, in return for being allowed to rebuild on the wall.[67]

In August 1313 Geoffrey returned to Dublin, having got a stay of execution until Christmas in respect of the murage, only to find himself summoned as defendant to the Dublin hundred court at the suit of the citizens. It must have been humiliating for him to appear as defendant in a court where he had once presided as mayor. We do not know what the charges were, but in December

63 NAI, KB 2/5 p. 9 (the surviving text is defective). **64** Ibid. **65** NAI, RC 8/9 p. 525.
66 NAI, KB 1/1, m. 96d. **67** *Hist. & mun. doc. Ire.*, pp 280–1.

1313 his humiliation was completed when he was forced to submit himself to the grace of the mayor and commonalty and to make amends for his offences at their will. He relinquished all actions of trespass and debt which he and Matilda had begun against the mayor and commonalty, and anyone associated with them, and most humiliating of all, he had to bind himself and his heirs in 500 marks of silver to be paid if at any time in the future he offended against the commonalty or any member of it, or harassed them, to the detriment of the liberty of the city.[68]

Geoffrey was still alive in June 1314 and seems to have died later in that year or early in 1315. It must have been particularly galling for him to witness the return to Ireland in May 1314 of his old adversary Richard Barford, this time as chancellor. We know nothing about Geoffrey's will, except that he did make one, indicating that he was ill or infirm shortly before his death. The executors were Richard de Morton, probably a relative, and his widow Matilda, and the main beneficiaries appear to have been Matilda and their two daughters Alice and Petronilla.[69] On his death, his goods were taken into the king's hands, because of outstanding debts owed from the murage and other accounts, but although we know that his family soon recovered them, there is no evidence as to how much was involved.[70]

In fact, Geoffrey's wealth is something of a mystery. We know that he was wealthy, and that the wealth was derived from legitimate trade as well as from extortions and sharp practices. He traded with Flanders, Gascony and Scotland, and was also involved in internal trade within Ireland and provided stones for building works at Dublin castle. Unlike Matilda's first husband, Robert de Bree, he does not seem to have invested in property in the city or the surrounding area – Robert had houses and shops in Dublin, and land in Oxmantown and Co. Dublin. All of the real property which we know Geoffrey had in Dublin – the tower at the bridge and the Fishhouse –came from Robert de Bree through Matilda, while his lands at Kilsalaghan in Co. Dublin were actually bought by Matilda before her marriage to Geoffrey. And while it is dangerous to argue from silence, there is no mention of any property described as belonging to Geoffrey in any of the collections of deeds which have survived from Dublin for this period. We know he spent money on the building works on the tower at the bridge and the adjoining walls. He may have been a benefactor of churches and religious houses, but if so, no record of it has survived. One suspects that he put his money to work to make more money. We know of one occasion when he entered into an agreement to finance a legal action for the recovery of an annual rent of 10 marks, on condition that the rent was made over to him if the

68 Ibid., pp 279–80.   69 NAI, RC 8/10 pp 140–3.   70 Ibid., pp 79, 98.

action was successful,[71] and there are indications that he may have been involved in money-lending.[72]

The optimism of Geoffrey's fellow Dubliners on his election in 1303 was soon replaced by embarrassment and apprehension as to the damaging effect that his activities might have on the city. This more than outweighed any approval of some of his actions, but relations were apparently reasonably cordial until 1309. Even then, there were apparently no objections to Geoffrey's application for licence to build houses adjoining the city wall near the bridge. It was Geoffrey's behaviour in obtaining the grant of murage and his extortions in collecting it, together with his encroachments on the walls that caused relations to break down. Geoffrey was too greedy in his attempts to enrich himself; he over-reacted to criticism and was disinclined to obey orders from royal officials. If anyone crossed him, he pursued his opposition to them to the limit. He obviously felt that he could get away with almost anything, because of his connections, and when things were not going his way in Ireland, he lost no time in rushing off to England to complain to the king and council or to pursue his case through the courts there. With hindsight, one might say that Geoffrey had cultivated the wrong people. If he had made friends of Richard Barford and the other exchequer officials, to say nothing of his fellow merchants, things might have turned out very differently for him.

---

71 *Cal. justic. rolls Ire., 1305–7*, pp 8–10. See also Hand, *Eng. law in Ire.*, p. 162, for the application to Ireland of legislation relating to champerty at this time.   **72** In 1301 or 1302 Peter de Bermingham of Tethmoy and Alan son of William fitz Warin acknowledged a debt of £220 to Geoffrey in the city of London (*Cal. close rolls, 1302 7*, p. 67). This may have had its origin in a loan made to them by Geoffrey during the Scottish campaign in which they took part , and it is possible that other smaller recognisances of debts owed to Geoffrey represent loans rather than debts relating to trade.

List of illustrations

BARRA Ó DONNABHÁIN
Figures